NATIONAL (

SURVIVING DEBT

The Consumer Law Practice Series

Debtor Rights
Fair Debt Collection
Consumer Bankruptcy Law and Practice
Student Loan Law
Repossessions
Access to Utility Service

Mortgages & Foreclosures
Mortgage Lending
Mortgage Servicing and Loan Modifications
Home Foreclosures

Consumer Litigation
Collection Actions
Consumer Class Actions
Consumer Arbitration Agreements
Consumer Law Pleadings

Credit and Banking
Fair Credit Reporting
Truth in Lending
Consumer Credit Regulation
Credit Discrimination
Consumer Banking and Payments Law

Deception and Warranties
Unfair and Deceptive Acts and Practices
Federal Deception Law
Automobile Fraud
Consumer Warranty Law

For more information on print and digital resources from the National Consumer Law Center, visit www.nclc.org/library.

NATIONAL CONSUMER LAW CENTER®

50TH
ANNIVERSARY EDITION

SURVIVING DEBT

Expert Advice for Getting Out of Financial Trouble

THE NATIONAL CONSUMER LAW CENTER®
America's Consumer Law Experts

For reprint permissions or ordering information, contact
Publications, NCLC, 7 Winthrop Square, 4th Floor, Boston MA 02110,
(617) 542-9595, Fax (617) 542-8028, E-mail: publications@nclc.org

Library of Congress Control No. 2018956037
ISBN: 978-1-60248-176-3

Cover design by Francisco Javier Rivera.

About the National Consumer Law Center

Since 1969, the nonprofit **National Consumer Law Center**® (NCLC®) has used its expertise in consumer law and energy policy to work for consumer justice and economic security for low-income and other disadvantaged people, including older adults, in the United States. NCLC's expertise includes policy analysis and advocacy; consumer law and energy publications; litigation; expert witness services; and training and advice for advocates. NCLC works with nonprofit and legal services organizations, private attorneys, policymakers, federal and state government, and courts across the nation to stop exploitative practices, to help financially stressed families build and retain wealth, and to advance economic fairness.

NCLC publishes a nationally acclaimed series of legal treatises on all major aspects of consumer credit and sales. The treatises, available individually or as a set, are available in print volumes and in continuously updated digital format on the NCLC Digital Library. Visit the NCLC Digital Library at www.nclc.org/library to subscribe to news and analysis from NCLC attorneys and to read the first chapter of each treatise for free.

www.nclc.org/library

Acknowledgments

Surviving Debt (11th ed. 2019) is the culmination of years of work and contributions from experts in the field. We also have received support from the AFL-CIO, the United Auto Workers, the Public Welfare Foundation, various church groups, and NCEE/AT&T Consumer Credit Education Fund. The views in this book are NCLC's and not those of any other entity.

NCLC attorneys contributing to this edition include: Jen Bosco, Carolyn Carter, Joanna Darcus, Charlie Harak, Brian Highsmith, April Kuehnhoff, Sarah Mancini, Andrew Pizor, John Rao, Geoff Walsh, Olivia Wein, and Chi Chi Wu. Also contributing are Ron Abrams of the National Veterans Legal Services Program, Pat Baker of Massachusetts Law Reform, Eric Dunn of the National Housing Law Project, Elizabeth Maresca of Fordham Law School, Cathy Schoen, and Claudia Wilner of the National Center for Law and Economic Justice.

Jon Sheldon authored the 1992 and this edition; Gary Klein authored the 1996, 1999, and 2002 editions; Odette Williamson co-authored the 2002 edition; John Rao co-authored the 2005 and 2006 editions; and Deanne Loonin co-authored the 2005 and 2006 editions and authored the 2008, 2010, 2013, and 2016 editions.

Although too many to thank individually, we also recognize the many current and former NCLC attorneys and other experts in the field for their assistance in this project through ten prior editions over the last 27 years.

Special thanks to Denise Lisio for editing this edition and for production management, Eric Secoy for editing a prior edition, Katie Eelman and Fabiane Best for editorial assistance, Julie Gallagher for typesetting, and Francisco Javier Rivera for cover design.

Contents

1

Six Essential Rules for Surviving Debt

TOPICS COVERED IN THIS CHAPTER

RULE #1: PRIORITIZE DEBTS WHOSE NON-PAYMENT IMMEDIATELY HARMS YOUR FAMILY

Non-payment of certain debts have sudden and dire consequences for your family. Deal with these debts immediately—either pay these debts first or otherwise follow advice in this book on how to manage these debts.

Never pay smaller, low priority debts just because you cannot keep up with high priority debts—"If I can't pay my mortgage, at least I will keep up with my credit cards." This is a bad idea. If you don't have enough money to make full payments on high priority debts, try to negotiate with the creditor to accept lower payments or save the money to be used later to get caught up, to cover the initial costs of moving to a new residence, or to pay for another car if your car is repossessed.

High Priority Debts Include:

- *Court judgment debt.* You have been sued on a debt and a court has ruled for the creditor. The creditor has rights to seize part of your wages, bank accounts, and even your home or other property. Chapter 21 explains your rights to protect your income and assets from the seizure and steps you should take to deal with court judgment debt.

- *Criminal justice debt.* Non-payment of debt arising from a criminal proceeding (such as fines, fees, and costs) can lead to immediate loss of your driver's license, loss of income or assets, or even incarceration. Chapter 22 explains how to deal with criminal justice debt.
- *Automobile loans or leases* can result in a creditor repossessing your car after you miss only a few payments. This is high priority debt, particularly if you need your car to get to work or for other essential transportation. Your rights to respond to a threatened or actual repossession are examined at Chapter 14.
- *Rent payments for your residence* (or for the lot on which your manufactured home sits). Swift eviction can result if you do not keep up these payments. Steps to deal with an eviction threat are set out at Chapter 20.
- *Utility bills.* Non-payment of utility bills can lead to termination of gas, electric, water, and other utility service. Chapter 15 explains how to stop a utility disconnection, reconnect service, and otherwise deal with utility bills. In some states, programs to help people avoid disconnection may make utility bills a somewhat more flexible priority in the short term.
- *Child support debts* will not go away and can result in very serious problems, including prison, for non-payment.

Debts That Quickly Become High Priority. Other debts can be put off for a few months, but at some point soon, they become just as high priority debts as those detailed above, and then must be addressed immediately. Most notable are:

- *Home mortgage delinquencies* (including non-payment of a debt to buy a manufactured home). Miss a month or two and you are unlikely to face foreclosure, but if you get behind by enough months, you face loss of your home. In some states this can happen without a court hearing. Chapters 17 and 18 provide advice on delaying and fighting a foreclosure, and even modifying your mortgage payments to make them affordable. Use these strategies months before a threatened foreclosure.
- *Real estate taxes.* If you do not have an escrow account with your mortgage lender you are responsible for paying your own property taxes. While non-payment of property taxes will not result in the immediate loss of your home, at some point your home will be subject to a tax sale. You should learn your rights in this area before it is too late, as set out in Chapter 19.
- *Federal student loans* are not in default until you are nine months behind on payments, but then you risk seizure of your tax refund and your Social

Security or other federal benefits, wage garnishment without a court order, and denial of new student loans and grants. Chapter 13 examines how to eliminate, delay, or reduce your student loan payments. These strategies work best when you are not in default, so focus on your student loans as soon as practical.

- ***Taxes owed to the IRS.*** Even if you do not pay your federal income taxes when due, always file your tax return on time, or file it by the deadline set by any requested extension. Then you can delay for a time paying taxes owed without serious adverse consequences. But at some point it will be critical to work out an arrangement with the IRS, because the IRS can seize your bank account, part of your paycheck and federal benefits, and even your home.

Lower Priority Debts. Lower priority debts should not be paid ahead of higher priority debts if this prevents you from appropriately dealing with high priority debts. Low priority debts become higher priority once you are sued in court on the debt. Some low priority debts include:

- ***Medical debt,*** such as payments due hospitals, doctors, other medical professionals, dentists, and ambulance companies. This debt does not affect your credit rating for six months, is unlikely to involve high interest rates or late charges, and it could take a year or two before you are sued, if you are ever be sued at all. Medical debt does not result in immediate loss of your property or income, unless you are successfully sued on the debt. More on medical debt is found in Chapter 11.
- ***Credit card debt.*** You will not be subject to seizure of bank accounts, income, or property unless you are successfully sued on the debt or there is a default judgment taken against you. Debt collection contacts can easily be stopped. This is discussed in Chapter 2. Interest and late charges may even stop after you are six months delinquent. Credit card debt is explored in Chapter 12.
- ***Debt owed friends and relatives.*** Non-payment is not going to harm your credit rating or result in lost property or wages, and you may not even be charged interest. Of course, you want to repay these debts, but your friends or relatives who lent you money are unlikely to want you to lose your home or car just to pay them back sooner.
- ***Private student loans.*** These loans typically do not involve collateral, and special remedies available to the government to collect federal student loans do not apply to private student loans. However, private student loans are difficult to discharge in bankruptcy. Student loans are discussed in Chapter 13.
- ***Debts you owe as a co-signer.*** If you co-signed for someone else's debt and put up your home or car as collateral for the other person's loan, the loan is

high priority. Other loans for which you are a co-signer but have put up no collateral are low priority. If others have cosigned for you, tell them about your financial problems so that they can make plans.

- *Deficiency actions after your car is repossessed.* If a creditor repossesses your car and sells it for less than the amount owed on the car loan, it may seek the difference from you, called "a deficiency." This is a low priority debt because you have already lost the car, your credit rating has already been damaged, and the creditor can do little other than sue you. If you are sued, you often have solid defenses that prevent the creditor from recovering any deficiency, as described in Chapter 14. If the creditor prevails in the lawsuit, the debt becomes high priority.
- *Charge accounts or other debts owed to merchants,* particularly if the merchant has not taken as collateral the goods sold.
- *Small loans even when they take household goods as collateral.* Non-payment is unlikely to cause you to lose household goods collateral because creditors rarely seize them. They have little market value, a court order is usually needed to seize them. It is time-consuming and expensive to obtain that court order.

RULE #2: DON'T LET DEBT COLLECTORS, CREDIT SCORE WORRIES, STRESS, OR OTHER FACTORS FORCE YOU INTO BAD DECISIONS

Don't Make Decisions Based on Debt Collection Harassment. A debt collector's job is to convince you to pay its debts first. Instead make your own decision as to which debt has the highest priority. The collector contacting you most aggressively is often collecting on a low priority debt. Do not be persuaded; just get the debt collector off your back. Chapter 2 sets out nine ways to stop debt collection harassment, including four different sample letters that typically will stop collectors from contacting you.

Worries About Your Credit Score Should Not Move Up a Debt's Priority. If you are behind on your bills, this almost certainly ends up on your credit record. You cannot stop this, short of always being current on your bills. Nevertheless, do not prioritize a particular bill first just because a collector is threatening to ruin your credit record.

Creditors routinely report the status of all of their accounts each month to a credit bureau. When the account is turned over to a collection agency, this also may be indicated on your credit report. By the time a collection agency is threatening you about your credit report, your report will already include the fact that the debt is a number of months delinquent and has been turned over for collection. The damage to your credit score has already happened. Paying now will not do much to improve your credit rating and failing to pay will not do much more damage. For more on your credit rating, including what a blemished credit rating does and does not mean for you, see Chapter 3.

Threats to Sue You Should Not Move Up a Debt in Priority Until You Are Actually Sued. Many threats to sue are not carried out. Even if they are, it may be years before you are actually sued. On the other hand, non-payment of rent or car loans may result in immediate loss of your home or car. It is hard to predict whether a particular creditor will actually sue on a past-due debt. How aggressively a collection agency threatens suit is no indication whether the creditor will actually sue, even if the threat appears to come from an attorney. Whether you will be sued and what to do if you are sued is covered in Chapter 4.

Worries About Creditors Withholding Services from You. Sometimes non-payment of a debt results in the creditor stopping doing business with you. Explain your financial situation and ask for understanding. If you are cut off, there should be other options in your community. A hospital cannot deny you emergency room services because you owe them money, as discussed in Chapter 11.

Feelings of Obligation. Your feeling that some creditors are more entitled to repayment than others should rarely be a factor in deciding which debts to pay first. Giving up the family home to pay off a creditor for whom you have good feelings is too big a sacrifice. If a creditor is sympathetic or has done you favors in the past, it is more likely to be patient as you work out your financial problems.

Stress. You are not alone if financial problems cause you embarrassment, panic, and stress. The pressure can cause disagreements, temporary separations, divorce, or even physical abuse. As you make the difficult choices associated with your financial problems, be aware of these emotional pressures.

Mental health counseling, family therapy, and marriage counseling may be useful. Health insurance may include free or low-cost mental health assistance and this help may be available from a variety of organizations on a sliding-scale fee basis or for free. Call your doctor, a trusted local credit counseling agency, or family services for a reference. Whatever course you choose, be aware of the additional stress you may be feeling and deal with it in the healthiest possible way.

RULE #3: STRETCH YOUR DOLLARS AND YOUR DEBT, BUT ALSO THINK LONG TERM

Stretching Out or Reducing Debt Payments. If you cannot pay all your debts, try to reduce your monthly debt payments. Even if you must pay the full amount eventually, delay can help, particularly if your financial problem is caused by unusual expenses or a short-term drop in income.

As described in Rule #1, low priority debts (such as medical, credit card, and private student loan debt) should be put off if payment endangers higher priority debts. This book sets out ways to spread out payment of higher priority debts, paying less each month, and even lowering your total obligation:

- *Mortgage payments.* You may be able to skip a few months mortgage payments, pay back-due amounts slowly over time, or otherwise reduce your monthly mortgage payment through programs offered for most mortgages. These are described at Chapter 17.
- *Federal student loans.* Chapter 13 outlines a number of ways to cancel your student loan, put off all payments for a year, or reduce your monthly payment to an affordable amount.
- *Real estate taxes.* Chapter 19 sets out ways to lower or delay payment of real estate taxes.
- *Utility debt.* Chapter 15 describes options to lower your utility rate, spread payments out more, or skip payments without the threat of disconnection.
- *Auto loans.* Chapter 14 provides advice on ways to reduce the size of your auto loan payments.
- *Court judgment debt.* A court judgment against you may lead to loss of wages, money in your bank account, and even your home or other property. Chapter 21 provides advice to reduce your exposure to these losses.
- *Criminal justice debt.* Chapter 22 explains that criminal justice debt can sometimes be stretched out through payment plans or even reduced if you can show financial hardship.
- *Federal income taxes.* Chapter 23 describes how to pay your back-due federal income taxes in installments and when you may be entitled to reduce the amount owed.

Paying Debts by Taking on More Debt. Borrowing from friends and relatives often makes sense. Interest rates are likely to be low or nonexistent, and you typically need not put up collateral for the loan. Problems arise when a friend or relative faces financial difficulties and asks for repayment, or when you are counting on further loans from that person.

Another option is borrowing against your home equity to free up money to pay other debts. Chapter 5 discusses the pitfalls and advantages of this approach. Interest rates are low, and you have years to repay. But non-payment can lead to loss of your home and the total cost of the loan—including closing costs and fees—can be much higher than you think. If you refinance your first mortgage and other debt into a new larger first mortgage, you may end up with larger monthly payments than you can afford and even larger than you expected because of pre-payment penalties, hidden charges, and the like.

One way to pay off your debts and avoid home foreclosure is to take out a reverse mortgage, as explained in Chapter 6. If you are at least 62 years old you can draw on your home equity to obtain cash. You have no loan payments until you move out of the home or pass away. But you still face foreclosure if you cannot keep up property taxes, insurance, repairs and other home expenses. There also are other downsides to a reverse mortgage. It is a complicated decision. Read Chapter 6, and then find expert help.

It is tempting to pay off debts using your credit cards or a cash advance through your credit card. Unless you can pay off the full card balance each month, this is a bad idea when dealing with medical debt (see Chapter 11), debts owed to the IRS (see Chapter 23), federal student loans (see Chapter 13), and other debts that you could spread out over time through working with the creditor. An advantage of adding charges to your credit card is that non-payment does not immediately lead to loss of your home, car, wages, or bank accounts. If you file bankruptcy, with certain exceptions, you can also get rid of the entire credit card debt. But interest rates and fees are high and if you are eventually sued on the credit card debt, you then face potential loss of wages, bank account assets, and other property.

Reducing Expenses. Pay family necessities first, such as food and unavoidable medical expenses if the medical provider requires pre-payment. (Do *not* pay old medical bills first.) But look to reduce these and other expenses, as discussed in Chapter 8. That chapter provides advice on lowering expenses for:

- Homeowner's, auto, and other insurance premiums;
- Medical and dental care;
- Food;
- Appliances and furniture;
- Check cashing and banking;
- Automobile, tax preparation, and other expenses.

The chapter also provides advice on reducing pressure-related shopping and reducing the winter holiday cycle of debt.

Other chapters in this book explain other ways to reduce expenses:

- Lowering your mortgage payments (Chapter 17);
- Lowering your student loan payments (Chapter 13);
- Lowering your real estate taxes (Chapter 19);
- Lowering your costs for heat, electricity, telephone and the internet (Chapter 15);
- Avoiding high cost loans and scams that prey on those in debt (Chapter 7);
- Reducing the size of fines, fees, and other criminal justice debt (Chapter 22);
- Reducing payment of delinquent income taxes (Chapter 23).

Increasing Income. Make sure you are not taking out excessive withholding from your paychecks. Also consider canceling voluntary disbursements from your paychecks. Chapter 9 sets out a number of ways you can increase your income by making sure you are taking advantage of benefits to which you may be entitled, including:

- The earned income tax credit;
- Unemployment compensation;
- Workers' compensation;
- Child support;
- Cash assistance for families with children;
- General assistance programs;
- Social Security based on age and disability;
- SSI benefits based on age and disability;
- SNAP (formerly food stamps);
- School lunch, school breakfast and summer meals;
- Woman Infant and Child Program (WIC);
- Other food programs;
- State and local emergency programs;
- Disaster relief;
- Veterans disability compensation and veterans pensions.

Long-Term Solutions for Long-Term Financial Problems. After stretching out debt payments, reducing expenses, and increasing income, you may find that you cannot in the long-term sustain your present living costs. To help determine this, write down for a few months your income, your expenses, and your debt payments, as discussed in Chapter 10. If you cannot sustain your living costs, you must consider steps such as moving to different housing or disposing of your car.

If you cannot afford your rent, consider moving to a less expensive unit. If you need to break your lease, Chapter 20 provides advice on how best to do that. If you own your home, you may have to sell it or give it up and move to lower cost housing. If your home is worth less than the amount you owe on your mortgage, Chapter 17 discusses how to work with your lender to best move to alternative housing. Chapter 14 reviews your options to work with your lender to get out from your auto loan.

If you recently entered into a rent-to-own contract to purchase furniture, appliances, or electronics, you may be better off turning the goods back to the store. There will be no penalty and you may save a lot of money by finding a cheaper way to purchase what you need. See Chapter 7.

These are difficult decisions. Once the choice is made, stop making payments on that debt in favor of other pressing items. It is not a good idea to continue paying a debt on property that you will eventually lose anyway. You can save the money to pay for alternative housing or transportation.

RULE #4: AVOID SCAMS AND OTHER RIP-OFFS PREYING ON THOSE IN DEBT

Many banks, creditors, and scam artists target those in financial difficulty for some of the worst abuses. They see consumers whose desperation may lead them to make bad choices, and look for ways to take advantage of these families. Chapter 7 describes scams to avoid, including:

- Debt elimination scams promise for a fee to eliminate your debts completely—these are all bogus.
- Debt settlement agencies charge high fees and rarely help you settle your debts with your creditors.
- Foreclosure rescue scams offer to save your house but end up stealing it.
- Reverse mortgages that do not meet federal "HECM" standards can get you into big trouble.
- Credit repair charge to clean up your credit record, but you can do it better yourself for free.
- Small loans such as payday, auto title, and installment loans have extraordinarily high interest rates. Walk away from any loan with a disclosed annual percentage rate (APR) more than 36%. Also watch out for loans that add charges for insurance. Auto title loans also put your car at risk.
- Refinancing or consolidation loans can put you further in debt, increasing the chances you will lose your home. You also lose rights if you consolidate federal student loans into private student loans.
- Student loan debt relief scams charge high fees to allegedly help with your student loans—help is available for free from your servicer or the U.S. Department of Education.

- Rent-to-own sales of appliances, furniture, and electronics have effective interest rates over 100%.
- Auto brokers offer to lease your car to someone else but may make matters worse for you.
- Subprime credit cards, with hidden fees and charges, end up being extraordinarily expensive.
- Using "overdraft protection" at your bank amounts to an astonishingly expensive short-term loan.

RULE #5: KNOW WHETHER AND WHEN TO FILE BANKRUPTCY

How Bankruptcy Can Help. Federal law provides you the right to file bankruptcy and this is a powerful tool to deal with your financial issues. Bankruptcy at least temporarily stops foreclosures, repossessions, utility terminations, garnishments, and other collection actions against you. Bankruptcy can restore your utility service. It allows you to keep your home or car by getting caught up on back-due payments slowly over time. For car loans you may even be able to lower your monthly payments. To keep your home and car, you still have to keep up with new mortgage and car payments creditor as they come due.

Bankruptcy gets rid of medical, credit card, and many other debts, but it cannot eliminate child support, alimony, most student loans, court restitution orders, criminal fines, some taxes, and debts you incur *after* you file for bankruptcy.

Bankruptcy is effective dealing with court judgments, stopping wage garnishment, bank seizures and enforcement of judgment liens. It protects household goods collateral. If bankruptcy discharges a debt whose non-payment led to suspension of your driver's license, you get your license back.

Bankruptcy Costs. It is best to hire an attorney help you file bankruptcy. Sometimes you can find a legal services or other attorney who will not charge you. The bankruptcy court charges a filing fee of more than $300, but you can spread this fee out over several months and in some cases it can be waived.

Common Misconceptions. Despite what you might think, typically you lose little or no property in bankruptcy. Bankruptcy may not hurt and may even help your standing with creditors. Your reputation in the community is unlikely to suffer. Housing authorities, licensing departments, and other government agencies cannot discriminate against you for having filed for bankruptcy.

When to File Bankruptcy. Bankruptcy is not really a "last resort" for those in financial trouble. Legal rights can be lost by delaying a bankruptcy. Get early advice about bankruptcy if you are concerned about saving your home or your car or protecting your bank account or wages from seizure.

On the other hand, if you do not face immediate property loss and will incur new unaffordable debts in the future, delay bankruptcy until you incur those new debts. Debts incurred *after* you file bankruptcy are *not* discharged in that bankruptcy case—you are obligated to repay those new debts in full.

For More on Bankruptcy. More on whether and when to file bankruptcy is found in Chapter 24. Chapter 25 summarizes the steps involved in filing either a chapter 7 or a chapter 13 bankruptcy.

RULE #6: GET HELP FROM A COUNSELOR OR LAWYER

Help from a Counselor. The federal Department of Housing and Urban Development (HUD) funds housing counselors to help you with home mortgage problems. To find a HUD-approved counselor, call 800-569-4287 (TTY 800-877-8339) or visit www.hud.gov. Counselors specializing in reverse mortgages can be located using that phone number or at www.hud.gov/offices/hsg/sfh/hecm/hecmlist.cfm.

For help with credit cards, you can contact a consumer credit counselor. There are pros and cons with consumer credit counselors. Even some nonprofit consumer credit counselors will just take advantage of you. So shop carefully. More detail is found at Chapter 11.

If you have cannot resolve federal income tax debt problems through normal channels, you can get assistance with from the IRS Taxpayer Advocate Service, an independent organization within the IRS. Send in IRS Form 911 (available at www.irs.gov) or call 1-877-777-4778.

Help from a Lawyer. Low-income families with limited assets may be eligible for free legal services. Find legal aid programs at www.lawhelp.org/find-help or http://lsc.gov/find-legal-aid. Other consumers can contact local bar associations for a referral to an attorney who may help at no charge.

The National Association of Consumer Advocates (NACA) can help you find an attorney to take your case to sue a debt collector, defend a collection lawsuit, deal with your credit report, or handle other debt issues. Members by state and specialty are listed at www.consumeradvocates.org/find-an-attorney.

For bankruptcy help, consult an attorney who is a consumer bankruptcy expert. Recommendations from family, friends, the neighborhood legal services office, or a volunteer lawyer project are useful. To find a consumer bankruptcy attorney in your area, you can use the "Find an Attorney" search at the National Association of Consumer Bankruptcy Attorneys, at www.nacba.org.

Help with disputes with the IRS is available from low-income taxpayer clinics, based at law schools and legal services offices. Clinics are listed in IRS Publication 4134: Low Income Taxpayer Clinic List, and at www.irs.gov/advocate/low-income-taxpayer-clinics/low-income-taxpayer-clinics-map.

For help with criminal justice debt, contact the lawyer who represented you in the criminal case in which the debt was imposed. That lawyer may represent you, counsel you about your options, or refer you to another lawyer. If you have a low income, you may be able to obtain free legal representation from a public defender, particularly if you are facing incarceration for non-payment. Legal services offices, pro bono attorneys affiliated with local bar associations, and other civil attorneys may also help.

Selecting and Working with an Attorney. Lawyers should provide a free initial consultation. Meet the attorney and make sure you are comfortable with the attorney and that the attorney answers your questions. You should have a clear idea of what the lawyer will do for you, what you will be charged, and how often the lawyer will communicate with you.

Price is not the only consideration when hiring a lawyer—although it is a factor. The cheapest lawyer will not necessarily be the best. Find someone who can help you with your specific problem. The attorney should also explain the potential consequences of doing nothing about your delinquent debt.

The attorney typically will ask you to sign a retainer agreement, a contract under which you hire the attorney, governing what the attorney proposes to do, and the fees for the proposed work. Read it carefully and make sure you understand what you are signing.

Determine whether you are paying an hourly rate or a flat fee. If a flat fee, get in writing what the fee covers. Some lawyers agree to a contingency fee where the lawyer keeps a percentage of your recovery if you win your case. If you lose, you owe the attorney nothing.

Even after you sign a retainer, you can still cancel if you are dissatisfied with the service you are getting. You will only pay for services you have already received. If you do not receive a refund that you are entitled to receive from the attorney, complain to the local disciplinary agency for attorneys.

2

Responding to Debt Collectors

TOPICS COVERED IN THIS CHAPTER

DO NOT LET COLLECTORS PRESSURE YOU

Do not let debt collection harassment force you into wrong decisions. Make your own choices about which debts to pay first based on what is best for you.

You are not a deadbeat—circumstances outside your control prevent you from paying all your debts. The most common reasons most people cannot pay their bills are job loss, illness, divorce, or other unexpected events. And, creditors and collectors know this. The debt collector's job is to try to convince you to pay their debt first. Your job, however, is to make the right choices for you and your family.

WHAT COLLECTORS CAN LEGALLY DO TO COLLECT ON A DEBT

Most debts, such as almost all credit card obligations, medical bills, and cell phone charges are "unsecured." You do not have to put up any collateral such as your home or car to secure repayment. An *unsecured* creditor collecting a debt that is not owed to the government (for example, tax debts or federal student loans) can only legally do the following four things if you do not pay their debt:

1. Stop doing business with you. A credit card issuer can cancel your card or a dentist might refuse to let you continue as a patient. Usually, even if one merchant stops doing business with you, you can find someone else who will do so, on a cash basis or even on credit.

2. Report the delinquent debt to a credit bureau. The fact that you are behind on your bills will likely end up on your credit record. You cannot stop this, short of always being current on all of your bills. While this is unfortunate, it still may not make sense to prioritize this particular bill first just because that collector is threatening to ruin your credit record.

Many creditors routinely report the status of all of their accounts each month to a credit bureau. When the account is turned over to a collection agency, this also may be indicated on your credit report. By the time a collection agency is threatening you about your credit report, your report may already include the fact that the debt is a number of months delinquent and has been turned over for collection. If that is true, the damage to your credit score has already happened. Paying now will not do much to improve your credit rating and failing to pay will not likely do much more damage to your credit rating. Moreover, if the creditor does not normally report information to a credit bureau, the creditor will not start with you.

3. Contact you to ask you to pay. Creditors will attempt to contact you to arrange for payments on overdue accounts. Your account may then be placed with debt collectors who also attempt to reach you. Traditionally most of these communications have been in writing or by phone, but some collectors now use email, text, or other types of communication. Below you will find several different sample letters that are effective in stopping a debt collector from contacting you if you want to avoid debt harassment. In addition, federal law prohibits third-party debt collectors from telling friends, relatives, employers or other third parties about the debt they claim you owe.

4. File a lawsuit to collect the debt. It is hard to predict whether a particular creditor will actually sue on a past-due debt. How aggressively a collection agency threatens suit is no indication whether the creditor will sue, even if the threat appears to come from an attorney.

If the creditor sues you, you have a right to respond and raise defenses. Doing so may stop the creditor from pursuing the case. However, failing to respond to a lawsuit or failing to show up in court when required may result in a win by default for the creditor.

If the creditor does pursue a lawsuit to its conclusion (or you do not respond to the lawsuit and the creditor wins by default) and the judge rules that you owe the debt, the unsecured debt becomes a court judgment. A court judgment is a higher priority debt than the previous unsecured debt. Post-judgment the creditor may be able to use powerful collection tools such as wage or bank account garnishment (depending on state law), as discussed in Chapter 21.

NINE WAYS TO STOP DEBT COLLECTION HARASSMENT

1. Investigate the collector. You may receive calls from scammers pretending to be debt collectors. Do not make any payments unless you are sure that the collector is legitimate. Investigate whether the person calling you is legitimate by asking for the caller's name, company, phone number, and business address. Simply asking these questions may discourage a phony debt collector from contacting you again.

Also check to see if your state licenses debt collectors and if the company that is contacting you is licensed. If your state does not license debt collectors, check the registry for a neighboring state. A few states also provide licensing information to the Nationwide Multistate Licensing System at www.nmlsconsumer access.org. That website will thus provide a few more states where the debt collector might be licensed.

2. The "stop contact" or "cease" letter. The simplest strategy to stop collection harassment is to write the collector a "stop contact" letter, also called a "cease" letter. Then the collector can only acknowledge the letter and notify you about legal steps the collector may take. This a federal right, however, and only applies to collection agencies hired by the creditor and does not apply to creditors collecting their own debts. But even creditors collecting their own debts will often honor such requests. Below is a sample letter:

[Your name]
[Your return address]

[Date]
[Debt collector name]
[Debt collector address]

Re: [Account number for the debt, if you have it]

Dear [Debt collector name],

I am responding to your contact about an alleged debt you are attempting to collect. You contacted me by [phone/mail], on [date]. You identified the alleged debt as [any information they gave you about the debt].

Please stop all communication with me and with this address about this alleged debt.

Thank you for your cooperation.

Sincerely,

[Your name]

Important: Even if debt collector stops contacting you because of the letter, you will still owe the debt.

Keep a copy of the letter and send the original by mail, return receipt requested. If a debt collector still continues to contact you, send another letter and once again keep a copy. Let them know that you are aware that they are violating the federal law by continuing to contact you. Keep a careful record of any letters and phone calls you receive after sending the letter, which will be helpful if you sue the debt collector.

You do not need a lawyer to send a cease letter. However, if a cease letter does not stop collection calls, a letter from a lawyer usually will. Collection agencies must stop contacting a consumer known to be represented by a lawyer, as long as the lawyer responds to the collection agency's inquiries. Even though this requirement does not apply to creditors collecting their own debts, these creditors usually honor such requests from a lawyer. A collector's lawyer is bound by legal ethics not to contact you if you are represented by a lawyer.

3. Stopping some types of collection contacts. Instead of stopping all types of collection communication, you may only want to stop some types of contacts and allow others.

If you are getting collection calls on your cell phone, these calls are probably being made by an autodialer. You can stop receiving such calls by clearly telling a live operator:

> "Please stop calling me at this number."

Both collection agencies and original creditors collecting their own debts have to stop calling your cell phone with an autodialer if you ask them to do so.

Whether you are being contacted on a cell phone or a landline, you can stop calls by collection agencies at inconvenient times or places by telling a live operator that the contacts are inconvenient. For example, you could say:

> "I am not allowed to receive this type of call at work. Please stop calling me at work."

> "Please don't call me before noon. Morning calls are not convenient."

> "Please don't call me at [phone number]. This location is not convenient."

Alternatively, you can tell a collector exactly when and how you would like to be contacted. For example:

> "Please only contact me at [phone number] after [time]. Calls at other times and numbers are not convenient."

You do not have to put these requests in writing. However, if you would like to do so, you can change the last line of the letter in #2 to tell the collector what type of communications are inconvenient or specify when and how you would like to be contacted.

4. The "exempt income" letter. If your only sources of income are state or federal government benefits, your income may be "exempt" or protected from collection. (See Chapter 21 for more information about whether your income is exempt.) If you inform the collector that government benefits are your only source of income, the collector may voluntarily stop contacting you about the alleged debt.

You can inform collectors over the phone if all of your income is exempt, and you can also send a letter like this one:

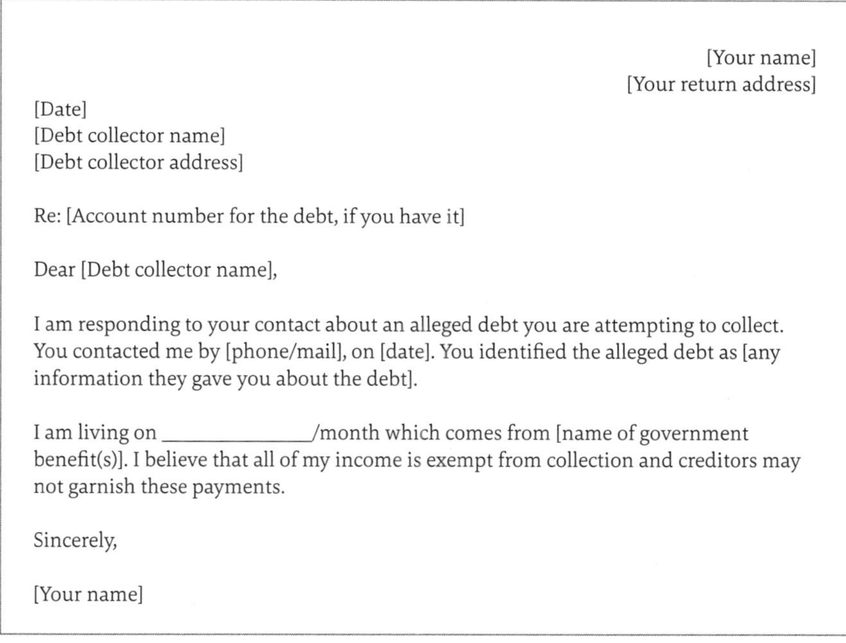

[Your name]
[Your return address]

[Date]
[Debt collector name]
[Debt collector address]

Re: [Account number for the debt, if you have it]

Dear [Debt collector name],

I am responding to your contact about an alleged debt you are attempting to collect. You contacted me by [phone/mail], on [date]. You identified the alleged debt as [any information they gave you about the debt].

I am living on ______________/month which comes from [name of government benefit(s)]. I believe that all of my income is exempt from collection and creditors may not garnish these payments.

Sincerely,

[Your name]

You may want to ask in the letter or a separate letter that the debt collector stop contacting you—see #2, above, for a stop contact or cease letter. Keep a copy of any letters that you send. It is best to send the letter by mail, return receipt requested.

5. The "verification" letter. Often it is not even clear what debt a collector is calling you about, and in that case you should never pay the collector, at least not until you obtain more information. Federal law gives you the right to obtain a verification of a debt from a third-party collector if you send a letter within thirty days of receiving the first written notice from the third-party collector. However, if you have questions, you can still send a verification letter even after the thirty-day period has passed. The collector may still respond.

This sample letter outlines some of the different types of information you might request about the debt—you typically do *not* need to ask for all this information:

[Your name]
[Your return address]

[Date]
[Debt collector name]
[Debt collector address]

Re: [Account number for the debt, if you have it]

Dear [Debt collector name]:

I am responding to your contact about an alleged debt you are trying to collect. You contacted me by [phone/mail], on [date] and identified the alleged debt as [any information they gave you about the debt].

Please supply the information below so that I can be fully informed about the alleged debt:

Why you think I owe the debt and to whom I owe it, including:
- The name and address of the creditor to whom the alleged debt is currently owed.
- The name and address of the original creditor and any other names used.
- A copy of the original contract or other agreement.
- The name of any other person that is or was required to pay the alleged debt.

The amount and age of the debt, including:
- Provide a copy of the last billing statement sent to me by the original creditor.
- State the amount of the alleged debt when you obtained it.
- State the date when you obtained the alleged debt.
- Provide an itemized list of any alleged interest, fees, or charges since the last billing statement from the original creditor.
- Provide a copy of any agreement expressly authorizing such interest, fees, or additional charges.
- Provide an itemization showing any payments since the last billing statement from the original creditor.
- State when the creditor claims this debt became due and when it became delinquent.
- Identify the date of the last payment made on this account.
- State when you think the statute of limitations expires for this debt, and how you determined that.

Details about your authority to collect this debt, including:
- Provide the number of any license to collect debt in [insert name of the state where you live] and the name of the issuing agency.

- Provide the number of any license to collect debt in the state where you are located and the name of the issuing agency.

Please treat this debt as disputed until you provide the information requested.

Thank you for your cooperation.

Sincerely,

[Your name]

Keep a copy of any letters that you send. It is best to send the letter by mail, return receipt requested.

6. The "dispute" letter. If you do not think the debt is yours, you should send the collector a dispute letter. Collectors make a lot of mistakes, and disputing the debt may resolve the matter. The letter also stops collection contacts until they send you more information verifying the debt. Here is a sample letter.

Your name]
[Your return address]

[Date]
[Debt collector name]
[Debt collector address]

Re: [Account number for the debt, if you have it]

Dear [Debt collector name],

I am responding to your contact about collecting an alleged debt. You contacted me by [phone/mail], on [date] and identified the alleged debt as [any information they gave you about the debt]. I do not have any responsibility for the debt you're trying to collect.

Record that I dispute having any obligation for this debt. If you stop your collection of this debt, and forward or return it to another company, please indicate to them that it is disputed. If you report it to a credit bureau (or have already done so), also report that the debt is disputed.

Thank you for your cooperation.

Sincerely,

[Your name]

Keep a copy of any letters that you send. It is best to send the letter by mail, return receipt requested.

You may want to ask the debt collector to stop contacting you in the same letter. Alternatively, you may wish to combine a dispute with a request for verification of certain information. See #2 and #5, above.

7. Negotiating work-out agreements. Too often consumers respond to debt harassment by agreeing to make payments to the collector. You should not pay even a little on a credit card, medical, or other unsecured debt if doing so means that you become delinquent on high priority debts like your rent or payments for a car that you need to get to work or have insufficient resources for essential family expenses like food.

Be wary of making a partial payment on old debts. You cannot be sued on a debt that is a certain number of years old (depending on your state). If you make even a small payment on an old bill, courts may treat this as starting the time period over again, and you can then be sued on the debt only because you made that payment.

Beware of debt settlement companies that promise to negotiate with the creditor on your behalf. These companies typically take large fees and often produce far less than promised. If you do decide to negotiate a payment plan for a reduced amount of the debt, you may get a better deal if you try to work with the creditor and not the debt collector.

Drive a hard bargain on any payment plan you agree to—ask them to reduce the debt. Be careful not to agree to pay more than you can afford. If you're uncomfortable negotiating on your own, ask a social worker, trusted friend, or relative to help you. Get any deal in writing. Also negotiate to get the creditor to help you with your credit report.

Determine, after reviewing Chapter 21, below, if you are judgment-proof. Being judgment proof means that if the creditor sues you, that creditor will not be able to seize your income or property because they are all exempt under your state law. If you are judgment-proof, offer the creditor little or nothing and just say that it is not worth pursuing you since you are judgment-proof. Also tell them to stop contacting you. See letters at items #2 and #4, above.

8. Complaining to the Consumer Financial Protection Bureau. Send a complaint about a debt collector to the Consumer Financial Protection Bureau at www.consumerfinance.gov/complaint. The agency will forward your complaint to the debt collector and work to get you a response, usually within fifteen days. You can also complain to the consumer protection division of your state attorney general's office. Some states offer mediation services for consumer disputes.

9. Bankruptcy. Filing your initial papers for personal bankruptcy instantly triggers the "automatic stay" that stops all collection activity against you. As a rule, a bankruptcy filing does not make sense where your only concern is debt harassment since you can stop the harassment with a cease contact letter (see #2, above). Save the bankruptcy option for when you have serious financial problems. For this reason, be wary of an attorney offering to file bankruptcy for you if the only problem is debt harassment.

ILLEGAL DEBT COLLECTION CONDUCT

The major law dealing with illegal debt collection conduct is the federal Fair Debt Collection Practices Act (known as the FDCPA). The FDCPA only applies to debt collectors (including collection attorneys), but state law may have similar requirements for the creditor's own collection efforts.

The FDCPA requires collection agencies to take certain actions, including:

- The collection agency must stop contacting you if you make a request in writing.
- The collection agency, in its initial communication or within five days, must send you a written notice identifying important information about the debt. If you raise a dispute in writing within thirty days of receiving that notice, the collector must suspend collection efforts on the disputed portion of the debt until the collector responds to the request.

The FDCPA also prohibits collection actions from engaging in harassing conduct, including:

- Communicating about a debt without your permission with your relatives, employers, friends, neighbors, or others. Collectors may contact attorneys, credit bureaus, cosigners, and your spouse. They can contact others only to locate you and cannot reveal that a debt is involved.
- Using any communication, language, or symbols on envelopes or postcards that indicate that the sender is in the debt collection business.
- Communicating with you at unusual or inconvenient times or places. The times 8:00 a.m. to 9:00 p.m. (in the time zone where you live) are generally considered convenient, but daytime contacts with a consumer known to work a night shift may be inconvenient.
- Contacting you at work if the collector should know that your employer prohibits personal calls.
- Contacting you if you are represented by a lawyer.
- Using obscene words, racial slurs, insulting remarks, or threats of violence.
- Telephoning repeatedly with intent to annoy, abuse, or harass.

- Falsely representing the character, amount, or legal status of a debt.
- Falsely stating or implying a lawyer's involvement.
- Stating that nonpayment will result in arrest, garnishment, or seizure of property or wages, unless such actions are lawful, and unless the collector fully intends to take such action.
- Failing to disclose in communications that the collector is attempting to collect a debt.
- Collecting fees or charges the collector is not entitled to collect.
- Depositing post-dated checks before their date.
- Creating the false impression that the collector is an affiliate or agent of the government.

Finding an Attorney to Sue a Debt Collector. You can sue debt collectors that violate your rights under federal law. If you win a lawsuit under the FDCPA, you can recover money for any injuries, up to $1000 in additional damages, and attorney fees.

The National Association of Consumer Advocates (NACA) is a good resource to help you find an attorney to take your case to sue a debt collector for illegal debt collection conduct. Members by state and specialty are listed at www.consumeradvocates.org/find-an-attorney. Families with low incomes and limited assets may be eligible to obtain free legal services from a neighborhood legal services office. You can find legal aid programs at www.lawhelp.org/find-help. Other consumers can contact local bar associations for attorney referrals.

What You Should Tell Your Attorney. Once you find an attorney, tell him or her how the collector's misconduct affected you and your family. Overcome any reluctance to discuss your feelings about the harassment, since the details will be critical in determining what kind of legal case you have. All symptoms of emotional distress should be discussed, including: anxiety, embarrassment, headaches, nausea, indignation, irritability, loss of sleep, and interference with family or work relationships. Did you consult a doctor? Were there illnesses brought on by the harassment?

Share information about out-of-pocket losses with your attorney, from loss of employment to loss of wages because of time taken off from work to try to resolve the dispute. In addition, telephone charges, transportation, medical bills, and counseling services could all be part of your actual damages. Keep a record of all expenses related to the collection effort.

Make a log of all collection contacts with as many details as possible for each contact: time, date, company, caller, and what was said. Abusive voicemail messages should not be erased, if at all possible.

3

What You Need to Know About Your Credit Report

TOPICS COVERED IN THIS CHAPTER

What Is a Credit Report and a Credit Score?

How Does Continued Non-Payment Affect Your Credit Score?

Who Sees Your Credit Report and Who Does Not?

How to Review Your Credit Report

Coping with a Bad Credit Report

Rebuilding Your Credit

Understanding how a credit report works and how it affects a family is critical in allowing families to make the right choices in dealing with their debts and other obligations. This chapter explains how information gets into your credit report, what information is in your report, who sees it, and how it affects your life.

WHAT IS A CREDIT REPORT AND A CREDIT SCORE?

Your credit report is a record of how you have borrowed and repaid debts. Almost every adult American has a credit file with each of the three major national credit bureaus: Experian, Equifax, and TransUnion. Many but not all creditors report each month electronically to one or more of the credit bureaus the status of each of their accounts.

Your credit report is a record of the history and description of the status of many of your credit accounts. It has basic personal information about you—Social Security number, birth date, current and former addresses, and employers. For many of your debts, the report will list the date you opened the account, the type of account (such as real estate, credit card, or installment), whether the account is currently open or has been closed, the monthly payment, the maximum credit limit, the latest activity on the account, the current balance, and any amounts that are past-due.

Each account includes a code that explains whether the account is current, thirty days past-due, sixty days past-due, or ninety days past-due, or if the account involves a repossession, charge off, turned over to a collection agency, or other collection activity. The report will also list under "inquiries" the names of creditors, employers, or insurers who have requested a copy of your credit report during the past year or two. It also includes creditors who have looked at your account to decide whether to send you an offer of new credit, but other creditors do not see this last item.

Many creditors will not even review all of this individual information in your account, but will only look at your credit score, which is a number that summarizes all the individual items in your credit report. There is no one scoring system that all credit bureaus and creditors use, but about 90% of the credit scores used by creditors are issued by FICO. A FICO credit score ranges from 350 to 900. FICO considers the following as detracting from your credit score:

- History of missed payments (about 35% of the score).
- High debt in comparison to your credit limits (about 30% of the score).
- Small number of years of credit history (about 15% of the score).
- Opening too many new accounts (about 10% of the score).
- All credit of the same type (about 10% of the score).

HOW DOES CONTINUED NON-PAYMENT AFFECT YOUR CREDIT SCORE?

Consumers are rightfully concerned about their credit score, but you should not respond to debt collector pressures by paying overdue low priority debts ahead of high priority ones just because of these concerns. An overdue bill may damage your credit score but very often the damage has already happened by the time a debt collector is threatening you.

For credit card debt and other debt payable on a monthly basis, the creditor will report the status of the debt to credit bureaus every month. The biggest impact on your credit score will be when the debt is reported as 30 or 60 days overdue. Once that happens, your score will not take that much more of a hit if you are 90, 120, or 150 days overdue.

When your account is referred to a collection agency, and the collection agency reports the debt to a credit bureau, your credit score will take another big hit. Continued non-payment after that will not change your score nearly as much. By the time you are being contacted by a debt collector, it is too late to do much about your credit score—rushing to pay the debt won't really help your score.

As a result, worry about your credit score should not be a reason to pay a late bill. Responding to the collector's pressure may not help your credit score, but it will put at risk payments on higher priority debts, whose non-payment will have far more serious consequences. Also, if you pay off a debt that was already reported by a collector, the collection item will show in your report as "paid," but your credit report will still show that the debt was in collection. If you want that information removed, you must get the collector's written agreement to delete it and not all collectors will agree to do so.

Typically, hospitals, doctors, and other medical providers will not report your debt to a credit reporting agency. It is only if and when a medical debt is turned over to a collection agency that many—but not all—collection agencies will report the overdue debt to a credit bureau. In addition, the three major credit bureaus have agreed not to include any report on medical debt if that debt has been outstanding for less than six months. Reporting of a medical debt over six months will hurt your credit score. But after that first report, continued non-payment to the collection agency will not affect your score much.

Most utilities will not report your delinquencies to a credit bureau until they say the bill is uncollectible. Until then there may be no adverse impact on your credit score to be late in paying gas, electric, landline telephone, or water bills.

Landlords are unlikely to report overdue rent to a credit bureau, but particularly larger landlords are likely to report problems with tenants to special tenant screening companies that landlords use to evaluate applicants. Thus your rent payments are less likely to affect your credit score than your ability to find another apartment.

In a significant development, the Big Three credit bureaus are not reporting the vast majority of public records, such as collection lawsuits, court judgments against you, and tax liens. Of course, the creditor or collector seeking payment may already have reported the overdue debt to the credit bureau, even if a public record about that debt (for example, judgment or lien) is not reported by the credit bureau.

Most negative information stays on your credit report for seven years, and then the credit bureau must remove it from your report. Bankruptcies stay on your report for ten years from the date of filing.

WHO SEES YOUR CREDIT REPORT AND WHO DOES NOT?

While your credit report will affect you in a surprising number of situations, it will not affect many other aspects of your life. You can expect that your report will be viewed by the following:

- *Creditors* when you apply for credit. A low score can mean you will be denied credit or pay a higher interest rate.
- *Employers* in most states to evaluate you for hiring, promotions, and other employment purposes. This is somewhat limited in a number of states and cities, such as California, Colorado, Connecticut, the District of Columbia, Hawaii, Illinois, Maryland, Nevada, New York City, Oregon, Vermont, and Washington.
- *Government agencies* trying to collect child support and when considering your eligibility for public assistance.
- *Insurance companies* using special credit scores for homeowners and auto insurance.
- *Landlords* when deciding whether to rent an apartment to you.
- *Utilities* are more commonly reviewing your credit score to determine whether to charge you a security deposit—not as to whether to provide you service.

Your credit report should not be a problem in the following situations:

- *Your application for federal student loans and grants.* Except for parents, graduate students, and professional school students applying for PLUS loans or anyone applying for a private student loan.
- *Your credit report will not damage your friends or relations, and need not even affect your spouse.* For example, a creditor is not allowed to look at your credit record if your spouse, child, or parent applies for credit and they are not relying on your income or assets.
- *Your reputation in the community.* No one can obtain your credit record for curiosity, gossip, or to determine your reputation. Your credit record is just between you and creditors—your neighbors and friends should never see it.
- *Divorce, child custody, immigration, and other legal proceedings.* Your credit report shouldn't be used in proceedings such as applications for citizenship or to register to vote.

HOW TO REVIEW YOUR CREDIT REPORT

The first step in learning about your credit report is to order copies from the three major credit bureaus and read these reports carefully. Because there can be differences between the three major national credit bureaus, you should order your report from all three. You are entitled to one free copy of your report every year from each of the three major bureaus, but you must order from the centralized request service, and not from the individual credit bureaus:

- Call 877-322-8228;
- Go to www.annualcreditreport.com and click on "request your report through the mail," print out and complete the Annual Credit Report Request Form and mail it to Annual Credit Report Request Service, P.O. Box 105281, Atlanta, GA 30348-5281; or
- Order online at www.annualcreditreport.com.

The ordering process may be more difficult online because you will be asked security questions based on information in your report, which some people find hard to answer.

For your free report from each credit bureau, you can order all three at the same time, or stagger the three throughout the year. You need to provide your name, address, Social Security number, and date of birth. If you have moved in the last two years, you may have to provide your previous address.

The credit bureaus are also required to give you an additional free copy of your report if:

- You have been denied credit within the past sixty days;
- You are unemployed and will be applying for a job within the next sixty days;
- You are receiving public assistance;
- You have reason to believe that the file at the credit bureau contains inaccurate information due to fraud; or
- You have requested a fraud alert.

For free reports based on these reasons, contact the credit bureau directly: Equifax at 800-685-1111, www.equifax.com; Experian at 888-397-3742, www.experian.com; Trans Union at 888-916-8800, www.transunion.com.

You can also purchase a credit report. Federal law limits this to $12 per report, and in some states the maximum is even less. Colorado, Georgia, Maryland, Massachusetts, New Jersey, and Vermont resident can get an additional free report.

Getting Your Credit Score. Your free credit report will *not* come with your credit score. You have to specifically request your score, you may need to pay for it, and it may not even be based on the same scoring system as the score that your creditors use. But if a creditor rejects you or charges you a higher price for credit based on a credit score, it must give you a copy of that score and related information. Mortgage lenders are also required to give you information about your credit score for free. When you get your score, you will be sent the top four factors that most affect the score.

Beware Credit Monitoring and Other Subscription Products. Avoid monthly or annual subscription packages sold by the credit bureaus for credit monitoring or identity theft protection. They provide limited value, are not as effective as security freezes at preventing identity theft, and are expensive and over-priced. You can sometimes find credit monitoring and other services available for free. Sometimes expensive subscription plans are advertised as being initially free, so be careful what you sign up for!

COPING WITH A BAD CREDIT REPORT

Avoid Credit Repair Agencies, also called credit services, credit clinics, or similar names. Signing up with these agencies is almost always a really bad choice. They charge a hefty fee and usually cannot deliver what they promise. You generally can do a better job cleaning up your credit record at no cost, these agencies may even make matters worse for you or cause you legal problems.

Correct Errors in Your Report. When you have unpaid bills damaging your credit score, the last thing you want is inaccurate information in your credit file making matters worse. It is amazingly common to find incorrect information in your credit file, and you can take steps to correct this information.

After reviewing the report you received from each of the three major credit bureaus, send a written dispute to each credit bureau that has reported incorrect information. The credit bureau by law must investigate the entry and correct the mistakes. You can also dispute the error with the creditor that supplied the incorrect information to the credit bureau, but you should always make sure you dispute it also with the credit bureau in order to preserve your legal rights. Even if the credit bureau told you they are making the correction, after a period of time obtain another credit report to see if the correction was actually made or whether it has popped up again. Also send the first bureau's statement of correction to the other two bureaus to ensure it is corrected there too.

You can also send a statement to the credit bureau explaining damaging items. Credit bureaus are required to accept these statements if they relate to why information in the report is inaccurate. They cannot charge to include this statement in your report.

Clean Up Your File with the Help of the Creditor. If the creditor insists information is accurate, the credit bureau is unlikely to change it in its files despite your written dispute. To prevail, you will have to convince the creditor supplying the information. Give the creditor whatever proof you have.

If your debt is in fact delinquent, you can try to improve your credit report by entering into an agreement with the creditor to pay all or some of the debt, up front or in installments. But you should get the creditor's *written* agreement to inform the credit bureau to delete any reference to the debt ever being delinquent—otherwise the fact that you were previously delinquent will stay on your report. Another option is for the creditor to agree not to affirm the debt after you dispute it with the credit bureau. The bureau must remove the information if the creditor who supplied it does not affirm it is correct.

Prevent Identity Theft. Just as you do not want inaccurate information on your report, you do not want negative information caused by an identity thief using your Social Security number and credit history to open new credit, cell phone, or other accounts, and then default on those accounts. Below are listed three ways to protect your credit report from identity theft.

The first way is to place a "security freeze" on your credit history, that prevents your credit history from being shared with potential creditors. If your credit files are frozen, a thief will probably not be able to get credit in your name. A new federal law makes security freezes free of charge. If you need to apply for credit, you can ask that the freeze be temporarily lifted.

A second way is to place a fraud alert on your credit report. A fraud alert is a statement added to your report asking creditors to check with you before issuing credit. It requires creditors to take steps to verify the applicant's identity. This is a less effective than a security freeze in preventing identity theft.

When a credit bureau receives your fraud alert request, it notifies the other major credit bureaus to also initiate a fraud alert. An initial fraud alert lasts one year. An extended alert lasts seven years and requires you to provide additional information, including an identity theft report from an appropriate law enforcement agency.

A third approach is to place a credit "lock" on your report. A credit "lock" is a product that prevents creditors from accessing your credit report, similar to a security freeze. However, it is a voluntary product not governed by federal or state law, so you have fewer legal rights if something goes wrong with the lock.

Shop Around for the Best Credit Offer. Predatory lenders look for consumers with blemished credit records to take unfair advantage with extraordinarily bad credit terms. Do not fall victim, but shop around. You will be surprised at how much better terms you may find even with your blemished credit record. The same credit score may be treated very differently by different creditors.

Don't be afraid to shop for the best credit because you are worried that too many inquiries will lower your credit score. For some types of credit, such as mortgages or car loans, the credit scoring systems count multiple inquiries during a certain time period, such as 14 or 30 days, as only one inquiry because the system assumes you are shopping around. Even when a credit scoring system counts a large number of inquiries against you, it will have only a small impact on your score. Getting affordable credit and paying it off each month will outweigh any harm caused by too many inquiries.

Explain the Reason for a Low Credit Score. When applying for a credit card for example, you will not have an opportunity to explain why your credit score is not representative of your creditworthiness. But other situations will allow you to do so, for example when applying for employment, for rental housing, for insurance, or for a mortgage. For example, you can explain that loss of a job due to an illness caused an old default, but you are healthy now and re-employed. Some businesses will listen to your explanations while others will not. Keep trying until you find someone who will accept your explanation.

Rely on Someone Else's Credit Score. If a husband and wife are seeking credit, and only one spouse has a bad credit record, you can apply in the name of the other spouse, relying exclusively on that spouse's income and assets. Then the creditor is not allowed to look at the other spouse's bad credit record. Another option is to apply for credit with a co-signer with a better credit score, but remember that the co-signer will be liable on the debt if you do not pay.

REBUILDING YOUR CREDIT

Do Not Rush Into New Credit Just to Build Your Credit Score. It is tempting to rebuild credit by getting new credit and making timely payments. You should not start trying to get new credit during times of financial difficulty simply to improve your credit report. This is likely to take your attention away from paying high priority debts first. Definitely do not obtain credit from a creditor advertising "easy credit" or "no credit history required." Many of these offers are rip-offs from lenders preying on consumers who fear that they cannot get traditional forms of credit. One of the most important steps you can take to cope with a bad credit history is to avoid getting deeper in debt during the bad times.

Stabilize Your Situation. In the long run, the most important thing for you to do to reestablish a good credit rating is stabilize your employment, income, and debts. This will prevent new delinquencies from being reported. While your past delinquencies can stay on your record as long as seven years, creditors are likely to ignore older debt problems if your situation becomes stable and if you start paying your present obligations.

Once you get back on track, each year your older debt problems will have less of an impact on your ability to obtain credit. Seven years will come around sooner than you might think, and then there will be no record of those past problems at all. If your financial problems are behind you, your credit record problems will not go away immediately. Be patient. Your credit profile will improve over time.

Establish New Credit Accounts (with Caution). You can improve your credit by getting new credit and paying it back on time. But be careful. Avoid causing yourself more problems by getting unaffordable high-rate credit. One way to avoid this trap is to wait until you are offered a credit card with reasonable terms. You may get credit card offers even though you have a negative credit history, but these offers may be for expensive subprime cards that offer little credit and charge high fees.

Another approach is to get a secured credit card, offered by some banks and other creditors. These cards require that you keep a cash balance with the card issuer and draw down on this amount. You need to be very careful in selecting a secured card because some offers are bad deals.

Finally, if you decide to get new credit, be sure that the creditor you use actually reports account information to a credit bureau. If not, your hard work to pay back the credit will not be reflected in your report.

4

Collection Lawsuits

TOPICS COVERED IN THIS CHAPTER

WILL THE COLLECTOR ACTUALLY SUE YOU?

If you are in default on a debt, the creditor *can* sue you to collect the money owed. The important question though is whether it *will* sue you. Often, the answer is "no," even in cases where the collector repeatedly threatens to sue. The following may indicate that a collector will *not* sue:

- If your home or car is collateral on a loan, the creditor is more likely to foreclose or repossess than sue. A lawsuit is slow, expensive, and may not even succeed in recovering money from the defendant. Home mortgage and auto lenders instead will seize their collateral and sell it.
- Many collectors rarely sue on debts under $1,000 and some don't sue unless a debt is much higher than that.
- If you dispute the debt and threaten to raise a reasonable defense. The collector not only has to factor in the value of your claim, but also the time and expense to resolve the case.

- When you are making small payments, even if they are less than the collector demands.
- When that collector has no history of filing suit. Check with the local court records to see if the entity that is collecting on the debt or its law firm file lawsuits to collect money from consumers.

CAN YOU WIN THE LAWSUIT?

You will lose any lawsuit if you do not respond to the lawsuit properly. If you do respond properly within time deadlines, and raise reasonable defenses, you have a good chance of winning or of the creditor dropping the lawsuit. The stronger your defenses, the better your chances.

One predictor of your chances of winning is whether you are sued by the original creditor or by a "debt buyer." Debt buyers purchase thousands of debts at a time from a creditor, and have little information about each account when they sue. Most people don't respond to debt buyer lawsuits—which can be filed by the thousand—so the debt buyer often wins by "default." But debt buyers are paper tigers. They may fold if you raise good defenses and counterclaims, force them to produce evidence that they own the debt, and force them to produce the credit contract and account statements.

Collectors also pay little attention when they file lawsuits to collect on consumer debt. Their paperwork is often sloppy or incomplete. Pointing out these errors can throw the lawsuit out. Whether brought by the debt buyer or original creditor, trying a case may cost the collector more than they could ever recover and just by contesting the case you can lead them to dropping the lawsuit.

HOW TO RESPOND TO A COLLECTOR'S LAWSUIT

Always Pick Up Your Certified Mail and Accept Notices About Court Actions. You will not escape the consequences of a lawsuit by hiding from notices about that action.

Get Professional Advice. Fighting back and raising legitimate defenses and claims against a collector can erase some or all of your debt, and a lawyer's involvement may significantly improve your outcome. Chapter 1 includes tips on finding an affordable lawyer.

If you cannot get the advice you need from a lawyer, see if a self-help manual has been written for your state on how to defend a lawsuit. Make sure you get a manual for *your* state. Check with the clerk of your local court, local library, or bookstore.

You may be able to get help from the clerk of the court. Court offices are not just for lawyers—you have as much right to ask questions as someone with a law degree. It is the court clerk's job to provide assistance, but in some busy courts, clerks may not be very helpful. While in others, the advice they give may not be accurate. You may find that the officers in the individual courtrooms are more accurate than the employees in the clerk's office. Ask several clerks the same question and compare their answers. Write down the clerk's name and the answer you received.

Some "Help" Will Just Get You into More Trouble. Unfortunately, some companies advertise bogus products to help you defend a collection action or otherwise deal with debt. These products are expensive, do not work, and worst of all, prevent you from properly defending the collection action.

For example, some companies offer—for a hefty fee—to explain how to eliminate any debt, such as by offering you a "bond for discharge of debt" or a "redemption certificate" or explaining that "monetized" debt need not be paid. These are all bogus. Other than a self-help book from the local bar association, a legal services office, or similar entity, do not pay for non-attorney help.

Be careful even with lawyers who advertise they can help you avoid debt. Some are not even licensed as lawyers. Many will take your money and do nothing. Others will file faulty responses to your lawsuit which, in some cases, may cause you to lose valuable rights and defenses. Contact your local bar association if you are unsure whether someone is really a lawyer and to see if there are complaints filed against the lawyer.

Carefully Read All Court Documents You Receive. The collector must file a document with the court to start a lawsuit. Usually, this is called "the petition" or "the complaint"—this chapter uses the term "complaint." The complaint asks the court to enter an order or judgment that you owe the collector a certain amount of money.

Along with the complaint, the collector usually must prepare another document to be delivered to you, informing you that a lawsuit has been filed against you. It is often called a "summons" or "original notice" and this chapter uses the term "summons." The summons usually tells you what the collector wants and the actions you must take to respond to the lawsuit, including the deadline for responding.

In some states a sheriff or constable must personally deliver the summons to you or an adult member of your household. In other states, mailing it to you is sufficient. Dropping the summons on your doorstep is not sufficient.

The summons tells you the steps to take to respond to a lawsuit *for that particular court.* Do not assume that a response that is appropriate for one type of court will be correct for another court or another type of case. Instead, read the instructions on the summons or seek help from the clerk's office. Be especially careful to meet the deadlines. The court may not accept responses received after the deadline.

To avoid the collector winning the lawsuit without your having a chance to defend it (called "winning by default"), you *must* follow the instructions on the summons and meet all deadlines, whether the deadline is to appear at a hearing, file an answer, or file an appearance. Often the collector has little or no evidence to present to the court, and is just hoping you will not respond, so that the collector can win by default. When the collector wins by default, the collector will be granted whatever it requested, even if it was not owed that amount.

Check Which Court Is Hearing the Case. Direct all questions and your responsive documents to the correct court—the court that issued the summons. Collectors usually sue in "small claims court," designed to decide claims for relatively small amounts of money. For example, the small claims court might only handle cases involving $5,000 or less. Other states have different limits. Small claims courts' procedure is usually simple and less formal and you do not need a lawyer. In a few states, lawyers are not even permitted. You should feel confident appearing in small claims court without a lawyer.

If the collector is seeking more money than the small claims court limit, the suit must be filed in the state's general, all-purpose court. These general courts have different names in different states, and follow more formal procedures. Collectors are represented by lawyers and formal legal rules apply. Although you may represent yourself in this type of court (this is sometimes called appearing "*pro se*" or "*pro per*"), your wisest course may be to hire a lawyer to represent you.

How to Answer the Summons. The summons tells you that you must appear at a hearing, file a written response, or file an appearance at the clerk's office. Pay special attention to any deadline for a written response in the summons. If the summons has both a deadline for a written response and a date to appear in court, you must file your written response by the deadline or you may risk losing by default and having your court date canceled.

If the summons requests you to appear at the hearing, it will usually specify a time, date, and place for the hearing. In more formal courts, a hearing typically will not be scheduled immediately, without allowing time for you to file a written answer. In some states, hearings are scheduled right away for small claims courts cases.

A summons often tells you to file a written "answer" to the summons (sometimes called an "appearance") within a certain number of days, usually less than thirty. Although the summons may say "appear and defend," this may not mean that you must physically appear on the date mentioned, but rather that only a written document must be filed with the court by that date.

Many small claims courts that require written answers will provide prepared answer forms, which only need to be signed and returned to the court clerk. The answer form states that the defendant (you) deny the plaintiff's (the collector's) claim. You should return these by the appropriate deadline if you wish to dispute the case. Other small claims courts require no written answer.

In more formal courts, there are usually no prepared answer forms, and the answer should usually be written by a lawyer and include reasons why you deny that you owe the money. You may draft an answer on your own without a lawyer, but you should do your best to follow the court's procedural requirements. Although answers not written by lawyers are accepted by courts, they may be found insufficient on technical grounds.

Most courts require that you send a copy of the answer and any other document you file with the court to the collector or the collector's lawyer. Indicate on the original court document filed with the court clerk that a copy was mailed to the collector or its lawyer. Keep a copy of the documents you file.

If you need more time to find a lawyer or to prepare an answer, a time extension is usually allowed, either by written agreement with the collector's attorney or by court order. If you reach an agreement for an extension of time (or any other type of agreement) with the collector's attorney, confirm the agreement in writing.

If you reach an informal agreement to settle the whole case with the collector, you should still file an appearance and answer. Collectors have been known to proceed with a case and take a default judgment despite having reached an agreement with you. Any agreement should be in writing and include a statement that the collector will drop its lawsuit. The safest course is to file a copy of the written agreement with the court clerk to be entered into the court record.

Promptly Answer a Collector's Requests for Admissions. A favorite collector tactic is to send you a document that asks you to admit to many facts about the case, including that you owe all the money it seeks. This is a trick, because if you do not answer within the time limit, the law says that you have admitted these requests to be true! That way the collector can win the case without any evidence and without even a hearing—even if you do not owe the money. Failure to respond to the request for admissions can mean that you have lost the case before it even started.

Respond to *all* questions in the request for admissions, respond by the time deadline, and deny any facts that are not true or where you think they might not be true. You can also say you do not have knowledge about a fact, so you cannot admit or deny it. If you miss the deadline to respond, ask the court to give you more time—the court may or may not do so.

COMMON DEFENSES TO RAISE

The facts of each case are different, and each state has its own laws. Here are some common defenses:

The Lawsuit Was Brought in the Wrong Court. If you are not sued in the county where you live or where you signed the contract with the creditor, the action is illegal because it was brought in the wrong court.

The Collector Has Not Proved It Owns the Debt. The collector has the burden to prove not only that you owe the money, but that you owe the money to this collector. If it cannot do so, you should win the case.

Many collection cases are not brought by the company to which you first owed the debt (such as a credit card issuer), but by someone who has allegedly bought the debt, called "a debt buyer." Ask that the debt buyer prove that your debt has been properly transferred to it. Amazingly, debt buyers often do not have that proof. It may produce a document indicating it bought thousands of accounts and state that the list of those accounts, including yours, is on a computer tape. This is meaningless until the debt buyer produces the computer tape and shows that your account is one of the accounts on that computer tape.

The Collector Has Not Presented Your Credit Contract in Court. Collectors often sue you based upon a contract you entered into with the creditor and then ask the court to make you pay not just the amount owed, but also interest, late charges, and attorney fees—all as provided for in the contract. To recover on the contract like this, the collector must produce the contract. Make sure the collector produces in court the actual contract you agreed to, and not some standard form agreement with no evidence that it was the one you entered into with the creditor. If the collector cannot do so, it may lose the right to collect attorney fees, late charges, and interest, and may even lose the right to recover on the debt.

If the collector cannot produce the actual contract, it may sue for money on some other theory. For example, it may say that it sent a statement of how much you owed and you did not object. An attorney will be helpful in advising you whether that theory is valid, but this theory should not allow the collector to recover attorney fees and interest based upon a contract, because no contract has been proved.

The Debt Is Too Old to Be Collected. Some debts are so old that they cannot be collected in court (in legalese, this referred to as "that the statute of limitations has run"). If you do not raise this with the court, the collector will win, even if the debt is too old. There is no one simple rule as to when a debt is too old to collect in court. The time period varies by state and even by the type of lawsuit being brought. The time period might be as short as three or four years, but it can be five or more years. On a very old debt, it is risky to make a partial payment or say in writing that you owe the debt, because this can start the time period running all over again.

Someone Else Incurred the Debt or You Are Only an Authorized User. You are only liable for your debts and not for someone else's (unless you are a co-signer or otherwise guaranteed payment.) This means that you are not liable if someone forged your name or used your credit card without your authority (under federal law, you may be liable only up to $50). You are not liable if you are only an authorized user on a credit card. You are not liable for the debts of a family member who passed away (although the debts may be deducted from any inheritance you receive). You may not even be liable for your spouse's debts, depending on state law.

You Have Already Paid, Settled, or Discharged the Debt in Bankruptcy. Virtually all debts are eliminated by a bankruptcy and this is a defense to the lawsuit, as is that you have already paid the debt, paid more than the collector claims, or if you already settled the debt with the collector or the original creditor. Present whatever evidence you can to support your claim.

Where Money Is Sought After Your Car Was Repossessed. When your car is repossessed and sold, the creditor may claim that the sale proceeds did not pay off the debt and seek in court additional payment. You can challenge that the repossession and sale were not "commercially reasonable." Then the collector must prove that every aspect of its notice to you and the sale was commercially reasonable.

COMMON COUNTERCLAIMS TO RAISE

A defense is a reason you do not owe the money being sought. A counterclaim is a reason why the person suing owes you money. If your counterclaims are large enough, they wipe out everything you owe and even allow you to recover money from the collector. *These claims often are available even if your claim relates not to the collector's conduct, but that of the seller or original creditor.*

Sale of the goods or services. Many debts arise from the purchase of goods or services. Anything unfair, deceptive, or defective in the sale may lead to a counterclaim (other than when purchased with a credit card). The same is true if warranties are not honored or if goods or services are not delivered. Counterclaims may exist even if the car or other goods are sold "as is."

Credit terms. Anything that you find to be outrageous, unfair, or deceptive about the credit terms may form the basis of a valid claim. High-pressure tactics should also be challenged. In addition several laws, including the federal Truth in Lending Act, state installment sales laws, and other state credit legislation, create requirements as to what the creditor must tell you about a loan. These laws are technical in nature and you may need the assistance of a lawyer.

Debt collection tactics. Chapter 2 discusses what types of debt collection practices are illegal. Illegal collection practices often provide excellent counterclaims.

SPECIAL RIGHTS IF YOU ARE ACTIVE DUTY MILITARY

If you are sued while you are on active duty with the military, or within the first ninety days after you get off active duty, you can ask the court for a postponement or "stay" of the case. The lawsuit will not be dropped, but the case will not move ahead while the stay is in effect. Once the stay ends, you have to defend the case.

To request a stay, send a letter to the court explaining how your military duties prevent you from appearing in court, when you will be able to appear, and include a statement from your commanding officer that your current military duties prevent you from appearing in court and that military leave is not authorized for you. Once the court gets this letter, it must order a stay for at least ninety days. If you need more time, ask for it in the original letter, or send a second letter that includes the same information as the initial request. If the court refuses to give you a longer stay, it has to appoint a lawyer to represent you. A JAG Corps attorney may be able to help you ask for a stay.

Courts also have authority to stay enforcement of judgments, including orders for attachment and garnishment, against servicemembers. A court may stay collection of a judgment if it finds that military service impairs the servicemember's ability to comply with an order to pay the debt.

GOING TO COURT

Attend All Court Proceedings and Respond to All Papers You Receive. Attend all hearings that are scheduled in your case. If you don't show up, a default judgment will be entered against you even if you filed an answer or appearance earlier. If you cannot attend, send someone else to ask for a delay (usually called a "continuance") and explain the reasons why you could not attend the hearing that day (such as illness, family emergency, preexisting and unavoidable work conflict, or unusual transportation problems). In small claims court, you usually only have to go to court once to resolve the case.

Whenever possible, let the collector or the collector's attorney know in advance if you have a good reason for not attending the hearing. Often, they will agree to a delay in the case. If a delay is agreed to, you should put it in writing in the form of a letter confirming the agreement.

Summary Judgment. In more formal courts, either side can ask for a judgment before the trial even begins if there are no important facts in dispute. This is usually called a "motion for summary judgment." If you receive a copy of a motion for summary judgment, you must respond to it or the collector may automatically win the case. Describe all facts that you dispute that relate to whether this collector has the right to obtain a court order against you for the debt. Most courts require the disputed facts to be stated in affidavits signed under oath by people who have first-hand knowledge of the facts. When you file a response, always send a copy to the collector's lawyer.

Preparing for a Court Hearing. At the hearing both sides tell their story to a judge or magistrate. In many small claims courts, the hearing is informal. Usually, the collector first explains why it is suing. Make sure the collector gives the judge a copy of the credit contract as well as the accounting records showing any missed payments. If the collector is not the original creditor to whom you owed the money, make sure the collector shows sufficient paperwork that it in fact is the current owner of the debt.

You then present your response. Be as prepared as much as possible, preferably with the advice of an attorney. Here are some tips to help you prepare:

- ***Bring all relevant documents.*** This is usually your only chance to present documents, and courts pay a lot of attention to written documents. Try to have extra copies available, because the court and the collector will keep copies of the documents you present.
- ***Bring witnesses if there are any.*** Witness testimony may be important, especially if the witnesses are not friends or relatives. For example, if the dispute is about an item which does not work properly, a mechanic or another witness can testify from their own experience in using that item.

- *Do not rely on written statements of your witnesses* because the court usually will not allow them into evidence. Have the witnesses attend the trial.
- *Consider going to court beforehand* to get a feel for where the courtroom is, how the court works, how people dress, when to stand, how to tell when your case is called, where you sit during the hearing, whether a microphone is used and how to use it, the judge's personality, whether an interpreter is available, etc.
- *Take a companion to the actual hearing* if possible to offer emotional support, to give you feedback and other help, keep track of your documents, and offer a second opinion if you must respond on the spot to a settlement offer.
- *Prepare a written chronological report of events in advance,* as well as a checklist of points to make and documents to give to the court, and bring these with you. Judges may be impatient if you are disorganized. Mention all of your defenses and counterclaims.
- *Assume that the judge has not read any of the documents* already presented to the court and does not know the facts of the case. Start at the beginning and tell your story in a clear and organized fashion in the order it happened.
- *Do not be afraid to be forceful, but do not make personal attacks on individuals,* including lawyers, witnesses, or the judge. A display of anger will usually hurt you more than it helps.

BE WARY OF DEALS YOU MAY BE ASKED TO MAKE IN THE COURT'S HALLWAY

The collector's attorney will not want to try the case and often will collar you in the courtroom hallway and try to work out a deal. The collector's attorney is only looking out for the collector's interest and not yours. No matter what the collector's attorney tells you, he is not there to help you and may be taking unfair advantage of you or even misrepresenting things to you.

In return for giving up your right to go to court and force the collector to try the case, expect a substantial reduction in the amount you owe. The more defenses you have, the greater the reduction. Also think about other settlement terms. You might ask the collector to help you clean up your credit record, by agreeing in writing that it will no longer report that you owe the money and that the collector will tell the original creditor to do the same.

If you reach an informal agreement with the collector, still go to court to file an appearance and answer. The safest course is to file a copy of the written agreement with the court clerk to be entered into the court record. No deal should include a judgment being entered against you unless you have no defense and the settlement is for only a fraction of the debt owed. A judgment being entered against you is a very dangerous thing—this can lead to your bank account being frozen and the amount owed whisked out of your account in no time.

If you are not represented by an attorney, you may need help to determine if a settlement is fair and reasonable. Never agree to anything you do not understand or which you think is unfair. Whenever possible, wait until you see the terms of the settlement in writing before you agree.

UNDOING A DEFAULT JUDGMENT

Not filing a written answer or appearance within the specified time, or by failing to attend the hearing, or by missing other deadlines may lose you the opportunity to raise your defenses. This is usually called a "default." Try never to lose by default.

If a default has been entered against you, you may be able to still get another chance to be heard by asking the court to "set aside" the default. A default can be set aside only for specific reasons and most often only within a short time after the judgment has been entered into the court records.

To set aside the default, act immediately, presenting reasons why you did not respond to the court case, such as that you never knew about the case or that there were unavoidable circumstances that made you unable to answer within the required time. In some courts, you will also have to tell the court briefly about your defenses or counterclaims so that the court will know that you have a chance to get a different result if the default is lifted. Usually, a request to "remove," "lift," or "set aside" a default has to be made to the court in writing. A copy of your request should be mailed to the collector's lawyer.

It is difficult to set aside a default. You can avoid the problem by instead responding on time to all deadlines.

YOUR APPEAL RIGHTS

If you lose the case, the court will issue a judgment against you, and this judgment may allow the collector to seize your money and other property. If you lose a lawsuit at the first court level, you can appeal to a higher level. For cases heard in small claims court, this usually means appealing to the state's trial court. If a case starts in a more formal trial court, the losing party can appeal to another court which has power to hear appeals.

Deadlines for filing an appeal are generally short and strictly enforced. You may need professional assistance in bringing an appeal. The costs of an appeal vary widely but can be significant. Typical costs include a filing fee, fees for a transcript of the trial, and posting a bond to cover the judgment being appealed. In some circumstances, a party unable to afford these fees can request that some of them be waived.

Appeals rarely involve a completely new presentation of the case. Usually, an appeals court will review the case only on the facts presented in the court below it.

5

Taking Out New Loans to Pay for Old Debts

TOPICS COVERED IN THIS CHAPTER

Borrowing from Friends and Relatives

Borrowing Against Your Home

New Credit Card Debt

Credit Union Loans

Loans to Avoid

You may be tempted to take out a new loan to deal with pressing debt, or to refinance some of your old loans into new loans that offer relief at least in the short run. This chapter examines when this makes sense and particularly when it does not.

Taking on new debt when you cannot make all your payments is a serious undertaking that can get you into a lot more trouble, so you must carefully consider a number of factors before deciding to do so. There are at least four guiding principles in deciding whether to take on a new loan to pay off old debt:

- ***How pressing is payment on the old debt?*** You should never take on new debt just to get a debt collector off your back. The debt collector's job is to push you into raising cash to pay them, whether it is in your interest to do so or not. There are easier ways to stop debt harassment, as described in Chapter 2. This book also has many other suggestions on dealing with specific types of debts to make them less pressing.
- ***Is your financial difficulty short-term or permanent?*** If you cannot pay off your debts today and your situation is not likely to change in the future, taking on new debt is almost always a bad idea. If you cannot make ends meet now, things will get even worse in the future when you have to pay off not only the amount you borrowed on the new loan, but also additional interest

and fees, which can be substantial. On the other hand, if extraordinary expenses or a temporary drop in income is the problem, you are more likely to be able to repay a new loan that gets you through a difficult time.

- ***Is the new loan a good deal or a rip-off?*** Predatory lenders target those in financial distress and offer credit at much worse terms than you could find if you shop around. Particularly because you are looking for a loan when you in difficulty, you have to look out for hidden fees, bogus broker fees, shady paperwork, and more. On the other hand, you will be ahead of the game if you can find a new loan whose total cost to you will be less than your existing loans, considering interest, points, fees, and the like.
- ***Does non-payment of the new loan get you in more trouble than non-payment of the old debt?*** Do not, for example, take out a home mortgage to pay for medical bills. Non-payment of the mortgage will lead to foreclosure of your home, while non-payment of the medical bills might only lead to debt collection (which you can stop) and a reduced credit score, where the damage to your score will be less than if there is a foreclosure.

BORROWING FROM FRIENDS AND RELATIVES

Borrowing from friends and relatives avoids some of the worst traps in borrowing from a lender. You are unlikely to be charged high interest rates or hit with hidden charges or have to put up your home or car as collateral. There is nothing wrong with asking for and accepting help to get you through a tough period. Of course, if your troubles are of a more long-term nature, both you and your friends or family will have to recognize the money is more likely to be a gift than a loan.

Problems also arise when your friends or relatives face their own financial difficulties and they either request the money back or refuse to loan you anything more when you have counted on their assistance. Debts can also cause tension between you and your friends or relatives.

Some creditors will push you to get a friend or relative to cosign on an account when you are facing financial problems. You should avoid this whenever possible. The person who cosigns will be on the hook with you. Your financial problems become theirs if you cannot afford to pay.

BORROWING AGAINST YOUR HOME

There are a number of ways in which you can be tempted to use your equity in your home to obtain new loans to help pay off old debt:

- ***Taking out a second mortgage on your home.*** You then have to make monthly payments both on your first and your second mortgage, and you can lose your home if you fail to make payments on either loan.
- ***Taking out a home equity line of credit.*** When you need cash, you draw on your line of credit, up to a set amount. You must make minimum payments each month and risk losing your home if you do not make those payments.
- ***Refinancing your existing mortgage loan with a higher principal balance, either with your existing or a different lender.*** If this increases your monthly payment, this also increases your risk of foreclosure.
- ***Borrowing through a reverse mortgage.*** Because of its complexity, this option is described in its own chapter, Chapter 6.

Borrowing against your home is risky, but might make sense in the right circumstances and with the right loan. Home mortgages tend to have lower interest rates and more years to repay than other types of loans. Drawing on your home equity may make sense if your financial situation is pressing. If you can refinance your existing mortgage with a new loan that reduces your net borrowing costs, you might even be able to borrow additional cash while not increasing your monthly payments.

On the other hand, even though interest rates may be relatively low, closing costs, points, fees, and the like may mean that your initial outlay on your mortgage loan will be quite expensive, and be a bad idea, particularly if you are soon going to sell your home (or lose it to foreclosure).

Taking out a new loan secured by your home also puts your home at risk for foreclosure. If you are in danger of losing your car, you may be tempted to pay off your car loan by taking out a second mortgage on your home. You may save your car temporarily this way, but you are putting your home in danger.

Avoiding the Wrong Mortgage Loans. Avoid predatory lenders that hide from you the true cost of their high cost mortgage loans. Be wary of anyone who initiates contact with you about a mortgage loan, particularly if the solicitation does not come from an established financial institution in your community. Definitely avoid anyone who solicits loans during a "door-to-door" visit of your home. It is very expensive to market anything door to door. The odds are that someone coming to the house to help bail you out of trouble will really get you deeper into it.

Another way to avoid scams is never to let a contractor or sales person arrange financing for you and to be wary of mortgage brokers. Some brokers will find loans for you which involve big commissions for them rather than good loans for you. If your regular banker or credit union cannot help you, odds are that lenders and brokers who advertise cannot get you a good deal either. Be wary also of a lender who claims that you will get a tax advantage from a mortgage loan. Most consumers will not be able to deduct their mortgage interest, particularly if it is a second mortgage.

When in doubt, check out the lender with your state's attorney general, banking commission, or consumer complaint hotline. Check both the business name and the names of any individual you are dealing with because some individuals change their company names repeatedly to avoid becoming well-known in the community. If you do check on a business, remember that the absence of complaints does not necessarily mean that the business is reputable.

Read and Understand the Mortgage Terms. Your lender should give you a closing disclosure with the final terms and charges. Read it carefully to see if it is consistent with what the lender promised you. You can always walk away before signing loan papers, even at the last minute. Definitely walk away if the lender tries to change the loan terms or costs from what you had originally discussed. Also be wary of a lender who refuses to put in writing any oral promises upon which you are relying.

Never sign documents without knowing what is in them. When in doubt, get help in reviewing the loan papers *before* you sign anything. A lender that is unwilling to let you get outside help before you sign the loan documents should not be trusted. You might contact a HUD-certified housing counselor for advice on the loan terms. You can find such a counselor by calling HUD at 800-569-4287 (TDD 800-877-8339) or by going to www.hud.gov.

Walk away from a bad deal even at the last minute. If loan terms are not favorable, shop around for another loan. Within three business days after receiving your loan application, the lender or mortgage broker must provide you with a loan estimate of closing costs. You should use this form to compare loans from different lenders. You can also negotiate with the lender by asking for something better.

A mortgage loan can involve great potential for hidden costs, fees, and other unfair loan terms. Even some reputable lenders make unfair loans. When you take out a home mortgage loan, you often have to pay points (one point equals 1% of the loan amount; for example, 1% of $100,000 equal $1,000), closing costs, a broker's fee, or other up front charges. Closing costs may include title services, the preparation of closing documents, obtaining credit reports and appraisals, property surveys, inspections, loan processing, and other similar charges. All of these fees provide lenders with an opportunity to take advantage of unwary borrowers by including excessive, duplicative, or unearned fees. The best way to avoid being ripped off is to shop around. By comparing the fees from different lenders, you'll be able to weed out those trying to charge excessive fees.

On the other hand, do not expect to get the best mortgage loan rates if you have a blemished credit score. If your credit score is under 670, most lenders will consider you to be a riskier borrower and will probably charge you more. Shop around even if your credit score is low. Do not assume that the deal offered by a particular lender is the best you can do. Up to one-third of all borrowers that end up with higher cost loans actually qualified for lower cost products.

Charges for Insurance. Watch out for unnecessary insurance added on to the mortgage. An example is credit-life and credit-accident and health insurance or similar products called "debt cancellation" or "suspension" contracts. These policies or contracts are supposed to pay off your loan or suspend your payments for a period of time if certain conditions occur, such as you are in an accident. Typically, you will be asked to initial a statement that you want this coverage. You should not do so. Only a small percentage of these insurance premiums or charges are ever paid out as losses to policyholders.

These policies or contracts also are often designed so that companies can deny coverage to you even when it appears that you have a valid claim. For example, the insurance may not cover many types of accidents that you would expect it to cover. Any benefits that are paid out are limited to the amount left on the loan, so you never actually receive much, if anything. You will be better off buying insurance from other sources.

When Refinancing, Are You Saving Money or Throwing It Away? You may be tempted to obtain a new mortgage loan that pays off your old mortgage and other debts as well. One question is whether—when taking all costs and charges into consideration—you are paying more on the new loan than you were paying on the old ones. This is important not just because it is a bad deal, but also because if you could not make payments on your old debts, how can you avoid foreclosure by consistently paying on a refinanced loan that is more expensive than what you were paying before?

It is not simply comparing the cost of your old mortgage and other debt with the cost of a new mortgage that refinances the old debt. Compare the stated interest rates you are paying under the old and new loans. And then it gets more complicated. Your new loan will likely include closing costs, title insurance, points, fees, and other charges that must be considered. These might have been included under your old loan as well, *but* you have already paid for those. The question is how much more you will be paying now that you have to pay all those fees and charges all over again for the new loan. The paperwork you get with the new loan will set out all the fees and charges and some of these will be included in the

"Annual Percentage Rate" or "APR" disclosed on the new loan. Is this higher than the stated interest rates on the old loans?

Next you have to consider any prepayment penalties for paying off the old loan early. These penalties are an added cost of the new loan. You also have to consider whether your old loan was at a fixed rate and your new loan at a variable rate (or vice versa). Fixed rate loans are safer because variable rate loans can suddenly increase your monthly payment. In addition, some variable rate loans are set up so that they will almost always increase the interest rate shortly after you take on the loan.

Another question to ask is whether you have taken on added risk with a refinanced home mortgage, because your monthly carrying costs secured by your home go up, and thus put you at risk of foreclosure. This is a bad idea if your increased payments on the refinanced loan (and increased risk of foreclosure) are caused by it paying off medical bills or credit card debt that are relatively low priority loans.

When You Change Your Mind About Taking Out a New Mortgage Loan. You can always back out of a mortgage loan before the papers are signed. Never feel embarrassed to walk away from a bad loan even if you are being pressured. Some lenders will threaten penalties or legal action if you do not sign papers that have already been prepared. These threats are false because you have no responsibility to pay until you sign the papers.

Except for the original mortgage to purchase your home, federal law gives you the right to cancel your mortgage loan for any reason for three business days from the date you sign the papers. If you wish to cancel, do so in writing before the deadline. The lender is required to give you a form for this purpose, but you do not need to use that form. You can just send a signed, dated letter indicating your desire to cancel. Keep a copy and send it return receipt requested.

NEW CREDIT CARD DEBT

One way you might be tempted pay off old debts is by increasing your credit card debt. This can be done directly by paying debt collectors using your credit card or by taking out a cash advance using the card. Some card issuers send you convenience checks which allow you to pay for your debts with the check. The hitch is that these checks come with high interest rates. Or you can pay for debts using the card indirectly by putting on your card necessities you usually pay in cash, freeing up cash to pay down your debts. If you have maxed out your card, this may involve taking out new credit cards.

One advantage of using a new credit card debt to pay off old debt is that it typically does not take your home or other property as security. You can avoid default by making the minimum payment each month, and even if you default completely, your income, bank accounts, and assets are not at risk until you are successfully sued on the debt. Even then your income, bank accounts, and assets may be partially or fully exempt from seizure. See Chapter 21.

Another advantage of using credit card debt, as opposed to taking out a loan with your home as security, is that you can eliminate the debt in bankruptcy. Nevertheless, this may not be the case if you run up big bills on your credit card or take cash advances just before filing. Creditors have argued with some success that if you use a credit card at a time when you did not have the ability to repay, you have committed a fraud which prevents the debt from being eliminated in the bankruptcy process.

The downside of adding charges to credit cards is that cards have interest rates over 20% plus late charges and other fees. The more you put on your card, the harder it will be to pay off your card. When you max out your card, you will not be able to use it in emergencies, and may have to resort to even more expensive forms of credit.

Definitely do not put medical debt on a credit card if you cannot pay off the card right away. As explained in Chapter 11, medical debt will have lower interest rates than credit cards, will have less of an immediate impact on your credit score, and you are more likely to find ways to reduce or delay payment of medical debt compared to credit card debt. Chapter 23 also explains that you should similarly not put debts owed to the IRS on your credit card.

Other of your debts, even high priority debts, can often be handled in a smarter way than putting the full amount on your credit card. Before using your card to pay down real estate taxes, federal student loans, or home mortgages, refer to the relevant chapters in this book about ways to reduce, delay, or even eliminate payments on those debts.

On the other hand, using your credit card is clearly better than taking out a payday, auto title, or similar high-interest small loan. In addition, use your card if that is the only way to pay for necessities or to pay high priority debt that cannot be otherwise delayed or paid out in installments.

Credit Cards to Avoid. Whatever the merits of using a credit card to pay off debts, you should definitely avoid certain cards that will just get you into trouble. Subprime credit cards, often advertised as helping those with "bad credit" generally come with very high interest rates, expensive fees often loaded onto your balance on card opening, and low credit limits.

It may make sense when it is time to build up your credit record to take on a secured credit card that allows you a credit limit up to the amount you have on deposit in a particular bank account. But such a secured card makes no sense if you are looking to borrow additional funds. If you are going to use the card to pay down your debts, it makes more sense to just take the money in your bank account and pay down the debt.

Avoid any credit card that takes your home as security. The more you put on your card, the more your home is at risk of foreclosure.

Credit cards offering zero interest should also be used with caution. No interest is charged during the promotional period, but the full balance must be paid off by the end of that period. If you do not pay the full balance by the end of the period, you are retroactively charged interest at a high rate for the whole promotional period. Suddenly you owe not only the remaining balance, but as much as an extra $1,000 or $2,000 on top of it.

No matter the type of card, also steer away from any card that charges high interest rates or high fees—late fees, over-the-limit fees, annual fees, membership fees, cash advance fees, balance transfer fees, even fees for buying lottery tickets with a card. No matter what card you have, make sure your monthly charges do not automatically include junk purchases, such as credit protection, credit report monitoring, travel clubs, and other similar offers. They will cost you a lot, but provide little benefit.

CREDIT UNION LOANS

Particularly where you have maxed out your credit cards, another option to obtain a new loan is from a credit union. Credit unions that have a federal charter are restricted to charging you a maximum of 18% interest. An exception is made for loans up to six months in length for amounts between $200 and $1,000. These loans can be made at 28% plus a $20 application fee.

Credit union loans are generally not secured by any of your collateral, and thus are safer than mortgage loans. They also have lower interest rates than payday, installment, or other predatory loan products found in the marketplace today. On the other hand, just as with a credit card, credit union loans should not be used to pay off medical debt or other low priority debt with low interest rates, and also should not be used to pay off even higher priority debt that can be handled in a better way.

LOANS TO AVOID

Chapter 7 lists ways to get into even more trouble when you are in financial difficulty. Described there are a number of types of loans that you should avoid, even if you have pressing debts:

- Payday loans;
- Auto title pawns;
- High cost installment loans and other high cost small loans;
- Disadvantageous refinancing and consolidation loans;
- Tax time loans;
- Overdraft loans;
- Subprime credit cards.

6

Reverse Mortgages

TOPICS COVERED IN THIS CHAPTER

OVERVIEW

For households struggling to pay all their bills, and where at least one of the homeowner's is 62 years old, one option to consider is a reverse mortgage. A reverse mortgage differs from a traditional mortgage because the borrower receives a lump sum or a stream of payments, but does not make monthly payments on the loan. Instead, over time the balance due on the reverse mortgage grows, as the monthly interest and other fees are added to the loan balance. The loan is called a "reverse" mortgage because the balance goes up over time, instead of going down. No payment is due on the reverse mortgage until the borrower dies or moves out of the home, at which time the full loan balance becomes due.

A reverse mortgage can provide cash to the homeowner, eliminate payments on a pre-existing mortgage, and allow the homeowner to remain in the home (as long as the homeowner can pay for property taxes, insurance, and necessary repairs). Contrary to some misconceptions, the borrower on a reverse mortgage is still the owner of their home, although the lender will be permitted to foreclose if the loan is not paid off within a period of time after the borrower's death.

Reverse mortgages are not for most homeowners. They are expensive—high closing costs and interest rates higher than standard prime mortgages. Once the equity has been drawn down through a reverse mortgage, it may not be possible to draw against the home again to pay for necessary expenses, such as home health care. Worst of all, some reverse mortgages are scams, so borrowers should get all the information up front and seek independent advice before signing on the dotted line.

This chapter explains who is eligible, how the reverse mortgage operates, the impact of others in the household, and whether it is a good idea.

WHO SHOULD CONSIDER A REVERSE MORTGAGE?

Most reverse mortgages are insured by the Federal Housing Administration (FHA) under its Home Equity Conversion Mortgage (HECM) program. There are only a very small number of reverse mortgage loans made by private lenders outside of the HECM program. You are only eligible for a HECM (government insured) reverse mortgage on your home if you meet *all* of these requirements:

- You are at least 62 years old.
- The home is worth significantly more than any outstanding mortgages on the home.
- The home must be your principal residence, where you reside the majority of the year.
- You are not delinquent on any federal student loans or other federal debt.
- You have the financial resources to make timely payments on property taxes, insurance, homeowner association fees, and the like.
- You have a counseling session with an independent HUD-approved counselor.

The home itself must be one of the following:

- A single family home;
- A manufactured home meeting FHA requirements;
- A HUD-approved condominium project;
- A two-to-four unit home and you occupy one of the units.

Even if you meet all these requirements, a reverse mortgage may not be right for you—depending on your financial situation, it may be the wrong choice. If after reading this chapter you are still interested in a reverse mortgage, the first step is to discuss it with a reverse mortgage counselor approved by the U.S. Department of Housing and Urban Development (HUD). This counseling is required before moving forward with a loan application with any lender participating in the

HECM program. Find a counselor by calling 800-569-4287 or by going to www.hud.gov/offices/hsg/sfh/hecm/hecmlist.cfm.

Counseling is required, but it is also important to help you understand the reverse mortgage product. A counselor will help you weigh other financial and loan options, the costs and benefits of a reverse mortgage, its impact on your eligibility for federal and state benefits, and how the reverse mortgage affects others in the household and your heirs. If you do not fully explore all these issues with the HUD-approved counselor, you should seek alternative counseling sources, because the reverse mortgage decision can be very complex and will have a significant effect on your future.

You should be highly skeptical of any reverse mortgage offered you that is not in the HECM program or that does not involve a HUD-approved counselor. In fact, California and a few other states require counseling prior to obtaining any reverse mortgage.

You also should be very wary of any reverse mortgage lender that is aggressively pitching to you through advertising or over the telephone. Lenders sometimes push reverse mortgages on borrowers without accurately describing all of the downsides of the loan. After talking to a HUD-approved counselor, reach out to a lender participating in the HECM program. A list of such lenders is available on www.hud.gov/program_offices/housing/sfh/lender/lenderlist.

HOW THE REVERSE MORTGAGE WORKS

A reverse mortgage loan is secured by your home, like any mortgage, meaning the lender can foreclose if the loan terms are violated. Unlike most mortgages, there are no monthly payments on the reverse mortgage loan. Instead the loan comes due (with interest) upon a triggering event, typically the borrower passing away or permanently moving out of the home.

There is a limit to how much you can borrow on your home, called the "principal limit." Your principal limit will be higher the older you are, the higher the value of your home (after subtracting current mortgage balances), and the lower current interest rates are. If you are married or own the home with another person, the principal limit is based on the *younger* of the two of you.

Your ability to obtain a reverse mortgage is much less tied to your credit score than a traditional mortgage, and you should not be refused a reverse mortgage or pay higher interest because you have low income or a blemished credit rating. Since there are no monthly payments on the loan itself, the lender is not concerned about your ability to make such mortgage payments.

The lender will be checking to see that you have the resources (either on your own or through the reverse mortgage loan) to keep up with certain "property charges"—your property taxes, homeowner's insurance, any homeowner association (HOA) dues, and necessary home repairs. You are required to pay these property charges during the term of the reverse mortgage. Failure to pay them will result in foreclosure and loss of the home. Many people have gotten into trouble on their reverse mortgage loan because they're not used to paying the property taxes or insurance once a year when they come due, especially if they had a standard mortgage previously that collected the money through an escrow. It is important to understand this obligation to pay the taxes and insurance yourself, and to set aside the necessary funds.

There are a number of ways you can receive the proceeds from a reverse mortgage loan. If you have a pre-existing mortgage on your home, the reverse mortgage loan proceeds first will be used to pay off that mortgage. If your present mortgage balance is high, paying off this mortgage will significantly reduce what is available to you from your reverse mortgage loan. On the other hand, the reverse mortgage will free up your cash since you will no longer have to make mortgage payments on the pre-existing mortgage. Remember, you will still have to pay property taxes, homeowner's insurance, necessary repairs, and other home-related expenses.

After paying off any existing mortgage and any other liens on the house, the rest of your reverse mortgage loan can be paid to you in any of the following ways:

- One large payment of the full principal limit given to you in cash. This almost never makes sense. Instead, delay receiving as much of your reverse mortgage proceeds as possible to help you pay for future expenses—such as unexpected home repairs, health care expenses, and other emergencies.
- A fixed monthly payment paid to you for a set period of time. This is called a "term" plan.
- A fixed monthly payment (smaller than the "term plan" amount) that will be paid to you like an annuity for as long as you survive and live in the home (called a "tenure" plan).
- As a line of credit to be drawn at your convenience. Only draw down what you need, and then interest and fees will only accrue on what you draw on. Not only will the remaining principal limit be available for you for future use, but that limit will increase over time. The line of credit option may also be combined with a term or tenure plan.

Your reverse mortgage loan balance (how much you owe) is based on how much the reverse mortgage lender pays you, including paying off your mortgage and any other loans. Also added to the loan balance are any upfront closing costs similar to a regular mortgage—origination fees, real estate closing costs, and an initial mortgage insurance premium. As the lender gives you more money, your loan balance with the lender goes up. The balance also goes up each month with interest charges, mortgage insurance premiums and servicing fees being added to the balance.

The loan balance eventually must be repaid either when you pass away or when you move out of the house. The balance can be paid off by selling your home, by refinancing, or by letting the lender foreclose. If it is sold at foreclosure for more than the reverse mortgage loan balance, your heirs get to keep the difference. If it is sold for less, your heirs will not have to pay anything, because the difference is covered by mortgage insurance.

You can also sell your home before you pass away or move out, and if you do, you would be able to keep the difference if the sale price is greater than the reverse mortgage loan balance at the time of sale. If the house is sold through a foreclosure or short sale for less than the loan balance, you will not owe anything, again because of the mortgage insurance.

REVERSE MORTGAGES ARE STILL SUBJECT TO EARLY FORECLOSURE

A reverse mortgage lender may foreclose on your home if you do not keep up with property taxes, homeowner's insurance, homeowner association fees, and the like. If you fail to pay these charges, the lender may pay them for you and, if you can't repay the lender in a relatively short time period, may foreclose. At the time you take out the reverse mortgage, if the lender determines that you do not have the ability or willingness to pay these property charges, they may require you to set aside funds from the available reverse mortgage's principal limit to pay these expenses during your expected loan term.

You must keep your home well maintained or risk foreclosure. Your lender will tell you, at the time you take out the reverse mortgage, which repairs you must make. The lender may even set aside some of your borrowing limit to ensure the repairs are made. The lender may then foreclose if you do not make the required repairs. You also later may have to keep the home up to standard if the home deteriorates over time or is later damaged. Where the needed repairs are caused by a fire or other covered incident, your homeowner's insurance should help pay.

Your loan comes due and the lender may foreclose if you are absent from your home for the majority of the year. If your absence is health-related, you can be absent for a full year before foreclosure can begin. For example, the loan will become due if you move to another home or permanently move to a nursing home.

In a foreclosure, the lender will sell your home. If it is sold for less than your current loan balance, you will not owe the difference. If it is sold for more than the loan balance, you or your heirs will get the surplus funds.

WHAT ABOUT MY SPOUSE OR PARTNER?

Usually you should add your spouse or partner as a co-borrower on the reverse mortgage. Then you both are responsible for the loan and both receive the benefits. As a co-borrower, your spouse or partner will be able to live in the home even if you no longer live there, such as if you have to move to a nursing facility. Even after you pass away, the co-borrower will be able to draw funds from an available line of credit (if the reverse mortgage is structured that way), as long as he or she remains in the house.

According to HUD rules (after August 2014), a spouse who is not a co-borrower on the reverse mortgage is still protected and can remain in the home after the borrower leaves the house or passes on. The spouse has to be living with you continuously from when you took out the loan until when you pass on or leave the home. Also you have to have been married before you took out the loan. Even then, a non-borrowing spouse cannot receive loan proceeds after the borrower dies, which is a problem if you have been relying on such payments to make ends meet.

IS A REVERSE MORTGAGE A GOOD IDEA?

A reverse mortgage is not for most people, and much depends on why you need the money. Reverse mortgages do not make sense to just pay off old credit card bills or medical debt, that may no longer even be charging interest and where the collector may never even sue you for the money.

On the other hand, the inability to pay your car loan, utility bills, or your regular mortgage can have devastating consequences, and the costs of a reverse mortgage may make sense if these risks are at play. But even then, this book provides you with other advice on dealing with these obligations, often making resort to a reverse mortgage unnecessary. A reverse mortgage might also be considered if you are in a cycle of paying hundreds of percent interest on a series of small loans that are adding up to thousands of dollars of interest being paid every year—a reverse mortgage is a far cheaper alternative.

Once you take out a reverse mortgage, you may not be able to borrow on that value again (depending whether home values go up), when in the future you might need that home equity to pay, for example, for home health care. Other potential drawbacks to a reverse mortgage include:

- Reverse mortgage closing costs can be very high. Shop around for the loan with the smallest total fees. A reverse mortgage will be most costly, relatively speaking, if you continue to live in your home for only a few more years after taking out the loan.

- The amount of cash you get may not meet your needs. A 65-year-old whose home is worth $50,000 after deducing the outstanding mortgages may get only around $150 per month on a tenure mortgage. (This calculation depends on a variety of factors, including interest rates, home value, and the amount of the closing costs.) You are still responsible for paying the property taxes, insurance, general up-keep of the property, homeowner association fees, utilities, and other home-related expenses.
- You are paying interest, insurance, and servicing fees on a reverse mortgage loan, so that even if you do not draw down a lot of money, over time this loan obligation will grow. Then if you want to sell your home, you have to pay off a surprisingly large loan balance. It may mean that when you decide to sell, you have almost no remaining equity.
- A monthly reverse mortgage payment is not considered income. But if the loan proceeds are taken as a lump sum, while that money is in the debtor's hands it can be treated as an asset that could affect eligibility for means-tested government benefits like Supplemental Social Security Income, Medicaid, or food stamps. (Social Security payments are not affected.) Check with your benefits provider before taking out a reverse mortgage loan.
- Some shady lenders offer very unfair reverse mortgages or conventional mortgages that look like reverse mortgages. Only work with a reputable lender in an established program. As a rule, only sign up for a HECM reverse mortgage.
- A reverse mortgage may make it difficult to pass your home on to your heirs after your death. If your heirs want to keep the home they will need to pay off the amount due on the reverse mortgage. This is different from a regular mortgage, for which your heirs could simply keep making the monthly payments. At the time of your passing, the balance of the reverse mortgage may have grown to the point where there is little or no equity left to leave to your heirs. Using your home equity now and leaving less for your heirs may be the right decision if you need money now, but be aware of what it may mean for the future.

HOW DOES A REVERSE MORTGAGE STACK UP AGAINST A TRADITIONAL MORTGAGE, REFINANCING, OR HOME EQUITY LOAN?

There are other options beside a reverse mortgage to use your home as collateral to obtain loans to pay off your obligations—refinancing a first mortgage, a first or second mortgage, or a home equity line of credit. A reverse mortgage's advantage is that there is no monthly payment and there is looser underwriting as far as your income and credit-worthiness. The lender is not concerned whether you can make mortgage payments, and just wants to ensure you can pay for property taxes and insurance, either out of the reverse mortgage loan proceeds or otherwise. Also, upon foreclosure, with a reverse mortgage there is no risk of you or your heirs being required to pay a deficiency if the home is worth less than the mortgage's outstanding balance.

Interest rates and mortgage insurance for a reverse mortgage are generally higher than for other types of mortgages. With the exception of your spouse or your co-borrower, once you pass on or leave the house, those remaining in the house cannot stay—the house will be sold.

7

Choices to Avoid at All Costs

Below are "quick money" strategies that you should avoid at all costs. An entire industry of unscrupulous businesses exists to pressure you into making costly mistakes. These businesses know that people in financial distress often make desperate or poorly informed choices. They also know that people who feel that their options are limited are likely to be willing to overpay for credit and other services.

Unfortunately, even reputable companies operate businesses that take advantage of consumers in financial trouble. You cannot assume that because a company is well known or because it advertises on TV that it will give you a fair deal. Also be suspicious of companies that use names which are designed to create confusion about their identity, such as using the name "United States." Some companies use names very similar to legitimate organizations just to confuse you.

There are two cardinal rules to follow:

- If it seems too good to be true, it probably is.
- If you are in financial trouble, be wary of anyone seeking you out and offering you a way out of your problems. Most legitimate options wait for you to contact them.

The following list warns you to avoid twenty practices that may increase your financial problems, not solve them. This is not a complete list of scams. New scams constantly emerge, and old ones change form. The main message is that services aimed at people with bad credit or other financial problems are often rip-offs. If the services seem too good to be true, they probably are.

Debt Elimination Scams. These are internet offers to totally eliminate your debt. They are bogus, will just cost you money, and will prevent you from taking the proper steps to deal with your debts. See Chapter 12 for more on debt elimination.

Debt Settlement Offers. A whole industry advertises the ability to settle your debts for less than what you owe. They claim that you put away money each month in a special account and at some point they will settle the debt for the money in the account. This rarely happens—they rarely settle your debts, always take a lot of your money in fees, and get you into trouble with your creditors. Since your payments are going into a special account and do not go to the creditor, you will be subject to debt collection, negative reports to credit bureaus, and even collection lawsuits. More on problems with debt settlement is found in Chapter 12.

Foreclosure Rescue Scams and Sale and Lease Back of Your Home. Some scam operators read published foreclosure notices, and then seek out the homeowner with a plan to "rescue" the home. Other companies advertise "We Buy Houses"—stay away from them as well. Often these scammers buy your home at a low price (or for nothing at all) and lease it back to you, with promises that you can get the home in the future. You may not even know that in the mound of paperwork that you have sold them your home. You will be overpaying them for rent, and may never get your home back.

Rip-Off Reverse Mortgages. As explained in Chapter 6, reverse mortgages are complex loans that have benefits and costs. Evaluating whether to take out a reverse mortgage is a difficult decision and requires consultation with a knowledgeable nonprofit counselor. Both your home and a sizeable amount of money are at stake. For this reason, the federal government creates standards for legitimate reverse mortgages, called HECM mortgages. Be *extremely* suspect of any reverse mortgage offer that is not a HECM mortgage, because you risk losing not only a lot of money, but even your home.

Credit Repair. Credit repair agencies, sometimes called "credit services" or "credit clinics," offer to clean up your credit record. They charge a hefty fee and usually cannot deliver what they promise. You generally can do a better job cleaning up your own credit record at no cost. These agencies may even make matters worse for you or cause you legal problems.

Payday Lenders. Payday loans go by a variety of names, including "deferred presentment," "payday advances," "deferred deposits," or "check loans," and operate out of check cashers, over the internet, and elsewhere. They all work in the same way. You write a check or sign an authorization for the lender to take money out of your account electronically. The amount on the check equals the amount borrowed plus a fee. The check is due to be cashed or the electronic debit due to be initiated on your next payday or receipt of a government check.

Too often you will find that when it comes time to repay the loan, you do not have sufficient cash in your bank account or you need the funds there for more pressing purposes. You then have no choice but to roll over the loan into a new loan with a new fee. The effective annual rate of the loan is often as high as 400% or 700% or even higher. As you roll this loan over each time, the balance quickly grows, making it more and more difficult to repay. You become caught in a spiral of rolling over the loan each month, accumulating ever more fees and interest at astonishingly high interest rates.

Auto Title Lending. Auto title lending, often called "auto pawn," "auto title," or "auto equity" loans, are legal in some but not other states. You borrow money at very high interest rates (for example, 240% or 500%) and put up your car title as collateral for the loan. If you are unable to repay the loan when it becomes due or pay another fee to refinance the loan, your car will be repossessed and sold. Automobile title lending is not as simple and hassle-free as the title lenders advertise it to be. You can borrow money elsewhere at lower interest rates without endangering your car.

High Cost Installment Loans. There is a growing industry offering high cost loans of anywhere from $300 to $3,000 or more that you pay off in monthly installments over anywhere from six months to five years. These loans come in all kinds of shapes and sizes. Some are by licensed lenders in your state and charge interest rates in the 30% to 60% range. On top of that they may sell you overpriced credit insurance. The real risk with these loans is that very often these loans are rolled over into new loans when you have trouble paying them off with their high interest charges, meaning that your indebtedness grows to much more than you originally owed, and keeps growing each time you roll over the loan. Not to mention that your car or home might even be taken as collateral.

Other installment loans are sold over the internet and seek to avoid state regulation. Then the sky is the limit as to interest rates, which can be as high as several hundred percent. Make sure to look at the Annual Percentage Rate (APR). Avoid any loan with a high APR number—certainly any rate above 36%. Some high cost loans today are claiming to have a zero percent APR, but then charge high fees based on your outstanding balance. This is a sure sign of a predatory lender to be avoided at all costs.

Refinancing and Consolidation Loans. Any offer to consolidate your loans or refinance existing loans must be carefully considered. Too often the end result is that you are worse off than before. Your old low interest or no interest loans are turned into high interest loans. Prepayment penalties to pay off your old loans early are added to the new loan. Closing costs and other up-front charges and fees are also added to the new loan. Be especially wary of anyone who sought you out for the new loan or anyone that is not an established lender in your community.

If you have federal student loans, it is generally not a good idea to consolidate them into a private student loan. Federal student loans come with all kinds of rights, including rights to cancel the loan, defer any payment for a year or more, and payment plans that match your income. These rights are generally unavailable if you consolidate into a private loan. On the other hand, there are good reasons to consolidate federal student loans into a federal student consolidation loan. For more, see Chapter 13.

Student Loan Debt Relief Scams. For-profit private companies charge high fees to assist you in dealing with your student loans, when what you should do is contact your servicer to obtain relief at no charge. These companies prey on students to recover large fees for unnecessary work. See Chapter 13 for your rights to cancel, delay, or reduce student loan payments you can obtain directly by working with your servicer or the Department of Education.

Rent to Own. Appliances, furniture, electronic equipment, and even used cars are offered on a rent-to-own basis where you do not own the item until you consistently have made years of weekly or monthly payments, and where the effective interest rate on the purchase can be 300% or even 500%.

Auto Brokers. When you are having trouble keeping up with your auto loan or lease payments, these brokers offer to lease or sublease your car for you for a fee. The practice is illegal in many states. Moreover, the broker may try to keep payments it receives from the person using your car and may not even obtain permission from your creditor or lessor for the arrangement.

Subprime Credit Cards. Some credit cards marketed to those with low credit scores charge so many initial fees that 25% of the credit limit is already taken up by fees, and very high interest rates are then applied to the fees as well as any purchases. As a result, the effective interest rate on your credit card charges is much higher than you think it is or than is indicated by the disclosed interest rate.

Bouncing Checks and Postdated Checks. It is tempting to write a check or authorize an electronic debit when you have insufficient funds in your account to cover it. At best, you may hope to make a deposit before the check is cashed. At worst, you may be deliberately using the check payment as a way to make the creditor leave you alone for a few days.

Avoid this temptation. Bouncing checks is never the answer. You will be charged a hefty fee, often by both the bank and by the creditor each time the check is presented for payment. And creditors may present the same check for payment a number of times. You could also face criminal prosecution for fraud. Although you may be able to defend yourself successfully if you are prosecuted, it is better not to have to deal with this problem at all.

When in doubt, look up your account balance before writing a check or authorizing an electronic debit. Your balance may seem higher than it really is because other checks you have written have not yet been deducted from your account. If you have a joint account, coordinate your check writing carefully with any other person who has power to write checks and make withdrawals.

You might also be tempted to write a "postdated check," that is a check dated later than the date on which you write it. You do this assuming it will not be cashed until the date written on the check, when you hope to have sufficient funds in the account. Despite what you may think, the check can be cashed immediately and the bank need not wait until the date written on the check.

Instead, delay payment until you are sure you have sufficient funds in the account. That way you are not surprised that the check is cashed early. If things change in the interim, it is not too late to direct your funds to something else more important. And you avoid the cost of bouncing a check.

Using Overdrafts As Credit. Many banks and other financial institutions permit you to deliberately overdraw your account. The bank will honor a check, debit card payment, or ATM withdrawal even if you do not have sufficient money in the account. This is often an incredibly expensive way to pay your obligations.

Banks charge high fees for each overdraft, up to $35 per transaction. Some banks also charge a fee of up to $5 every day or $30 every few days until you repay the overdraft. Banks pay themselves back the amount of the overdraft and fees out of your next deposit, before you can use the money for other essential bills like your mortgage or utility payment. A $100 overdraft with a $30 fee has an interest rate of 780% if the overdraft lasts two weeks.

For ATM or one-time debt card transactions, the bank can only honor the payment and charge you a high fee if you affirmatively consent or "opt in" to this arrangement. Do not do so and revoke your consent if the bank already has gotten you to opt in.

Selling or Giving Away a Creditor's Collateral. You may have a car or other property that serves as collateral for a loan from one of your creditors. It is a bad idea to give away or sell a creditor's collateral without the creditor's permission. This is called "conversion" of collateral.

You may of course sell collateral if the sale price you receive is enough to pay off the existing loan. If the collateral is a car, typically you will need to pay off your loan and have the lender release the lien in order to give good title to the buyer. If you are selling the car to an individual, you may need to work with the lender to determine the amount of the payoff and the release of the lien in order to transfer title.

If you have already lost, given away, or sold collateral, you may be prosecuted for a criminal offense. A defense to a criminal prosecution is that your conduct was not intentional, that you did not understand that the property was collateral or that you did not know the consequences to the creditor of disposing of the property. In addition, most such prosecutions and lawsuits can be ended by payment of the value of the collateral either in installments or in a lump sum if you have it. Jail time is rarely or never imposed. Still, this is not a risk worth taking.

Get-Rich-Quick Schemes. Many products and jobs are advertised with the promise that you will make a lot of money quickly. These are almost always scams.

For example, real estate investment seminars are sold with the promise that you can make a bundle by buying and selling investment property. The reality is that the only one making a bundle is the person selling you the seminar. When seminars of this type are offered for free, the person running the seminar will usually aggressively try to sell you something very expensive.

A similar problem involves jobs which are offered with the promise of making quick financial returns. A common example is an advertisement with a bold heading such as **"Make up to $1,000 a week immediately—working at home."** The vast majority of these offers require payment of substantial "set up" or "one-time start-up" fees to a person or company that promises you a money-making plan in return. The company keeps these fees and you end up with no real way of making money.

8

Reducing Your Expenses

TOPICS COVERED IN THIS CHAPTER

Tips to Reduce Expenses Described Elsewhere in This Book
Saving Money on Insurance Coverages
Medical and Dental Care
Food Expenses
Appliances, Furniture, and Electronics
Check Cashing and Banking
Pressure-Related Shopping
Winter Holiday Cycle of Debt
Other Expenses

Cutting expenses is hard work and takes a lot of commitment. Work together with your family to understand the situation and to figure out ways to cut expenses. Think about putting away your credit cards, at least for a while, keeping only one to use for emergencies.

TIPS TO REDUCE EXPENSES DESCRIBED ELSEWHERE IN THIS BOOK

Important ways to save on expenses are described throughout this book, including:

- Lowering your mortgage payments (Chapter 17);
- Lowering your student loan payments (Chapter 13);
- Lowering your real estate taxes (Chapter 19);
- Lowering your costs for heat, electricity, telephone, and the internet (Chapter 15);
- Avoiding high cost loans and scams that prey on those in debt (Chapter 7);
- Reducing the size of fines, fees, and other criminal justice debt (Chapter 22);

- Delaying payment of low priority debts (Chapters 1, 11 and 12);
- Paying income taxes in installments (Chapter 23).

SAVING MONEY ON INSURANCE COVERAGES

Make sure you are not paying for automobile or homeowners insurance purchased by your lender when the lender thinks you do not have your own coverage. This lender-placed insurance is very expensive and offers less protection than insurance you purchase yourself. Cancel lender-placed insurance after binding your own insurance.

Unless your mortgage lender objects, reduce the cost of your homeowner's insurance by increasing your deductible, making sure your home is not insured for more than it will cost to replace, and by taking advantage of discounts the insurer offers for alarm systems or the like. Check with your agent about ways to reduce costs or shop around for a different insurance company.

Unless your auto lender objects, lower your premium by raising deductibles and getting rid of coverages you may not need, such as towing or alternative transportation, or even physical damage coverage for a very old car. Do you qualify for any insurance savings plans? Consider canceling and getting a refund for overpriced service contracts, GAP insurance, or other vehicle add-ons.

Private mortgage insurance (PMI) is usually initially required if the down payment on the loan used to purchase your house is less than 20% of the sale price. The insurance offers no protections to you—only to the lender. Once your home is worthy significantly more than your mortgage loan balance, the lender does not need PMI and it should be cancelled. Check with your servicer to see if you still have PMI and whether it should be cancelled.

Look into your life insurance and other insurance coverages with the help of a trustworthy insurance agent. You might convert a whole life policy to a term life policy in order to save money. Some policies may be "capped" or may include an option for deferring payments for a temporary period.

MEDICAL AND DENTAL CARE

Cut down on medical costs by obtaining low cost or no cost insurance that not only pays for some of your medical bills, but also reduces the size of your bills—medical providers charge insurers far lower rates than they charge an uninsured consumer.

Medicare. If you are 65 or older, make sure you are getting available Medicare benefits. A Medicare prescription drug program for seniors, Medicare Part D, is voluntary and lets you shop for a prescription drug provider from a number of private insurance companies. Selecting a plan that is favorable for you could save you a lot of money on drug costs. For those below 150% of the poverty line, Medicare Part D provides subsidies for premiums and co-payment for drugs. A number of programs also supplement Part D coverage.

For more information, visit www.medicare.gov. Both Justice in Aging (202-289-6976; www.justiceinaging.org) and the Center for Medicare Advocacy (860-456-7790; www.medicareadvocacy.org) are other excellent resources.

Subsidized Exchange or Marketplace Coverage. Many people are eligible to purchase health insurance in a marketplace called an "Exchange" or "Marketplace." Families with incomes up to 400% of the federal poverty level (in 2018, $64,920 for a family of two or $100,400 for a family of four, and higher in Hawaii and Alaska) receive tax credits to make this coverage more affordable. People in families with incomes up to 250% of the poverty line who are enrolled in certain Marketplace silver level plans receive subsidies to help them pay for out-of-pocket health care costs, such as deductibles and co-insurance.

For information on plan choices in each state, how insurance coverage works, and how to apply, visit www.healthcare.gov. There is one open enrollment period each year, but anyone losing their job, aging out of coverage under their parent's policy, or losing coverage because of other life events can enroll at any time during the year.

Medicaid. Apply for both subsidized Marketplace coverage and Medicaid coverage at the same time by going to www.healthcare.gov or calling 800-318-2596. You can also apply for Medicaid at your local public assistance office. If initially denied enrollment, you have appeal rights.

Eligibility for Medicaid varies from state to state and depends on family income and may also depend on family resources. Some states limit Medicaid to certain groups of people, such as pregnant women and children. However, people in many states automatically qualify as long as their income is 138% of the poverty line or below.

Sometimes you can get Medicaid for your children, even if you don't qualify. Medicaid's Early and Periodic Screening, Diagnostic and Treatment (EPSDT) requirements mandate coverage of a broad array of diagnostic, preventive, and treatment services for beneficiaries under age 21.

Children's Health Insurance Program (CHIP) and Other State Programs. CHIP provides health insurance to children in families with incomes that are above the Medicaid limit, often to 200% of the poverty line or higher. Each state program has its own rules. Check with your state health department to find out more information. Apply for CHIP at www.insurekidsnow.gov, www.healthcare.gov, or by calling 877-543-7669. In most states, you can apply for CHIP at the same time and location that you apply for Medicaid. If you have insurance coverage through your job but qualify as low income, your children may still be eligible for CHIP coverage.

Health Insurance for Young Adults. Health plans that offer coverage to the insured person's children must generally make coverage available until the children turn 26 years old. Children can join or remain on their parent's plan even if they are married, not living with their parents, or are financially independent.

Keeping Your Health Insurance After Losing Your Job. If you have recently left work at a private employer with more than 20 employees and were covered by your employer's health insurance, you may be able to keep that insurance, although you must pay the premium. This program is called COBRA. When your old employer contacts you about COBRA, you have 60 days to decide whether to pay the premium to keep the coverage. State-based insurance navigators can help you compare COBRA and Marketplace options to make an informed choice.

Other Medical Care Options. Some states have plans to assist with major medical expenses. When medical bills exceed a certain percentage of an applicant's household income, the balance of the bill above that percentage is reimbursed. Local service clubs also sometimes have programs designed to meet particular needs. The best known is the Lions Club, which helps to purchase eyeglasses for children.

Medical Prescriptions. When receiving a prescription, ask whether a less expensive generic drug can be substituted. Many states have programs to assist seniors in paying for prescription drugs. Medicaid covers some prescriptions for most beneficiaries and, as discussed above in the Medicare section, a Medicare prescription drug program, Medicare Part D, provides subsidies if you qualify as low income.

Doctors may have free samples of medication available. Most drug companies run programs which provide reduced cost or free medication for those in need. Search online for patient assistance programs based on the name of the specific drug or the drug's manufacturer. Hospitals run by the Department of Veterans Affairs generally provide medicine to veterans for a small fee.

Low Cost Dental Care. Some dental care may be covered by your health insurance policy, and some state Medicaid programs include dental coverage for adults.

All must provide children's dental checkups. Community college dental hygiene programs and university dental schools may provide free or low cost services as part of their teaching program. Some hospitals have low cost oral surgery clinics.

Avoiding Out-of-Network Medical Providers. If you have insurance, make sure that, for non-emergency care, your medical provider is within your insurance network, and thus covered by your insurance. Confirming in-network status is complicated because individual doctors, surgeons, or other medical service providers (such as radiologists, anesthesiologists, or pathologists) may be out-of-network even if a hospital is listed as in-network. A few states have protections for out-of-network charges in certain situations, such as emergency room care or for health maintenance organization (HMO) patients.

Financial Assistance/Charity Care. Nonprofit hospitals have a duty to provide charity care or financial assistance to low-income patients because of their tax-exempt status. The Affordable Care Act requires all nonprofit hospitals to have a written financial assistance policy that explains who is eligible and how to apply for financial assistance.

FOOD EXPENSES

You can save money on food in all kinds of ways, including:

- Use coupons to save money on products you would generally buy.
- Shop at different stores to get the best prices.
- Plan menus ahead of time instead of at the grocery store.
- Try not to shop when you're hungry.
- Shop without your kids if possible.
- Buy cheaper store brands.
- Eat at home whenever possible.
- Pack a lunch for school or work rather than eating out.
- Bring coffee to work or drink free coffee at your office if it's available.
- Check out food pantries.
- Determine your eligibility for food stamps (SNAP), WIC, and free and reduced school lunches. (See Chapter 9.)

APPLIANCES, FURNITURE, AND ELECTRONICS

A trap you can fall into when purchasing appliances, furniture, electronic items, or the like, is to use a rent-to-own company. You might think that this is the only way you can purchase these items, when in fact it is by far the most expensive possible way. Rent-to-own contracts have hidden interest rates of hundreds or even thousands of percent interest. You may even unknowingly be paying for used goods. Miss one payment and you could forfeit the item completely.

Credit card interest rate even as high as 25% are much better deals. If you have maxed out your cards, shop around for a store that will give you credit. The best approach might be to put away money each month until you can purchase with cash the product while it is on sale. The store might even have a layaway policy that might work for you. Shop around instead of falling victim to rent-to-own.

CHECK CASHING AND BANKING

If you regularly use a check-cashing service and also frequently purchase money orders or certified checks, it is amazing how fast these costs can add up. You may have good reasons not to use a bank—difficulties opening an account, no bank in your community, fear of high bounced check and debit card fees, not to mention other bank fees, and the threat that a creditor could seize your bank account.

Some of these problems can be solved. Avoid bank overdraft fees by not writing checks, instead using your debit card, and making sure the bank has not signed you up for an overdraft plan that hits you with big fees while it honors your ATM or debit card purchases even with insufficient funds in your account. Look also for credit unions and smaller banks that often have fewer fees than bigger banks. Social Security and many other federal benefits are generally immune from seizure by creditors, as described in Chapter 21.

Another option is prepaid cards. Social Security and Supplemental Security Income can be deposited to the Direct Express prepaid card. Call 888-741-1115 or visit www.USDirectExpress.com to sign up. For other government benefits, including unemployment insurance and child support payments, ask the program office if a prepaid card is available. Some larger employers also offer payroll cards as a way of directly depositing wages to employees without bank accounts. Ask your employer if one is available. Other prepaid cards are network-branded (such as Visa, MasterCard, or American Express) and can be used to make purchases, get cash back from a purchase, and withdraw cash at an ATM just like bank accounts. However, like bank debit cards, these are *not* credit cards.

With all these cards, your benefits or wages are automatically added to the card each month and you can mostly use the card just like a debit card. There will be no check writing privileges. Typically, you can obtain a prepaid card even with a poor credit history.

Shop around for cards that have low fees (including low fees to use an ATM machine), figure out how money will get onto the card if it is not being directly deposited by your employer or the government, determine how to check the balance on your card, and never sign up for overdraft "protection."

PRESSURE-RELATED SHOPPING

Don't respond to financial pressures and anxiety by going shopping, buying items you don't need, or overspending. Spending for unnecessary items or through credit card cash advances can be a problem if you later file for bankruptcy. You may lose your right to erase those debts in bankruptcy if the creditor can prove that you ran up your credit cards knowing that you could not pay them back.

Counseling groups in many communities can help you address uncontrollable spending habits. A credit counselor can usually point you in the right direction. Try to think about what influences your decision to shop and what to buy. Pause before you buy, creating a "cooling off period" or "time out" before you spend.

WINTER HOLIDAY CYCLE OF DEBT

Many consumers overspend on credit for Christmas or other winter holidays, hoping to repay their debt through their tax refund. This can be costly. When you are paying someone to loan you money early against your tax refund or when you put the purchases on your credit card and then you don't get the refund you were expecting, you may then carry a large credit balance for months.

In addition, you may be better off having higher take-home pay through the year so you do not get behind on important payments each month, rather than waiting to get a tax refund early the following year. Try also to be careful about holiday presents. Can you, for example, work out an agreement with your relatives that you will only buy gifts for the children, not for the adults? Or that you will all limit the amount you spend on gifts to a certain amount?

OTHER EXPENSES

Automobiles are expensive. Between car payments, gas, repairs, and insurance, an automobile in some communities can be as expensive as a home. If you can get by without a car (or with one fewer car than you have) temporarily or permanently, you will save hundreds of dollars a month.

Save on tax preparation services by going to a Volunteer Income Tax Assistance (VITA) location. VITA sites provide free tax preparation to low-income and moderate-income taxpayers. They are sponsored by the IRS, and can be found in libraries, community centers, and other locations during tax time. For the nearest VITA site, contact the IRS (800-906-9887 or www.irs.gov). AARP also operates

Tax-Aide sites that can be found at www.aarp.org/applications/VMISLocator/searchTaxAideLocations.action.

You may feel obligated to adult family members or friends who share your home with you. However, if that person has income, it is fair to ask for a contribution to the household expenses. Alternatively, it may be time to politely ask that person to find somewhere else to live permanently or temporarily. If you continue to pay the expenses of people who can manage on their own, this may stretch your budget to the point that everyone loses their home.

If you have children in private school, consider a change during a period when you are experiencing financial problems. Family counseling may help with these difficult transitions. If you feel your children must stay in private school, speak with a school official or a financial aid officer. Special assistance programs may be available for families having temporary financial difficulties.

If religious contributions are stretching your budget, consider talking to your clergy. More often than not, special efforts will be made to help you through a tough financial time without affecting your membership or standing in the community.

Many community-based social service programs offer assistance for free or on a sliding scale. Low cost counseling on a variety of issues is widely available if you are persistent in looking for it. These programs are designed to help people in your situation in a confidential and effective way. You should not be embarrassed to get help.

9

Options for Increasing Your Income

TOPICS COVERED IN THIS CHAPTER

Wage-Related Options
Income Assistance
Food Assistance
Emergency Programs
Veterans Benefits
Reporting Change in Income If You Receive a Needs-Based Benefit
Other Ways to Increase Income

WAGE-RELATED OPTIONS

Eliminating Unnecessary Payroll Deductions. If your income has gone down, you may be having excessive amounts deducted from your pay for income taxes. Check with your employer or with an accountant if necessary. If you are having trouble meeting your obligations, you are better off having the income now rather than getting a tax refund next year.

You may also have agreed to a payroll deduction, such as savings plans, voluntary pension contributions, vacation clubs, credit union deductions, optional but inessential health coverages, charitable contributions, or voluntary wage assignments to creditors that you have decided are not a high priority. Check to see if these deductions should be temporarily reduced or eliminated.

The Earned Income Tax Credit. The "Earned Income Tax Credit" is a frequently overlooked means of increasing your income if you are employed. If you have not qualified for this credit in the past, a change in your income or a lay-off may make you eligible during a year in which you have financial problems.

The amount of your tax credit is based on the amount of your income and the size of your family. If you are employed and your total income falls below a certain amount, you qualify for the credit even if you do not have to pay any taxes that year. You can get money back even if you pay little or no taxes. You can also get advance payments on your earned income tax credit if your employer provides that option.

You should check with a tax professional to determine if you qualify. (See Chapter 8 for tips on saving money on tax preparation and Chapter 1 for free assistance with tax issues.) Obtaining the earned income tax credit will require that you file the necessary tax returns.

INCOME ASSISTANCE

Unemployment Compensation. You should always think about unemployment compensation when you have lost your job for any reason or when your hours have been significantly reduced. You should apply as quickly as possible after your employment is terminated or reduced.

Unemployment benefits are most commonly available after a layoff. You may not be eligible for benefits if you have been fired for cause or if you voluntarily quit. However, in some cases, you may still qualify for benefits even if your employer told you that you were fired rather than laid off. Similarly, you may qualify in some circumstances even if you quit your job. In general, it can't hurt to apply, although if you were fired or if you quit, you may first want to learn more about your state's benefit program.

Each state administers its own program with guidelines established by the federal government. You should check with your state about extended benefits programs available during times of high unemployment.

Some free legal services and also private lawyers and other professionals specialize in this area. (See Chapter 1 about finding a lawyer.) In addition, there are several books and pamphlets available which discuss unemployment compensation. Call the personnel office of your former company, the state labor department, or your state's unemployment office. If you are a union member, ask the union if it provides help with unemployment compensation applications. The National Employment Law Project (NELP) has a number of useful publications on unemployment compensation. Visit www.nelp.org.

Workers' Compensation. If you were seriously injured on the job, or if you suffer from serious job-related medical conditions, you probably are entitled to workers' compensation benefits. These may include medical benefits and monthly income payments until you are able to go back to work. If you are a union member, the union may help you qualify. Otherwise, contact the workers' compensation board in your state directly. Your doctor's assistance in this process will be helpful. If you are having difficulties qualifying, you may wish to contact a lawyer specializing in workers' compensation cases.

Child Support. If you are a custodial parent, you may be owed current or back child support. If you apply for your state's version of TANF (described below), the TANF state agency will usually take on child support enforcement activities for you to establish a child support order and collect support.

If you are not receiving TANF and cannot obtain an attorney to press your claim for child support, most states have state agencies tasked with child support enforcement who should help you to collect. Contact the local department of revenue or public assistance office to see which state agency assists families in the collection of child support and what type of assistance they can offer.

If you owe child support but have lost a job or lost wages, you can find out how to modify a child support order in light of lost income from the same agencies.

Cash Assistance for Families with Children. All states administer some form of cash and other assistance to families with children through the Temporary Assistance for Needy Families (TANF) block grant program. States have great flexibility in setting eligibility requirements and benefit levels. Most states require you have assets below a certain level. Many states require that the family include a minor child or a pregnant woman.

Applications for this assistance can be made at a local public assistance office, sometimes called a department of public assistance, department of social services, or department of human services. You will need to provide proof that you are eligible.

If you qualify for the program, the amount of your benefits will be based on your other income and family size as well as other factors. Some states require at least in some cases job training, work requirements, time limits, and/or cooperation with paternity identification and child support enforcement. All children who receive or live with a child who receives TANF are automatically eligible for free school meals (see below) and most states automatically provide Medicaid with TANF.

Local legal services offices can provide more information about these programs and/or represent you if benefits are denied or cut. Go to www.lawhelp.org for more information.

General Assistance for Individuals. Some states have other emergency assistance or have state and/or locally funded programs often called "general assistance," "general relief," or "home relief." These programs are typically for seniors and persons with disabilities pending approval of SSI, Social Security, workers' comp or other disability-based benefits. The state will usually require individuals to reimburse the state for "interim assistance" paid from the first SSI or other benefit check they receive once approved.

Benefits and eligibility requirements vary tremendously among states, but the programs are usually available only to people who don't qualify for any other form of assistance and who have few or no resources.

Some general assistance programs are available only to certain groups, such as children not living with relatives, homeless individuals, or persons with disabilities. Some programs provide benefits for only a limited number of months each year. Most programs require that employable people participate in a work or job search program. Local legal services offices can provide more information about these programs and/or represent you if benefits are denied or cut. Go to www.lawhelp.org for more information.

Social Security Based on Age. If you have sufficient work history, at retirement age you are eligible for Social Security. The retirement age to qualify for your *full* amount of Social Security retirement benefits for people born in 1955 is 66.2 years. For people born after that, it gradually increases until it reaches 67 for people born after 1959.

If you are not yet 66, but are 62 or over and in financial distress now, it is a good idea to opt for "early retirement" Social Security benefits, instead of waiting until you are over 66 years old. You will receive benefits now, but they will not be as high as if you waited until you were 66 or 67. Nevertheless, you will have years of extra income you would not have if you waited until you were 66 or 67. Considering the high interest charges you may incur now to borrow money and some of the consequences of non-payment of your debt, you are almost always better off receiving your Social Security benefits early if you are having financial problems now.

Social Security Based on Disability. You may be eligible for Social Security Disability Insurance benefits (SSDI) if you are severely disabled and have sufficient work history. Covered disabilities take many forms. Illnesses, physical and mental limitations, extreme pain, and depression or anxiety all qualify as disabilities. To qualify, the impairment or combination of impairments has to have lasted or be expected to last a year or more or result in death, and also prevent you from engaging in substantial gainful activity in light of your age, education, and work experience.

Many applicants who are initially denied disability benefits succeed on appeal. Make sure to file an appeal at each stage and consider contacting a lawyer or other advocate who specializes in disability benefit cases. Many private attorneys and some legal services offices provide legal representation to individuals having difficulty getting these benefits. In addition, many U.S. Congressional and Senate Offices have constituent staff who are able to problem-solve for constituents.

Sufficient Work History to Qualify for Social Security. Both retirement and disability Social Security benefits are available only for those who have been employed a sufficient number of years (40 quarters of work credits—roughly 10 years' worth of work) in covered jobs. That means jobs that provided contributions to the Social Security fund (your FICA). To learn about how Social Security calculates the 40 credits of work and how many work credits you have, visit https://www.ssa.gov/planners/credits.html.

Social Security and Dependents and Survivors. The dependents or survivors of an insured worker may also be eligible for Social Security benefits upon the worker's death, disability, or retirement. Dependents typically receive Social Security at 50% of the beneficiary's benefit rate, also known as "auxiliary benefits."

For More Information and to Apply for Social Security. To learn more about Social Security benefits and how to apply, call 800-772-1213, visit Social Security's website at www.ssa.gov, or go to your local Social Security district office.

SSI Benefits Based on Age or Disability. If you do not have sufficient work history to receive Social Security retirement or disability benefits, or if you Social Security retirement benefits are low, you may still be eligible for Supplemental Security Income (SSI). To qualify for SSI based on age, you must be 65 or older and either do not qualify for Social Security or your Social Security benefits are low, and your income and assets fall below established guidelines.

SSI disability benefits are based on the same disability criteria as Social Security disability benefits described above. Many applicants who are initially denied disability benefits succeed on appeal. Make sure to file an appeal at each stage and consider contacting a lawyer or legal services advocate who specializes in disability benefit cases. Go to www.lawhelp.org for more information.

FOOD ASSISTANCE

Supplemental Nutrition Assistance Program (SNAP) (formerly known as Food Stamps). SNAP benefits can supplement your monthly food budget. To qualify, your income must be below a gross income threshold that varies by state and depends on your household size. Emergency or "expedited" benefits are available to very low-income/no-income and migrant households. The state is required to provide the first allotment of SNAP benefits within 7 days of application, with minimal verification.

You apply for SNAP by filing an application with your state SNAP office—either in person or by mailing in a SNAP application. Most states also offer an online application process. State and local SNAP offices often administer cash and medical assistance (Medicaid) benefits as well. To find out how to apply for SNAP in your state, the application procedures in different states can be found on https://www.fns.usda.gov/snap/apply. Some states have given SNAP a different name, like "CalFresh" in California, "Food Share" in Wisconsin or "3 Squares VT" in Vermont, but these are all the same federal SNAP program.

Children who receive SNAP, or live with a child who receives SNAP, are automatically eligible for free school meals. (See School Meals below.) Your SNAP eligibility may also, depending on the state, allow you to enroll in certain other benefit programs without proof of income.

The SNAP program does require applicants have an interview with a SNAP worker, but most states will do the interview by phone unless you prefer an in-person interview. Don't delay on filing a SNAP application if you do not have all the required proofs, because SNAP benefits are paid retroactive to the date you first applied if you later are found eligible.

Sometimes, the agency improperly denies an application because of confusion about eligibility requirements or because of arithmetic mistakes. Do not take a denied application or termination of benefits as final. Consider making an appeal before the required time deadline expires. Most legal services programs provide free assistance with these appeals for eligible clients, resources permitting. Go to www.lawhelp.org for more information.

For more information, contact the Food Research and Action Center at 202-986-2200, www.frac.org or the U.S. Department of Agriculture at www.fns.usda.gov.

School Lunch, School Breakfast, and Summer Meals. All low-income school age children in public schools and most charter schools are eligible for free or reduced-price school meals. Children who receive or live with a child who receives SNAP food assistance or TANF cash benefits automatically qualify for free school meals. The family does not even need to file an application and the school should enroll the child from information the school gets from the state.

All children not getting TANF or SNAP who live in families with gross income under 130% of the federal poverty level are eligible for free school meal status and children in families between 130%–185% FPL are eligible for "reduced-price" meal status, which is a $0.40 co-pay for lunch and $0.30 co-pay for breakfasts. Families typically file a paper application for free or reduced-price meals at the start of the school year, and can also file any time during the school year if income changes (loss of a job, wage earner leaves family).

Low-income children who live in school districts that offer summer meals or after-school programs also qualify for these food benefits. For more information on child nutrition programs, contact your local school district, the state School Nutrition Association, or visit the Food Research and Action Center's website at http://frac.org/programs/national-school-lunch-program or the U.S. Department of Agriculture's website at www.fns.usda.gov/school-meals/child-nutrition-programs.

Women, Infants, and Children Program (WIC). If your family includes a pregnant woman or a child under five, you should inquire about assistance from the WIC program. Typically, WIC is administered by local public health departments and provides vouchers for supplemental foods important to the health of mothers and to the early development of their children. Eligibility for this program is based on family gross income and on whether the women, infants, or children in the family are at nutritional risk. Public assistance offices or health departments can provide information about WIC. The National WIC Association also provides resources, including where to apply for WIC benefits based on your zip code at https://www.nwica.org/apply-for-wic and follow the link to http://signupwic.com/.

Other Food Programs. Many unions, faith-based organizations, and nonprofit community groups have community cupboards or food pantries that distribute food commodities for home preparation. Food pantries often receive food commodities from regional food banks that receive funds and food commodities through the federal Emergency Food Assistance Program (TEFAP) as well as donations.

Faith-based organizations, homeless shelters, and other social service organizations such as the Salvation Army may also offer community meals to which families and individuals can turn. These programs can be located by contacting local church offices, United Way offices, or other social service agencies. Many food banks are affiliated with Feeding America. For more information, call 800-771-2303 or visit their website at www.feedingamerica.org.

EMERGENCY PROGRAMS

Emergency Programs. Some states, communities, and private organizations, such as the United Way, Salvation Army, and the American Red Cross have emergency funds available to help with basic needs, such as food, shelter, medical care, clothing, or transportation. Often, these programs provide referrals to agencies, repurposed furniture, and clothing and/or provide vouchers for one-time needs rather than direct cash.

The American Red Cross often provides immediate shelter in hotels and motels, food and other emergency resources for local disasters (fires, floods, etc.), as well as a first responder team for major national disasters. See http://www.redcross.org/about-us/our-work/disaster-relief.

Private social service groups and charitable and religious organizations sometimes have small funds available that provide limited grants or short-term loans to families lacking other available resources.

Most states have hotlines, emergency shelters, safe homes, and other support services for domestic violence survivors. A national hotline, 1-800-799-7233, TTY 1-800-787-3224, www.thehotline.org has trained advocates available 24 hours a day, every day of the year to speak confidentially with anyone experiencing domestic violence seeking resources, information, or other assistance.

Disaster Relief. The Federal Emergency Management Agency (FEMA) is the main federal agency that is supposed to coordinate state and federal government disaster benefits. You may also be eligible for expedited or replacement food assistance or disaster-related unemployed benefits. In some cases, private creditors will agree to impose moratoriums on credit card payments or offer other relief for disaster victims. Time deadlines are often critical for these programs.

In the event of a federally declared disaster, the Department of Agriculture authorizes states to provide "Disaster-SNAP" benefits to low-income households, using a higher income threshold and minimal verifications for initial emergency benefits. Your local public assistance agency should have more information about Disaster-SNAP should your state or region experience a natural or other disaster. Even without a widespread federally declared disaster, SNAP households can qualify for "misfortune" SNAP replacement benefits to replace food lost (or becomes unsafe to eat), due to a local fire, flood, power outage, or other household "misfortune." Contact your local SNAP state agency for how to request replacement SNAP benefits.

You can get more information from your local legal services office or from FEMA's website www.fema.gov or by calling FEMA at 800-621-3362 (FEMA) or 800-462-7585 (TTY).

VETERANS BENEFITS

Veterans Disability Compensation. The Department of Veterans Affairs (VA) offers a service-connected disability benefit paid monthly if you suffer from a disability incurred in or aggravated by your military service. You are eligible if you have an honorable or general under honorable conditions discharge. The VA decides eligibility on a case by case basis for veterans with other than honorable discharges. Those with dishonorable discharges are not entitled to compensation benefits.

The VA evaluates service-connected disabilities from 0% to 100%. A veteran with a 0% evaluation gets no monthly benefit for that condition. A veteran without dependents with a 10% evaluation is paid $136 per month. A veteran with a 100% evaluation receives $2,973 per month. Additional benefits are paid if you have a spouse and/or child (under age 18 or 26 if the child is in school). These benefits are tax free.

Disabilities that affect a veteran's lifestyle may result in higher monthly payments. For example, additional benefits above 100% are paid to veterans who are housebound or are in need of aid and attendance because of their service connected conditions. Extra benefits, called "special monthly compensation," are paid to veterans who through service lost one or more limbs or hearing or eyesight. Veterans who are not evaluated as 100% disabled can be paid at the 100% rate if the VA determines that their service-connected conditions, without consideration of their age or non-service-connected disabilities, cause them to be unable to perform substantial gainful employment.

The VA encourages you to apply online at www.vets.gov. Submit copies of military and civilian medical evidence, your discharge paperwork, and anything else you may think is necessary. For fastest service, apply using VA Form 21-526 EZ.

Non-Service-Connected Disability (or Age) Pension. Veterans who served during congressionally defined wartime and who are permanently and totally disabled from a cause or causes *not* solely related to their military service may be eligible for pension benefits. Being aged 65 or over is defined for purposes of a VA pension as being totally disabled.

VA-recognized wartime periods to determine eligibility include:

- Gulf War (August 2, 1990–through a future date to be set by law or Presidential proclamation);
- Vietnam era (February 28, 1961–May 7, 1975 for veterans who served in the Republic of Vietnam during that period; otherwise August 5, 1964–May 7, 1975);
- Korean conflict (June 27, 1950–January 31, 1955).

Pension benefits are awarded based both on disability and income. Pension pays much less for a total disability than the above-described Veterans Disability Compensation program pays. The VA also reduces the VA pension payment dollar-for-dollar for any countable income you may have.

There are five eligibility requirements for a pension:

1. You must be discharged under other than dishonorable conditions.
2. If you enlisted in military service for the first time on or after September 8, 1980, you must have completed a minimum period of service, either twenty-four months of continuous active duty or the full period for which you were called or ordered to active duty. You must also have active service that included a total of ninety days during one or more periods of war; ninety or more consecutive days, one of which was during a period of war; or at least one day of wartime service that resulted in a discharge for a service-connected disability.
3. You must have limited income and a net worth that does not provide adequate maintenance (referred to as "the need test").
4. You must be permanently and totally disabled at the time of the application for pension. Veterans age 65 and older are considered permanently and totally disabled for VA pension purposes.
5. The permanent and total disability must not be due to willful misconduct of the veteran.

The maximum annual pension rate for a single veteran is $13,166. If the veteran is so disabled that he or she needs aid and attendance, the maximum annual rate is $21,962. Other income you may have is deducted from those amounts dollar for dollar. If a veteran's income is above the maximum pension rate, the pension claim will be denied. In computing your income, the VA will deduct some medical expenses.

You can apply by filling out VA Form 21-527EZ, Veteran's Application for Pension. If available, attach copies of dependency records (marriage and children's birth certificates) and current medical evidence (doctor and hospital reports). You can also apply online at www.vets.gov/pension/application/527EZ/introduction. For assistance call 800-827-1000.

For more information. Visit www.nvlsp.org to learn more about entitlement to VA disability benefits. Another good overview is the National Veteran Legal Services Project's *Online Basic Training Course* available online for purchase at https://nvlspbasictrainingcourse.com. The National Veterans Legal Services Project also authors a 1900 page comprehensive review of VA benefits, the *Veterans Benefits Manual,* published by LexisNexis.

REPORTING CHANGE IN INCOME IF YOU RECEIVE A NEEDS-BASED BENEFIT

If you are receiving a needs-based benefit, such as SNAP, TANF, Medicaid, SSI, certain veteran's benefits, or receiving unemployment compensation, report to the agency administering the needs-based benefit any changes in income that may affect your eligibility. Examples could be increased wages from overtime, a temporary job, or renting out part of your home. Failure to do so could result in a fraud determination or a requirement that you return overpayments. Check with a legal advocate if you have questions about what and when to report changes.

OTHER WAYS TO INCREASE INCOME

Other ways to increase the family income include taking a second job temporarily, increasing overtime, or collecting debts owed to you by others. Consider also whether you have space in your home which you can rent or whether you have a marketable skill which you are not using. If you have made a voluntary decision not to work, financial difficulties create an opportunity to reconsider. Any choice to return to the workforce in this circumstance must be weighed against the potential increased costs of child care, taxes, and other expenses.

10

Keeping Track of Income, Expenses, and Debt

TOPICS COVERED IN THIS CHAPTER

Why Keep Track. When facing financial problems, keep track of your income, expenses, and debt on a monthly basis. This has a lot of value. It gives you a realistic view of where you stand and how much you can allocate to debt payments. When you know that, you can decide which debt payments you can afford to make and which you cannot. Then refer to Chapter 1 to see which debts to pay first.

This book explains how to spread out debt payments for specific debts. But it does no good to lower your monthly payment on a debt if you cannot afford to make even that lower monthly payment. The creditor is likely to give up working with you if you cannot keep up your end of a deal that lowers your payments. Keeping track of your income, expenses, and debt obligations gives you a realistic idea of how much you can promise a creditor that you will pay each month.

Sometimes, in working with a creditor to set up a plan to lower your payments, you will need to show the creditor your income, other debts, and other information. You can have this already in hand if you keep track of your financial condition in an organized fashion. A list of your debts and income is also needed if you file for bankruptcy. Reviewing your expenses each month can also help you identify areas where you can reduce costs. Chapter 8 discusses ways to do this.

How to Keep Track. Keep a list of your actual income, expenses, and debt payments for the past month, and do the same for at least a number of months. There is no one required way to do this.

This chapter includes a filled-in form as a sample list. This form can also be seen at www.nclc.org/keepingtrack, which includes a version of the form in MS Word format that you can adapt in any way you wish and then print out. The form is only a sample; keep track in whatever way works best for you and makes sense for you.

Keep the lists for each month in a safe place. Using a notebook for this purpose is another way to do this. You can keep track on a computer or your smart phone if that is something you are used to doing. After you have made a monthly list for several months, start comparing months and see what is typical and how you are doing.

Corporations increasingly push to send you credit card, bank, and loan statements electronically instead of on paper. Some people prefer electronic statements. Companies may also try to slip you into electronic-only statements without your realizing it. If you receive electronic-only statements, you should have the ability to read them electronically and in fact do read them regularly. Otherwise, request paper statements.

Keeping Track of Income. Your income listing should include all present sources of income that month for each family member. List the amount separately for each source of income and then total them all up.

For employment income, use take-home pay and not gross pay. If you do not work on salary, list your earnings in the last month and also list under your expenses any self-employment and federal and state taxes you should pay on that income. If your income is higher or lower than usual that month, make a note of that.

Include in income additional cash you receive on a regular basis, including Social Security, unemployment compensation, food stamps, other public benefits, child support, alimony, pensions, and the like. Do not include as income money you draw down from your bank or savings account or cash from loans you took out that month. Do not list money friends or relatives lent you if you have to pay it back. If you are unlikely to pay it back, you could label it as a gift and treat it as income. Also do not treat as income any one-time, very large cash payment such as an inheritance, sale of property, or an insurance payment.

When you prepare your income list, evaluate whether you are maximizing your income. A number of ideas to increase your income are discussed in Chapter 9.

The Expense Listing. Your expenses should list separately each category of your monthly expenses, such as food, housing, utilities, clothing, transportation, and medical expenses. Some ideas for categories are listed below and on the sample form, but use whatever categories work for you. For example, it might be easiest for you to break down expenses by the type of store you go to, rather than the exact nature of the goods purchased there, such as "purchases at Walmart."

Listed below are some ideas for categories. Some of these categories are used in the filled-in sample form, which can also be seen (and adapted) at www.nclc.org/keepingtrack. But you should use whatever categories work for you.

- Rent or manufactured home lot rent or mortgage payments (first and second mortgages);
- Property taxes and homeowner's insurance if not included in your mortgage payments (make a note that these are billed only a few times a year);
- Condo or homeowner association fees and assessments;
- Home maintenance and repairs and landscaping;
- Furniture, appliances, electronics, or other goods;
- Gas and electric utilities, heating oil, propane, or wood;
- Water, sewer, and trash;
- Land line telephone and/or cell phone, TV, and internet;
- Groceries and related items;
- Eating out, including lunches not brought to work;
- Products and services related to personal appearance and hygiene;
- Clothing and footwear, laundry and cleaning;
- Medical insurance premiums, medical expenses not covered by insurance, and prescriptions;
- Dental expenses;
- Auto loan or lease payments, car insurance, gas, and maintenance;
- Buses, other public transportation, Uber, taxis, Lyft, etc.;
- Student loan payments;
- Religious and charitable contributions and organization dues;
- School-related expenses;
- Entertainment, newspapers, videos, video games, books, etc.;
- Alcohol, cigarettes, etc.;
- Hobbies, sports equipment, health clubs, and the like;
- Pet expenses;
- Alimony or child support;
- Other insurance (beside auto or homeowners);
- Taxes on self-employed income (where withholding not taken out from income);
- Tax preparation;
- Credit card minimum or other small payments.

HOW TO REMEMBER YOUR EXPENSES

It is often difficult to remember exactly where all your money goes. One way to remember is to look at monthly statements for all the ways you pay your expenses. If you use a credit card, review your monthly statement. As long as it covers a period of about 30 days, don't worry if the credit card statement straddles two months. Use all of the expenses you see on your June statement for your June expense listing even though the statement and the listing will include charges from May.

If you use your bank account to make payments—whether it is with checks, a debit card, or electronic transfer, these should all be on your monthly bank statement. If something is unclear, ask your bank for more information. Just like the credit card, don't worry if the bank statement straddles two months, as long as it covers a period of about 30 days. If the bank statement you receive in June covers part of May and part of June, just count all the expenses listed there as June expenses.

Expenses may be harder to keep track when you use a prepaid card. Contact the prepaid card issuer to see how and in what form you can get statements. These may be mailed to you, provided over the phone, or available in electronic fashion. Also keep receipts of money orders and similar payments.

Add up how much cash you receive each month—from an ATM, check casher, cash-back at stores when using your debit card, and the like. Try to remember what you spent the cash on and see if what you remember totals up to the total amount of cash you received that month. An estimate is better than not recording an expense.

Treat as an expense the amount you must pay each month on loans you used to purchase your home, goods, or services—such as student loans, home mortgages, or auto loans. List the amount due as an expense for the month it is due, even if it that month's payment is made late, early, or skipped. One exception is if you pay off your credit card obligation each month, since you already have listed what you bought on the card as an expense. But if you only make the minimum or other small payment on the card, treat this as an expense.

Listing of Debts. Separate from your listing of expenses and income, it is a good idea to also keep track of your debts. A filled-in sample is found in this chapter and you can see the filled-in sample and a MS Word version you can edit and print out at www.nclc.org/keepingtrack.

This shows you whether you are getting yourself deeper into debt or getting yourself slowly out of a hole. Describing your debts will help you plan which debts to pay first, how much you can pay on your debts, what type of plan you should seek from your creditor to deal with a debt, and the like.

For each debt, list the outstanding balance reported to you in that month's statement and the monthly payment due. There is value also in determining for each debt the interest rate and by when the loan is supposed to be fully paid off. Include as debts your credit card obligations, short-term loans, loans from friends and family, car loans, mortgage loans student loans, and all other loans.

SAMPLE LISTING OF MONTHLY INCOME, EXPENSES, AND DEBTS

These sample forms can be edited and printed for your actual use by visiting www.nclc.org/keepingtrack.

Monthly Income

This is a sample listing of a family's last month's income. Your income may include other sources than those listed here, such as workers' compensation, unemployment compensation, food stamps, other public benefits, or pensions. For wages, use take-home pay. If self-employed, include all income and also list under expenses any income taxes and self-employment taxes you pay in a given month.

NOVEMBER INCOME	RECIPIENT	MONTHLY AMOUNT
Take Home Pay	Maria	$2,070
Social Security	John	$2,733
VA Pension	John	$121
Total		$4,924

Monthly Expenses

This is a sample listing of monthly expenses. Your expenses may include other categories or you may wish to use different categories than the ones listed below. Estimate as best you can all your actual expenses during the prior month.

NOVEMBER EXPENSES	AMOUNT
Rent or mortgage payments (include both first and second mortgages. If property taxes and insurance not included in mortgage payments, list them as a separate expense)	$1,412
Home maintenance and repairs	$175
Furniture, appliances, electronics, or other goods	$135
Gas and electric utilities	$180
Water, sewer, and trash	$190
Internet, TV, cellphones, landline telephones	$185
Medical insurance	$553
Medical and dental expenses, prescriptions	$250
Groceries and other items purchased at market	$390
Eating out, coffee, snacks, and lunches at work	$115
Haircuts, personal care and products	$55
Clothing and footwear	$90
Gas, car repairs, car insurance, tolls	$245
Auto loan or lease payment	$356
Alcohol, cigarettes	$140
Pet expenses	$78
Health club	$58
Credit card payments (do not include if pay off most or all outstanding balance each month)	$469
Small loan payments	$275
Total	$5,351

Debts Outstanding

This is a sample listing of a family's debts that are still due in the current month. The source of your debts, amounts and interest rates will be different than in this sample. For credit card debts, include either the minimum payment due or another amount if that is what you regularly pay each month.

DECEMBER DEBTS	MONTHLY PAYMENT DUE	CURRENT BALANCE	INTEREST RATE	PAID OFF BY
1st Mortgage	$388	$32,763	5.1%	July 2027
2nd Mortgages (include all 2nd mortgages)	$1,024	$63,123	8.5%	Dec. 2025
Car loan or lease payment	$356	$13,344	7.4%	July 2021
Discover Card	$271 minimum payment	$14,821	24%	
Visa Card	$198 minimum payment	$9,980	21%	
Payday Loan	$275	$275	400%	Next payday
Medical Debt	$770	$770	0%	Past Due
Loan from Brother	$0	$2,000	0%	?
Total	$4,233			

11

Medical Debt

TOPICS COVERED IN THIS CHAPTER

DON'T PAY MEDICAL DEBT AHEAD OF OTHER DEBT OR BORROW TO PAY MEDICAL DEBT

Most families encountering financial difficulty have overdue medical debt. You should treat medical debt as a low priority debt to be paid only after you pay more pressing types of debt, such as your mortgage, car loan, or criminal citations. Almost any other type of debt will be more pressing—medical debt should typically be your lowest priority.

Similarly, never pay medical debt by incurring other debt. The worst thing you can do is take out a second mortgage to pay off medical debt. Also don't put medical debt on your credit card, even a "medical" credit card, unless you can pay the card and all your other obligations that month.

Unlike credit card debt, medical debt will typically carry low or no interest payments and late charges. While the medical debt may eventually end up on your credit report, it will not show up for at least six months. Delinquent credit card debt affects your credit score immediately. You are also less likely to be sued on medical debt than credit card debt. Medical debt can go unpaid for long periods of time without any significant adverse consequences.

Nonprofit hospitals have written policies to reduce or even eliminate certain medical charges if you are eligible for financial assistance. Many states have laws that reduce or even eliminate medical debt for eligible families. Whether or not you qualify for such financial assistance, health care providers are often more willing to reduce the amount of a delinquent debt where you can show financial hardship. Once you put medical debt on your credit card, you lose all of these opportunities.

Some doctor or dentist offices may encourage you to sign up for a special credit card to pay your medical bills, but these cards are usually not a good choice for paying medical bills. The credit cards often have high interest rates or unfavorable terms. You lose the option of negotiating with your health care provider over the bill. Using this type of card turns your medical debt into credit card debt.

Medical debt's status as a low priority debt does not mean that one should ignore medical debt. You have special rights concerning medical debt, and it is important to know these rights to be able to reduce the amount of your medical debt and its adverse consequences.

DEBT COLLECTORS AND MEDICAL DEBT

Hospitals and other health care providers are quick to turn over medical debt to debt collection agencies—some will do so after a month or two, while others may wait six or more months. The job of these debt collectors is to try to get you to pay medical debt even if this is not in your best interest.

They will push you to put medical debt on your credit card—don't fall for that. They will try to get you to pay these bills ahead of more important bills, such as your rent or home mortgage. They will threaten to ruin your credit rating, but they may not even report the collection effort to a credit reporting agency. If they do report the debt, the reporting agency will not even include the debt in its reporting unless it is over six months old. Just as importantly, paying your medical bill instead of your mortgage or car loan will end up damaging your credit report a lot more than not paying your medical bill.

Debt collectors also will call you and constantly press for payment. But this is easy to stop, particularly for medical debt. Few hospitals and health care providers will be collecting on their own debt, but will instead hire third-party collection agencies. Under federal law these agencies must stop contacting you if you simply send them a letter telling them to stop, as explained in Chapter 2, above.

Another approach to avoid debt collection harassment is to contact the hospital or health care provider early about your inability to pay, before the matter is turned over to a collection agency. Explain that you are unable to pay at present and that you will not pay the collection agency either. Since the health care provider must pay the agency, the provider may be better off waiting for you to pay the provider directly when your financial situation improves. Preventing your debt from going to a collector will also help your credit standing because typically only collection agencies and not medical providers report your debt to a credit bureau.

LIMITS ON CREDIT REPORTING OF MEDICAL DEBT

Virtually no medical provider will report your debt to a credit bureau. Instead, when your debt is eventually handed over to a collection agency, that collection agency may (or may not) report the debt to a credit bureau.

In addition, in almost all cases, your credit rating is determined by one of the three major national credit bureaus. All three of these agencies have agreed *not* to include any medical debt in your credit report if the debt is less than 180 days delinquent when reported to them. This means that medical debt will not affect your credit rating unless a provider's collection agency makes a new report to a credit bureau after the debt is over 180 days old.

For more on credit reporting, see Chapter 3, above.

CAN A HOSPITAL TURN YOU AWAY IF YOU OWE IT MONEY?

If medical debt goes unpaid for a period of time, a hospital or other health care provider may decide to stop providing you services. In some areas, you may have few other options for medical care, but in other locations you should be able to find other health care providers to take care of your family. That you own money to one hospital or one health care provider should not prevent you from obtaining services from other hospitals or providers. This will particularly be the case with public hospitals and community health centers.

Even if you owe a hospital for past-due bills, the hospital cannot turn you away from its emergency room. This is your right under a federal statute called the Emergency Medical Treatment and Active Labor Act (EMTALA).

If you request financial assistance from a nonprofit hospital, the hospital cannot deny you care in any part of the hospital because of an old bill until it determines whether you are eligible for financial assistance. You usually have about eight months (240 days) from when you first received the old bill to request such financial assistance.

If you are a Medicaid recipient and you owe a doctor or other health care provider for co-payments or deductibles, Medicaid prohibits health care providers from denying you future services.

CORRECTING YOUR MEDICAL BILLS

One way to reduce a medical debt is to review it carefully for errors and unauthorized charges. Also review any explanation of benefits (EOB) form you receive from your insurance company to see if it is consistent with the medical bill. If you see errors, contact the health care provider or your insurance company to have the erroneous charges taken off your bill.

Check also for charges based upon unauthorized balanced billing. The EOB may disallow a portion of the health care provider's bill, pursuant to its agreement with the provider. Balance billing is when the health care provider bills you for the disallowed portion of the bill. Balance billing is prohibited in certain states.

If you have Medicare or Medicaid, providers are usually not allowed to bill you for rates higher than what these programs are willing to pay. They can only bill you for copays and deductibles. If you have both Medicare and Medicaid coverage and are enrolled in a Qualified Medicare beneficiary program, providers are usually not even allowed to bill you the Medicare co-pays and deductibles.

If you receive a bill that you believe should be covered by insurance, Medicaid, or Medicare, contact your insurer to find out why the service was not covered. You may need to contact your health care provider also. If the insurance company made an error, they might be able to fix it when you call.

If your insurance company, Medicaid, or Medicare will not pay for a service that you needed, you have a right to appeal. Call your insurer and tell the insurer that you want to appeal their decision. Do this as soon as you can before the deadline for requesting an appeal. Contact your state insurance commissioner or state attorney general's office if you need assistance.

REQUESTING FINANCIAL ASSISTANCE

Federal law requires nonprofit hospitals to establish policies for offering patients financial assistance, such as free or discounted medical services for eligible patients. The policies and how to apply for financial assistance must be in writing and available from both the hospital and on the hospital's website.

Hospitals often charge an uninsured patient high "retail" prices for services, but charge significantly less for the same service to a health insurer, Medicare, or Medicaid. If you are eligible for financial assistance from a nonprofit hospital, the hospital should not charge you the "retail" price but instead should charge a price similar to what it charges insurance companies, Medicare, and Medicaid. The hospital even has to go back and reduce bills you received even before you established eligibility for financial assistance.

Federal law does not otherwise specify standards for financial assistance, but about half the states have medical debtor protection laws that specify who, based on family income, is eligible for financial assistance and what type of assistance a hospital must offer. For example, the hospital may have to offer an interest-free installment plan, reduced cost medical care, or even free medical care. The hospital's financial assistance plan will set out exactly the type of financial assistance that it provides to those who are eligible.

In at least some states you can also apply for Medicaid and if you are found eligible, Medicaid will cover retroactively medical bills incurred over the last three months. This retroactive coverage is not available in every state.

Other hospitals or health care providers may agree to reduce bills based on your financial hardship even if not required to do so by federal or state law. Explain your financial situation and that you will pay when you are financially able. You can ask for a payment plan, but do not agree to a payment plan if you cannot afford the payments.

Chapter 8 discusses ways before you incur a medical bill to obtain medical and dental care at reduced prices, such as applying for Medicaid or obtaining low cost dental care from a dental school. But even after you have incurred medical bills, there are charities and other programs that may help pay for some of your medical bills.

WILL A HEALTH CARE PROVIDER SUE YOU FOR UNPAID BILLS?

A hospital or other health care provider is less likely to sue you to collect on an overdue bill than are most other creditors, such as credit card companies. This is particularly the case for relatively small medical bills. In addition, if you request financial assistance from a nonprofit hospital, the hospital cannot start a collection lawsuit against you until it determines whether you are eligible for financial assistance.

If the hospital does sue you, you may be able to defend the lawsuit by arguing the medical bills are not reasonable. In most cases, patients do not agree to a price for medical services ahead of time, and the hospital or physician bills you for whatever price it decides to charge. Some judges may be sympathetic to your argument that the hospital charged you a higher price than the hospital charges to insurance companies, Medicare, or Medicaid. If you raise this in the lawsuit, the hospital or other health care provider may even settle with you for less rather than try to prove that its charges are reasonable.

See Chapter 4 for how to defend a collection suit. See also Chapter 21 detailing your rights even if you lose a collection lawsuit.

12

Credit Card Debt

TOPICS COVERED IN THIS CHAPTER

WHEN TO PAY ON YOUR CREDIT CARDS AND WHEN TO USE THEM

Credit card debt is relatively low priority debt. If you do not pay it, you do not face immediate loss of your car, home, wages, bank account, or other property. If you do not have enough money to pay all your bills, you should generally not make significant payments on your card debt ahead of your mortgage, car loan, utilities, food, medicine, and the like. Keeping this priority in mind, this chapter provides advice on paying down your credit card debt.

Just because credit card debt is low priority does not mean that you should pay off other debts with your cards. As described in the chapter on medical debt, you should not pay off medical debt with a credit card if you will have trouble paying these credit card charges, no matter how much a debt collector is hounding you to do so. You have better choices concerning your medical debt than you do concerning your credit card. Similarly, you should not opt for a special credit card offered by your medical provider—as described in the prior chapter, you are better off owing your provider than this card issuer.

Chapter 23 below also explains why you have better options for paying back-taxes to the IRS than putting the tax obligation on your credit card. You can get a better deal with more flexible terms from the IRS.

On the other hand, it may be a smart choice to put necessities on your card (or use your card for a cash advance) if that is the only way to free up cash to make your mortgage, rent, car, or utility payments. Similarly, paying a criminal citation with a credit card (if available) is better than losing your driver's license or even being incarcerated for non-payment.

You may find that delinquent credit card debt is your biggest headache because the lender or its collectors will be the most aggressive in contacting you. There is a reason for that—they don't have better tools, unlike a mortgage company that can take your house. The key point here is to think strategically about your card as to when it is best for you and your family to pay it and to use it. Do not let debt collectors make this decision for you. There are far better ways to stop debt harassment than giving in to the collector and making a bad decision. The next section gives you a realistic view of how non-payment on your card affects you and your family.

HOW A DELINQUENT CREDIT CARD ACCOUNT AFFECTS YOU

In making judgments about paying and using your credit card, you should understand what does and does not happen if you fail to pay your credit card. You are only required to make the required minimum payments on your credit card, but if you do so it will take many years to pay off your debt and you will likely pay thousands of dollars in finance charges. Nevertheless, if you consistently make the minimum payment, you will be avoiding late charges and your credit report will show your payments are on-time and current. The card issuer cannot raise your interest rate on charges you have already incurred if you keep current on your minimum payments. It is unlikely that you will lose the ability to use your card—assuming you have not maxed out the card.

If you stop making even the minimum payments, then your overdue credit card payments will almost certainly show up on your credit report, first as overdue, then 30 days overdue, then 60, then 90, etc. Your credit score will likely take its biggest hit when the card is 30 and then 60 days overdue. After the card is 60 days overdue, the card issuer can then increase the interest rate on your card even for existing charges that you have already made.

At some point, the card issuer will revoke your card privileges so that you cannot use the card any more—while you cannot use the card, you will still remain obligated on the debt. Not being able to use the card may not be the worst thing because you will not be ringing up more debt. Nevertheless, there are times when a credit card is very useful or even necessary. Nevertheless, there are alternatives to a credit card that perform similar functions. If you have a bank account, you can get a debit card. You can obtain a prepaid card even if you do not have a bank account.

At 180 days, the card issuer is likely to "write-off" or "charge off" your debt. This does not mean it will stop trying to collect on the debt or that you do not owe on the debt. It just means the card issuer will treat the card account differently for their internal accounting purposes. Most card issuers at 180 days will stop sending you statements and also stop assessing new interest or new late charges. They will cancel the card if that has not happened already and turn the account over for collection if that has not already happened.

At 180 days, when the card is written off, your credit score is likely to take another hit, but after that date your score will not be affected much even if you continue to not pay on it. Similarly, when your account is sent out to a collection agency (either before 180 days or at 180 days), the collector likely will report the account under its own name, which will also result in another hit to your credit score.

Being contacted by a debt collector is never fun, but you can stop the collector from contacting you (see Chapter 2, above). The debt collector may also threaten to ruin your credit score, but by the time the account is turned over to the collector, your score has already been lowered a lot. Not paying the collector will have little additional effect on your score, no matter how much the collector threatens to ruin your credit rating. Also, if you pay off a debt that was already reported by a collector, that collection item will show as "paid" but will not be removed from your credit report—if you want it removed, you must get the collector's written agreement to delete it and not all collectors will agree to do so.

At some point the credit card company or a debt buyer will decide whether to sue on the debt, but this may be years after you stop paying on the card. Moreover, particularly if the amount is relatively small, you may never be sued on the credit card debt. If you are sued, and you contest the lawsuit, the creditor may drop the case, particularly if the case is brought by a debt buyer or the amount is relatively small. See Chapter 4 on defending such a lawsuit.

If you are sued and the judge rules for the creditor, then the debt becomes much more serious. You do not have to pay the debt all at once. But it is possible part of your wages will be garnished, your bank account seized, or even some of your property sold. The extent to which you are vulnerable to these creditor post-judgment remedies is examined at Chapter 21, below.

Even if you lose the lawsuit, you may not have to pay the debt all at once. If your income and bank accounts are protected by law, you may not even have to pay anything on the debt. For more information on what may or may not happen when you lose a collection lawsuit, see Chapter 21, below.

SPECIAL CARDS CREATE SPECIAL PROBLEMS

The above description of the implications of a delinquent credit card applies to most credit cards. But a few special types of cards create additional concerns when you are delinquent.

Some cards are specially marketed to people who have low credit scores or no credit history. Beware of these cards! They come loaded with high fees that can eat up to 25% of the credit line. In some case, you may even need to pay a fee to apply for the card. These cards usually do more harm than good for your credit score.

Stores selling electronics or furniture and even some medical providers advertise credit cards at zero percent interest. The interest rate, though, is only zero percent interest if you pay the whole balance by the time the promotional period ends. If not, you will suddenly retroactively owe all of the interest that would have accrued during the promotional period as if you were charged interest at a high rate, such as 25% or 30%, all along. That means that when the promotional period ends, all at once you will be hit with a huge interest charge if you have not paid off the balance.

Some credit cards are marketed as helping you reestablish credit, and are secured by a certain amount of funds in your bank account. You cannot withdraw that amount from the account and your card's credit limit matches that amount. If you do not pay the card, the card issuer just seizes that amount from your bank account. These cards can be helpful in establishing credit, but only if you're careful not to max out and to make the minimum payment every month.

INTEREST RATE REDUCTION FOR MEMBERS OF THE MILITARY ON ACTIVE DUTY

While you are on active duty in the military, you should only pay 6% interest on your credit cards for those card charges that you or your spouse incurred *before* you entered active duty. Since credit card interest rates are typically several times this amount, this can result in you saving thousands of dollars if your card balance was high enough when you entered active duty and if you were slow in paying that amount off. Any higher rate interest assessed against you while you are on active duty that should have been assessed at 6% must be credited back to you. This 6% limit applies to many types of debts, not just credit card debt.

To get your interest rate reduced, notify your creditors in writing that you are on active duty and that you want your interest rates reduced. You should also send them a copy of the orders calling you to active duty or extending your active duty. It is important to notify your creditors as soon as possible, but you must let them know no later than 180 days after your period of active duty ends. If you notify them within that period you will get back a credit for all the interest charged at the higher rate that should have been charged at 6%.

To qualify for this protection, you must be a member of the Army, Navy, Marine Corps, Air Force, or Coast Guard, or a commissioned officer of the Public Health Service or the National Oceanic and Atmospheric Administration. Members of the Reserves or National Guard who are called to active service also qualify. You can get more information from a judge advocate. For example, the U.S. Army's Judge Advocate General's Corps has information at www.jagcnet.army.mil.

NEGOTIATING TO REDUCE YOUR CREDIT CARD DEBT

Often a credit card company will agree to reduced payments or accept payments in installments. But if you need all your money to pay your high priority obligations and other necessities, don't enter into negotiations with the credit card issuer on reducing your payments. Instead just tell the card issuer you cannot pay at present. If you *can* meet your other more pressing obligations and still make partial payments on your credit card debt, here are some tips about negotiating with the credit card company.

Decide whether you want to negotiate now or wait until you are sued. Negotiating now may help your credit score some, but waiting may give you more time to see whether your financial situation improves or gets worse. In addition, you may never be sued, and thus never have to repay the debt. If you are eventually going to file for bankruptcy, it also probably does not make sense to pay even part of the debt now.

Only agree to terms you can afford to pay. If you fail to meet your promised payment plan, the card issuer will most likely not negotiate reduced payments with you again. Get any deal you reach in writing and keep a copy. If you are uncomfortable negotiating on your own get a social worker, trusted friend, relative, or other person to help. The creditor might prefer a lump sum payment, but that might be impossible for you. Instead you can offer to pay in installment payments, but only make this offer if you plan on making these payments regularly.

As part of any negotiation, consider your credit report. You can ask the card issuer to remove from your report that you were ever delinquent. In the alternative, you can dispute with the credit bureaus that the debt was ever delinquent (see Chapter 3, above) and get a promise from the credit card company not to verify with the credit bureau that the debt was ever delinquent.

Paying someone or getting a counselor to help you negotiate with the credit card company is tricky business. We discuss this in the next two sections.

AVOID DEBT SETTLEMENT AND DEBT ELIMINATION COMPANIES

You may hear about companies that claim they can help you reduce your debts or eliminate them. These companies are a total rip-off. Never use them. Some say they can send you documents or sell you tips that will eliminate all your credit card debt. They offer a "bond for discharge of debt," "a declaration of voidance," or a "redemption certificate." Or they tell you that "monetized" debt need not be paid. Other times, they claim to be "sovereign citizens" or offer to set up sham arbitration proceedings to eliminate the debt. These are totally bogus offers. They will cost you money, and just make matters worse.

Another scam is often called debt settlement. The company claims that it can negotiate with your creditors so you can pay off your debts for less. They may even advertise examples of how they have saved people thousands of dollars. Some debt settlement companies claim that they have a special certification by the Better Business Bureau or other organizations. But this is all meaningless. Debt settlement is actually illegal in some states and a bad idea everywhere.

Typically, debt settlement companies instruct you to put money away in a special account each month. When there is enough in the account, they claim they will use it to settle your credit card debts. Some want to be paid upfront and others say they only get paid if they settle your debts. But they always manage to charge you monthly fees even if they never settle your debts. Or they may settle one or two small debts and claim their fee. But this still leaves you with your bigger debts—which often grow even larger while you wait for the company to do something. These companies have no special connection to card issuers and some credit card companies even refuse to talk to debt settlement firms.

While you are putting money in the special account, nothing is going toward to your card companies; interest and late charges are mounting; the total amount you owe is growing; the non-payment is being reported to credit bureaus; and you are likely being harassed by debt collectors or even sued on the debt. Even if the company eventually settles some debts, your total amount of debt will be bigger than when you started, especially after all the fees you must pay to the company.

CREDIT COUNSELING AND DEBT MANAGEMENT PLANS

Credit counselors offer budgeting advice. Sometimes they also offer debt management plans. The difference between a debt management plan and debt settlement is that a debt management plan requires you to pay all of your debt. While you usually get a discount on the interest rate and late fees, you are still paying the full bill. It may take years to pay off your credit card debt under a debt management plan—are you prepared to continue to make payments to the credit counselor for that long a period? In addition, most credit counselors require you to stop using any of your credit cards that have not already been cancelled. Some counselors will allow you to keep one card only for emergencies.

You must also still pay a monthly fee to the credit counselor, but this should be far less than what debt settlement companies charge. Legitimate credit counselors only charge small fees and are nonprofit organizations. They do not make grand promises; they offer budgeting assistance; and they provide consumer financial education. If you cannot afford their fee, a legitimate credit counseling agency will help you for free. Sometimes they recommend a debt management plan, but only if you can afford it. Shop around; do not go with the first company you see and certainly do not go with the first company that reaches out to you or that you see in advertising. You might even go to an agency in person to see what it looks like.

Nevertheless, even legitimate credit counselors work closely with credit card companies and may even receive funding from those companies. They may not be quick to recommend a bankruptcy option even when that makes sense for you, and are unlikely to consider the fact that you should pay your rent, mortgage, and car payments ahead of credit card debt. Typically, they offer you no help on these other types of debt, although sometimes a credit counselor will be affiliated with a housing counselor.

Being a nonprofit organization is not enough to make a credit counselor trustworthy. Avoid any credit counseling agency that charges high fees or promises you it has special methods to reduce your debt that no one else has. Even when advertised as nonprofits, these agencies are not legitimate credit counselors and are trying to make as much money off you as possible. They will not help you in the long run. Another tip-off for a shady credit counselor is if it only offers to work out a payment plan with your credit card company and does not offer budgeting or financial education services.

Even a legitimate credit counseling agency is not for you if you are having trouble paying your rent or mortgage, car payments, utilities, student loans, or other higher priority debt. Most credit counselors only help with credit card debt and require you to make payments that only go to the card companies. You shouldn't devote money to credit card debt when you have more important obligations to deal with.

On the other hand, if all you are worried about is credit card debt, a legitimate credit counselor may make sense. They should help you work out a realistic budget that meets your living expenses and higher priority debt before they recommend a debt management plan. If you cannot pay your basic expenses and high priority debt, do not sign up for a debt management plan.

THE BANKRUPTCY OPTION

Bankruptcy is an option that can legitimately eliminate all your credit card debt. A chapter 7 bankruptcy can wipe out all of the typical credit card debt (unless you go on a shopping spree just before filing bankruptcy). A chapter 13 bankruptcy can reduce how much you pay and spread payments over three years or more—it is more typically used if you want to protect against the loss of your home or car.

While many people file for chapter 7 bankruptcy to get rid of crushing credit card debt, do not rush into bankruptcy with just a minor credit card obligation. There are limits to how often you can file bankruptcy and this option is best saved for when you are having trouble paying many of your debts and not just a relatively small credit card debt, and when the total amount of your debt is substantial.

Bankruptcy is also not free. If you are very low income and file under chapter 7, you may be able to waive the bankruptcy filing fee. Otherwise, as of 2018, you will pay $335 to file a chapter 7 bankruptcy or $310 to file a chapter 13 bankruptcy. You can pay these fees in installments. It is also highly recommended that you file with the help of an attorney who may also charge a fee.

Bankruptcy will, however, give you a fresh start without the credit card debts hanging over you. Your credit report will show that your credit cards are not delinquent, because the bankruptcy has cancelled them out and many creditors may find you more creditworthy for having passed through bankruptcy rather than being buried under debt. On the other hand, the fact that you filed bankruptcy will be on your credit report for ten years, while the credit card delinquency stays on your credit report only for seven years.

A good rule of thumb might be that it is too soon to file for bankruptcy when you just have a relatively small amount of delinquent credit card debt, but that it may make sense to file once the creditor has won a lawsuit against you and you have wages or bank accounts you want to protect from seizure.

13

Student Loans

TOPICS COVERED IN THIS CHAPTER

First Step: Identify What Kind of Loan You Have

Rights to Cancel Your Federal Student Loan

How to Reduce or Delay Your Payments

What to Expect If You Are in Default on Your Student Loan

Getting Out of Default

More Help with Federal Student Loan Problems

Private Student Loans

Most student loans are backed by the federal government. The federal government has extraordinary powers to collect defaulted student loans if you don't pay. It can seize tax refunds, deny you new federal student loans and grants, garnish a percentage of your wages without a court order, charge you very large collection fees, and even take a portion of your Social Security benefits. To make matters worse, there is no time limit for collection on federal student loans. The government can keep trying to collect for twenty, forty, or even more years.

Consequently, federal student loans require your immediate attention, both because of the federal government's special collection powers and because of the special rights you have to cancel, reduce, or delay your payment obligations. However, these special rights require you to take action to request them—you cannot wait for the government or the loan collector to offer these options to you.

These special collection tactics and student rights apply only to federal student loans and not loans made by your school, a bank, or another financial institution without any backing from the federal government. Those are called private student loans. How you deal with private student loans will differ greatly from how you deal with federal student loans. Private student loans are discussed at the end of this chapter.

FIRST STEP: IDENTIFY WHAT KIND OF LOAN YOU HAVE

Your rights and strategies will vary depending on the type student loan you have. Access information about your federal loans at the Department of Education's National Student Loan Data System (NSLDS), by going to www.nslds.ed.gov or calling 800-4-FED-AID, TDD: 800-730-8913. When first using the online system, create a user name and password, supply an e-mail address, and provide other identity information. The NSLDS will provide your approximate loan balance, the type loans you have, who is servicing those loans, and other loan details.

You can also determine what type of loan you have by checking your loan agreement papers. If you do not have copies, request them from your loan holder. If the loan is federal, the name of the federal loan program will be written at the top of the loan document and also on the loan application and billing statements. Your credit report will also have information about your loans.

Direct Stafford Loans are the most common student loan. Since 2010, nearly all new federal student loans are Direct Loans, made directly from the federal government to you, with the school's assistance.

Federal Family Education Loan (FFEL) Stafford Loans are similar to Direct Stafford Loans, but were given out by banks or other financial institutions, administered by state and nonprofit guaranty agencies, and ultimately backed by the United States. Before 2010, many student loans were made under the FFEL program (also known as guaranteed loans), and many borrowers are still making payments on these loans or are subject to collection on old FFEL loan debts.

PLUS Loans are loans for parents to help finance their children's education and also for graduate and professional students. Since 2010, PLUS loans have been issued under the Direct Loan program, but were mostly FFEL loans before that.

Consolidation Loans allow you to combine one or more federal loans into a new loan that has different, hopefully better, terms—now issued only through the Direct Consolidation Loan program though some borrowers continue to repay old FFEL Consolidation Loans.

Perkins Loans were made directly from the school you attended. If you stop paying the school, the loan may eventually be turned over to the U.S. Department of Education for collection. Perkins Loans have a fixed interest rate of 5%.

Private Student Loans are increasingly offered to students. These loans have no government involvement but are offered by banks or other private institutions. If your loan is not listed in the NSLDS, it is probably not a federal loan, unless it is a very old federal loan. Other ways to identify a private student loan include:

1. If the loan was made since 2010 and has the name of a bank on it, it is a private loan.

2. If the interest rate is 10% or higher, it is most likely a private loan.
3. If there is a co-signer on a loan, it is probably a private loan.
4. If, when you took out the loan, you received a disclosure statement that looks somewhat like the statement you get when you take out a car loan, then it is probably a private loan.

Most of the discussion in this chapter applies to federal loans only. A separate section at the end of the chapter discusses private student loans.

RIGHTS TO CANCEL YOUR FEDERAL STUDENT LOAN

If there were serious problems with the school, if you are disabled (or have passed away), even if you are in default on the loan, you may be able to apply to have your federal loan discharged—that is cancelled—by submitting paperwork to your loan servicer, debt collector, or directly to the Department of Education. This is an administrative process. Ask whoever is holding your loan for the appropriate discharge request form. The forms are also available at https://studentaid.ed.gov. Be prepared to meet resistance and delay, insist on your rights, and consider seeking assistance from an attorney. You may also have rights to cancel the debt by filing bankruptcy.

A successful administrative discharge may not only completely wipe out the current loan, but may allow you to get back money you paid on the loan *and* any money that was taken from you through tax refund intercepts, wage garnishment, or other collection methods. In some cases, the government is also required to delete negative references on your credit report.

This section summarizes your rights to cancel your loan. More information is available from the https://studentaid.ed.gov, from NCLC at www.studentloanborrowerassistance.org, and NCLC's *Student Loan Law* (5th ed. 2015), *updated at* www.nclc.org/library.

Closed School Discharge. If your school closed while you were enrolled or within 120 days of your leaving the school, your loans can be discharged. (In a few cases, the 120-day period may be extended.)

Unpaid Refund Discharge. You are eligible to discharge all or a portion of a loan if you left school and the school failed to pay you a refund you were owed.

Borrower Defense to Repayment Discharge. You may seek to discharge all or a portion of a loan if your school misled you or otherwise violated state law regarding your loans or education. You should provide information identifying the law that your school violated and evidence showing the violation.

False Certification Discharge. A false certification discharge application form is available if any of the following happened to you (or to the student, if you're a Parent PLUS borrower):

- At the time of enrollment, state law disqualified you from getting a job in the occupation for which you were being trained (for example, you were enrolled in a truck driving program even though you had a physical disability that prevented you from obtaining a truck-driving license).
- You did not have a valid high school diploma or GED when you went to the school, and your school did not ensure that you met the applicable alternative financial aid eligibility criteria (such as through an ability-to-benefit test).
- The school forged your name on the loan papers or check endorsements, and you never went to school for the times covered by the forgery.

Disability Discharge. You can discharge your loan if the Department of Veterans Affairs, the Social Security Administration, or your physician certifies that you have a total and permanent disability. Parents with PLUS Loans may apply for discharge based on their own disabilities, not those of their child. If two parents have a PLUS Loan and only one becomes disabled, the other must still repay the loan.

The first step to apply is to notify Nelnet (a company hired by the Department of Education), by calling 888-303-7818 (8 a.m. to 8 p.m. EST, 7 days a week), e-mailing DisabilityInformation@Nelnet.net, or applying at www.disabilitydischarge.com. You can designate a representative to apply on your behalf, but you first must fill out the representative designation form available at www.disabilitydischarge.com. Additional details about applying are available there as well.

Death Discharge. Your estate will not have to pay back your student loans. Your estate should submit an original or certified copy of the death certificate to the loan holder. The death of both parents with a PLUS Loan (assuming both took out the loan) is also grounds for the "death discharge," but not the death of only one of two obligated parents. A parent can also apply for discharge of a PLUS Loan if the student for whom the parent received the loan dies.

Other Grounds for Loan Cancellation or Forgiveness. The Public Service Loan Forgiveness program allows Direct Loan borrowers employed in certain occupations to discharge any remaining loans after making 120 qualifying payments (the equivalent of ten years of payments). Certain teachers who have taught for five consecutive years are also eligible for at least partial loan forgiveness. Perkins Loans also may be partially or completely cancelled for borrowers who work in certain fields. Be sure to review the details about all of these programs at https://studentaid.ed.gov.

Bankruptcy. It is very difficult, but not impossible, to discharge a student loan in bankruptcy. You must prove that repaying the loan would cause an "undue hardship" for you and your dependents. Courts generally interpret this to mean that you must have serious financial problems which are likely to persist for reasons beyond your control. It is usually better to ask the bankruptcy court to make this determination at the time of the bankruptcy filing, but if you fail to do so, the bankruptcy court can make that determination later when collection attempts on the student loan are renewed.

HOW TO REDUCE OR DELAY YOUR PAYMENTS

If loan discharge, cancellation, or forgiveness is not currently available to you, the government also offers options to lower your monthly payments, so you don't default. Even if you do default, you can get out of default and qualify for one of these lower payment plans (see **Getting Out of Default** later in this chapter).

The typical federal student loan repayment plan, called the Standard Repayment Plan, generally gives you up to ten years to repay your student loan (up to thirty years for consolidation loans). Other repayment plans may lower your payments (at least initially). These plans do not reduce your total obligation, but they let you pay it off more slowly. This means that additional interest will be added to the loan, and you could end up paying more interest in exchange for more affordable monthly payments.

Extended Repayment Plan. This option allows you to extend repayment over a longer period (usually no more than twenty-five years), thus lowering your monthly payment. These plans are generally available only if you have loans totaling more than $30,000.

Graduated Repayment Plan. Payments start out low and increase every two years. In most cases, however, the loan still must be paid over a ten-year period.

Income-Sensitive Repayment Plan. If you have an FFEL and do not want to or cannot consolidate into a Direct Loan, you best option is one of the income-driven repayment plans (discussed below) or possibly an income sensitive plan. Income-sensitive repayment allows for reduced monthly payments due to your financial circumstances. Payment is calculated based on your total gross income, rather than your discretionary income. There is no loan forgiveness under this plan even after several years of repayment.

Alternative Repayment Plan. If no other plan is affordable, Direct Loan borrowers who have "exceptional circumstances" can submit documentation to apply for a repayment plan that is affordable. High medical expenses or private student loan payments could be among the expenses you provide to your loan servicer. There is no loan forgiveness under this plan.

Income Driven Repayment Plans. In recent years, the government has created a range of income-driven repayment (IDR) plans. These plans calculate your monthly payment after considering your income, rather than basing the plan on your loan balance. By lowering monthly payments—in some cases to zero—these plans help you avoid default, which prevents tax refund intercepts, wage garnishment, seizure of benefits, and high collection costs.

For these IDR plans, your loan servicer or lender will check with you every year to determine your income. If you fail to respond you will be dropped from the payment plan and your monthly payment will usually increase by a lot! In some instances, your balance continues to grow even though you make monthly payments, as interest will continue to be added to your loans. However, the government may pay a portion of the interest, depending on your loan type and repayment plan. Also, if you stay on an income-driven repayment plan for twenty or twenty-five years (depending on the plan), any remaining debt is forgiven, though some borrowers may owe taxes because of the forgiven debt.

Brief descriptions of these plans follow below. Detailed information about each of these repayment plans and a calculator to compute your payment amounts is available at www.ibrinfo.org or https://studentloans.gov. Pay special attention to which loan types qualify for which of these repayment plans. FFEL and Parent PLUS borrowers can only access some of these plans.

Pay As You Earn (PAYE) Repayment Plan. This is often the best option for borrowers who qualify, particularly if you would otherwise have high student loan payments relative to your income. PAYE is only for those who had no student loan obligations as of October 1, 2007, and then received a Direct Loan disbursement on or after October 1, 2011. You pay 10% of your "discretionary income"—the amount by which your adjusted gross income exceeds 150% of the poverty line for your state and family size.

In 2018, 150% of poverty was $1,517/month for a one-person household, $2,057/month for a two-person household, and $3,137/month for a four-person household. (The numbers vary in Hawaii, Alaska, or with different family sizes.) For example, if your monthly income is $120 above 150% of the poverty line, you only pay $12 a month.

If you are married, your spouse's income is included in this calculation only if you file a joint tax return. Your monthly payments can't go higher than your payments on the Standard Repayment Plan. After twenty years of payments on PAYE, your remaining student loans are forgiven.

Revised Pay As You Earn (REPAYE) Repayment Plan. REPAYE incorporates many of the benefits of PAYE and makes them available to borrowers no matter when they took out their loans. Under REPAYE, you pay 10% of your discretionary income toward your student loans. However, if you are married, then your spouse's income is included in this calculation even if you file separate tax returns. (The only exception is for spouses who are separated and borrowers who cannot reasonably access their spouse's income information.)

Under the REPAYE plan, there is no cap on your monthly payment so that higher income borrowers could end up with payments higher than on the Standard Repayment Plan. If you only have loans from undergraduate studies, the remaining loan is forgiven after twenty years of payments. Forgiveness for loans from graduate or professional school is not available until after twenty-five years of payments.

Income-Based Repayment (IBR) Plans. There are different IBR plans based on how recent your student loans are. If, on July 1, 2014, you had a zero balance on any loans and then took out a Direct Loan after July 1, 2014, your rights are almost exactly the same as under a PAYE plan. Because PAYE offers more flexibility in switching plans, you may choose to use PAYE (or REPAYE) instead of IBR. However, PAYE and REPAYE are not available for FFEL loans, but those loans are eligible for IBR.

For older loans, IBR is not quite as generous as IBR is for newer loans. Your payments are 15% of the difference between your income and 150% of the poverty line, and forgiveness occurs after twenty-five years. In either case, as with PAYE, your spouse's income is only included in the payment calculation if you file joint tax returns.

Income-Contingent Repayment (ICR) Plan. ICR usually requires higher payments than PAYE and REPAYE. But it is essentially the only income-driven repayment option for Parent PLUS borrowers. If you have an FFEL Parent PLUS Loan, you can consolidate it into a Direct Consolidation Loan to become eligible for

ICR. The calculators at https://studentloans.gov estimate what your monthly payment will be on ICR.

Deferments. If you cannot manage your monthly payment using one of the repayment options listed above, you may choose to seek a deferment instead. A loan deferment lets you temporarily delay repaying your loan, usually for up to a year, though sometimes longer. You can often renew the deferment if it ends, but if not, you must resume making payments. Deferments are not available if you are already in default, typically defined as missing nine payments. To benefit from deferment, you must first get out of default, as described later in this chapter.

Benefits from deferment depend on whether your loan is subsidized by the government. Subsidized loans are given out based on financial need. As of July 2012, graduate and professional students were no longer eligible for new subsidized loans.

For subsidized loans, the government makes interest payments for you during the deferment period. Your loan balance will be no higher after the deferment period than before. When you defer an unsubsidized loan or a PLUS Loan, you will later have to pay back the interest that accrued during the deferment period. If you can afford it, you should consider paying the interest while you are in a deferment period.

You have a legal right to a loan deferment under specified conditions. For most loans that you got after July 1, 1993, the available deferments include:

- Unemployment deferments (for up to three years);
- Economic hardship deferments (granted one year at a time for up to three years);
- In-school deferments for at least half-time study;
- Graduate fellowship deferments;
- Rehabilitation training program deferments;
- Military service deferments (there is no time limit, but eligibility ends 180 days after demobilization or the end of active duty service); and
- Post-active duty deferments for borrowers who are enrolled in school when they are called to active duty and plan to re-enroll after their service is completed.

FFEL and Perkins Loans have somewhat different deferment rules than those for Direct Loans.

Forbearances. If you cannot qualify for a deferment, you can still request loan "forbearance," meaning you do not have to pay for a while, and no adverse action will be taken against you during the forbearance period. Even for a subsidized loan, the government does not pay interest for you. You will eventually have to repay the full loan amount and all accrued interest. In some cases, you should be able to get a forbearance even if you're already in default. This will not get you out of default without further action.

In some circumstances, you have a legal right to a forbearance. For example, you have a right to forbear an FFEL or Direct Loan if your total student loan payments exceed 20% of your income even if you are many months delinquent. There are limits to how many times you can automatically get this and most other forbearances. If you don't have a right to a forbearance, loan holders still may grant you one, especially for health or other personal problems that affect your ability to make your monthly payments.

WHAT TO EXPECT IF YOU ARE IN DEFAULT ON YOUR STUDENT LOAN

The government has a number of aggressive collection tactics it can take if you are in default on a federal student loan, which usually means you have not made payments for at least nine months. The next section describes methods to avoid those tactics completely by getting your loan out of default status.

Denial of New Student Loans and Grants. If you're in default, the government can deny you new federal student loans and grants.

Your Credit Report. Most student loan defaults appear on your credit report for seven years. Perkins Loans may be reported until repaid in full, and then for seven years from the date of default.

Aggressive Collection Agency Contacts. Most student loan debt collection is by private agencies hired by the government or other loan holders. Private debt collectors are likely to be aggressive and to not inform you of options that would help you out, such as loan cancellation rights or affordable repayment plans. In general, you have the same rights to deal with student loan debt collectors as with any other debt collector—as detailed in Chapter 2. Complain about problems with student loan debt collectors to the Department of Education at https://feedback.studentaid.ed.gov/ and the Consumer Financial Protection Bureau at https://consumerfinance.gov/complaint/.

Collection Fees. When you are in default, a large portion of anything you pay to a collection agency on the loan is applied to high collection fees and not to pay off your loan—fees can be as high as 25% of your payment (less in some cases). Fees on Perkins Loans can be as high as 40%.

Tax Refund Offsets. When in default, the government can intercept your tax refund, including your earned income tax credit. The only sure-fire way to avoid this is not to have a tax refund due by lowering your withholding or any estimated tax payments you make. If your joint tax refund is seized, your spouse can recover some of the amount by filing IRS Form 8379, a simple form available at www.irs.gov.

You have the right to be notified before your tax refund is taken. You can contest the taking by checking appropriate boxes on the form (for example, the school closed or the school failed to give you a refund), by returning it immediately and by asking for a hearing. Send the form back return receipt requested as proof that you sent it. Do this every year that you get a notice. If you receive notice only after your tax refund is offset, you can contest the offset after the fact.

Wage Garnishment. When in default on a federal student loan, the government can garnish part of your wages *without first obtaining a court judgment.* The first $217.50/week of "disposable pay" (basically your take-home pay) is protected from garnishment. If your disposable pay is less than $256/week, the government can take the amount that exceeds $217.50/wk. If you make more than $256/week, it can take 15% of the pay.

There are a number of ways to stop student loan garnishments:

1. Request a hearing and explain why you think you need not repay the loan.
2. Ask for a repayment agreement, especially before the wage garnishment begins.
3. Explain you lost your old job against your wishes and have not been continuously employed in a new job for a full year.
4. If you enter a rehabilitation plan (discussed later in this chapter), the garnishments stop after your fifth on-time rehabilitation payment.

Federal Benefit Offsets. The government can seize part of certain or your government benefits, including Social Security, Social Security Disability, certain railroad retirement benefits, and Black Lung Part B benefits. Some benefits are exempt from seizure, including Supplemental Security Income (SSI), Veterans benefits, and Black Lung Part C. To find out which benefits can be seized or are protected, go to www.fms.treas.gov.

For benefits the government can seize, the government cannot touch the first $750 a month. If your monthly benefits are under $832 a month, it can seize the amount that is left after $750 is protected. If your benefits are over $832 a month, it can seize 15% of your benefits.

You should also receive a notice warning you that your benefits are going to be taken, with information about your right to request a hearing with the agency that is collecting the money. Request a hearing if you think you have defenses to repayment or if you are facing financial hardships.

Lawsuits. There is no time limit for the government to sue you to collect on federal student loan debt. If you are sued, you may have defenses and you can resolve the lawsuit by getting out of default (as discussed below) and resuming payments, or by applying for loan cancellation or discharge.

License Revocations. Some states allow professional and vocational boards to refuse to certify, certify with restrictions, suspend, or revoke your professional or vocational license, or even fine you if you default on a *state*-guaranteed student loan. Some states may allow for suspension or revocation of your driver's license, too. Some states also apply these policies if you are in default on federal student loans.

GETTING OUT OF DEFAULT

As described in the prior two subsections, after you default on your federal student loan by missing nine months of payments, you may be subjected to harsh collection tactics and lose access to some of the most generous repayment plans and deferments. It is greatly to your advantage to get out of default. One way is to cancel the loan as described earlier in the chapter. Three other ways are described below, but these do not happen automatically—you must press for your rights and initiate the request.

Reach a Settlement to Pay Off Your Loan Balance. You can get out of default by negotiating a settlement with your loan holder or the Department of Education to pay a lesser amount to pay off the loan. It can be difficult to negotiate a "good" deal, and you probably will need a large, lump-sum amount to offer. Get any settlement in a writing that confirms that you no longer owe anything, then pay on time, and request a satisfaction letter as proof of your payment in case someone attempts to collect further from you. Consult with a tax professional about any tax liability from your settlement.

Loan Consolidation. Loan consolidation is taking out a new federal Direct Loan that repays at least one Perkins, FFEL, or Direct Loan. Your consolidation loan, being new, is not in default. Being a Direct Loan, it is eligible for plans to reduce your payments not available to those with FFEL or Perkins Loans. Consolidation can also simplify repayment if you currently submit payments to multiple servicers.

You can apply online and need not deal with debt collectors or servicers. You can consolidate your loans only once, although there are a few exceptions to this, such as if you are adding new loans that were not included in the first consolidation. Consolidation is not an option if your wages are presently being garnished to repay your student loans. (You can still consolidate if the government is taking part of your Social Security benefits or other income, though.) If you consolidate loans in default, collection costs may be added into the consolidation loan, increasing your loan balance by as much as 18.5%. Since the consolidation is a new loan, you may lose the right to raise defenses you have on the old loans.

You must either pay the consolidation loan through enrollment in an income-driven repayment plan (such as PAYE, described above) *or* by first making three consecutive reasonable and affordable monthly payments. Because you need to do only one or the other, do not believe a collection agency that tells you that you have to make three payments on your old loans before you can consolidate. Consolidation also extends your repayment term and, therefore reduces monthly payments if they are not otherwise reduced through enrollment in a payment plan that takes your income into account.

Distinguish Direct Consolidation Loans from private loan consolidation products. It is dangerous to consolidate federal loans into a private consolidation loan. If you consolidate into a private loan, you lose the rights you have under the federal loan program, including rights to cancel or reduce your loan payments. Private lenders may even offer you bonuses if you agree to consolidate with them, but this may not be the right choice for you. Read the fine print!

More information about consolidation loans can be found in NCLC's *Student Loan Law* (5th ed. 2015), *updated online at* www.nclc.org/library, at www.studentloanborrowerassistance.org, by calling 800-557-7392, or by visiting www.studentloans.gov.

Loan Rehabilitation. This section explains how to get out of default by "rehabilitating" your Direct or FFEL Loan—the rules are slightly different for Perkins Loans. Loan rehabilitation requires you make nine payments within 20 days of the due date during a period of ten consecutive months. After five consecutive payments, wage garnishments stop. If needed, call the collection agency or your loan holder to remind them to stop the garnishments. Once you make six consecutive payments, you re-establish eligibility for new federal student loans and grants. You must complete all nine payments, and then a Direct Loan gets out of default. For an FFEL Loan, the loan holder must also sell your defaulted loan to a new lender. If you don't make all of your payments, you have to start the rehabilitation process all over again.

Rehabilitation payments need not be at your old payment amount, but can be at a "reasonable and affordable" amount. Request lower payments and the collector should offer payments equal to 15% of the difference between your income and 150% of the poverty line. In 2018, 150% of poverty was $1,517/month for a one-person household, $2,057/month for a two-person household, and $3,137/month for a four-person household. (The numbers vary in Hawaii, Alaska, or with different family sizes.) For example, if your monthly income is $120 above 150% of the poverty line, you only pay $18 a month.

If the amount is still too high, try to negotiate a lower amount based on your income and expenses. The minimum monthly payment for rehabilitation is $5—even if your income is below 150% of the poverty line, you still have to pay $5 each month during rehabilitation.

After a successful rehabilitation, you are no longer in default, the default notation is removed from your credit record, and a new repayment schedule is established, but you are still paying on the same loan. You should have access to all of the flexible and income-driven repayment plans that fit your loan type, and you regain eligibility for deferments and forbearances you have not exhausted. The amount of your rehabilitated loan increases as much as 16% to reflect collection costs. Once you rehabilitate your loan, you will not be able to do it again if you end up back in default.

Pros and Cons of Consolidation vs. Rehabilitation. Weigh the pros and cons between consolidation and rehabilitation; do not be pressured by a debt collector to choose one or the other. Make sure that you can afford to make the new payments for the option you choose so that you don't end up back in default.

Consolidation gets you out of default as soon as the loan is consolidated; rehabilitation requires nine payments in ten months; and for FFEL loans, there must be a buyer for your loan. Consolidation removes all loans from default with the one consolidation; rehabilitation requires you to separately deal with each loan. If you have an FFEL or Perkins Loan, only consolidation into the Direct Loan program gives you access to some of the newer income-driven repayment plans. Consolidation allows you to apply online; rehabilitation requires you to work out a payment amount with debt collectors. When you consolidate, you choose your new servicer, but you don't have that option when you rehabilitate a loan.

Rehabilitation's main benefit is that if you successfully complete the rehabilitation process, the default notation on your credit report is erased, but any other negative information still remains. After consolidation, the credit report notes that you had a defaulted loan for a period of time, but that the loan is paid in full. If you have claims and defenses concerning your federal student loan, you may lose the right to raise them after consolidation, but not after rehabilitation.

MORE HELP WITH FEDERAL STUDENT LOAN PROBLEMS

Free information to help you with all types of student loan problems is available at NCLC's website, www.studentloanborrowerassistance.org. NCLC's *Student Loan Law* (5th ed. 2015), *updated online at* www.nclc.org/library, has even more detailed information. The best Department of Education website to use for general information is https://studentaid.ed.gov and for information about your loans or how to manage your loans, you can use https://studentloans.gov. Also helpful is www.ed.gov. Useful publications to download from these websites, available in English and Spanish, include *Do You Need Money for College?, The Guide to Federal Student Aid,* and *Federal Student Loans: Basics for Students.*

Borrowers can submit problems online at https://feedback.studentaid.ed.gov to the Department of Education's Federal Student Aid Ombudsman or by calling toll-free 877-557-2575. Many guaranty agencies and private lenders also have ombudsman or customer advocate units. Another source to receive complaints is the Consumer Financial Protection Bureau at https://consumerfinance.gov/complaint. You can also contact your state or local consumer protection agency to make a complaint or seek assistance.

PRIVATE STUDENT LOANS

Dealing with Your Private Student Loans. Private student loan payments are lower priority than paying your mortgage, rent, utilities, car loan, or even your federal student loans. Private student loans should be treated like your credit card or medical debt—the only difference being that, as with federal student loans, it is very difficult to discharge most private student loans in bankruptcy.

Private student loan lenders or collectors may be willing to negotiate because they do not have as many collection tools as the federal government. They cannot intercept your taxes, seize your Social Security benefits, seize your wages before going to court, or deny you future government loans. A defaulted private loan may, however, show up on your credit report.

Private lenders often hire collection agencies. You have the same rights as with any other debt to fight back against any collection harassment or abuse. See Chapter 2.

If a number of years have passed since you last made a payment or requested a deferment or forbearance, consult an attorney before you contact the lender or start making payments again. A "statute of limitations" may have already expired on the loan, meaning the lender can no longer sue you on the debt. Payment now or even a new promise to pay may suddenly give the lender the right to sue you for years into the future.

It can be complicated to determine the number of years before the statute of limitations prevents suit on a debt, hence the need for legal help. In many places, the number of years is six after your default, but in some states and for certain loans it may be only three or four years, or even as long as twenty. The attorney will want to see a copy of the loan agreement to help determine this. If you do not have a copy, request one from the lender whose contact information may be on collection letters or your credit report. If you reach out to the lender, avoid making payments or promises to repay, and don't contact the lender unless you are prepared for them to follow up with collection efforts.

Private student loans do not have the same flexible repayment, loan cancellation, and other borrower protections that federal student loans have, but there may be steps you can take to help. See if the loan agreement says anything about relief if you are having trouble making payments. If the statute of limitations has not expired, you may choose to negotiate for lower payments or even principal reduction.

The borrower or the borrower's estate will generally be liable for the loan even if the borrower becomes permanently disabled or dies, but some private student loan lenders voluntarily cancel the debt in these circumstances. For loans extended after November 20, 2018, the lender cannot declare a default and ask for the immediate payment of the full loan amount from either the student or a co-signer just because the student has declared bankruptcy or dies. For loans extended after that date, a co-signer's legal obligation is also released upon the student's death. Even for loans extended before November 20, 2018, lenders may voluntarily implement the same protections.

You cannot consolidate private loans into federal loans. You *should not* consolidate federal loans into private ones. But you can look into consolidating higher interest private loans into a lower interest private loan. Also, if your private student loan's interest rate is more than 6%, and you go on military active duty after taking out the loan, you have a right to reduce the interest rate to 6% while you are on active duty. If the lender does not adjust your rate automatically, notify it of your active duty status.

In general, the ability to discharge private student loans in bankruptcy is subject to the same difficult standard as applies to federal student loans. But there is an important exception. If the school you attended (such as an unlicensed vocational school) is not eligible to participate in one of the federal student financial assistance programs, then you can discharge the private student loan in bankruptcy just like any other unsecured debt.

Defending Against a Private Student Loan Collection Lawsuit. Private student loan lenders do not have the collection tools available to the government, so that they are more likely to sue on an unpaid debt. But you have a number of defenses to such lawsuits.

If the school itself initially gave you the loan or referred you to a private lender, then you can raise as a defense to the collection law suit any claim or defense you have against the school. A viable defense might be that the school misrepresented graduates' employment prospects or the overall quality of the program, or engaged in other serious misconduct, but not that the math teacher was too tough.

Look carefully at any collection fees the private lender is seeking. The right to those fees must be stated in the loan agreement, and state law may further limit collection fees.

If you have a dispute or questions, it is prudent first to contact the lender. Private student loan lenders may have an ombudsman or other customer advocate unit. The Consumer Financial Protection Bureau has a complaint system for borrowers experiencing problems with private student loans. To ask a question or file a complaint, go to https://consumerfinance.gov/complaint or call toll-free 855-411-CFPB. You can also contact your state or local consumer protection agency to make a complaint or seek assistance.

14

Car Loans and Repossessions

TOPICS COVERED IN THIS CHAPTER

When buying a car on credit, you almost always must put up the car as collateral for the loan. Sometimes consumers also use their cars as collateral for an unrelated small loan. Most of these are high cost auto title or "auto pawn" loans, which are legal in some states but illegal in others.

If your car is collateral for a loan and you get behind on your payments or violate other loan terms, you risk the immediate repossession of your car. Miss one or two payments and your car may be gone.

A repossession agent may break into your car and drive or tow it away. The process is called "self-help" because the creditor is not required to go to court to get permission from a judge to repossess your car. In most states, the creditor does not even have to notify you that a repossession is about to take place.

There are important exceptions to a creditor's right to use "self-help" repossession:

- The creditor must have taken the car as collateral or the car must have been leased to you. For example, if you do not pay a medical debt or a credit card debt, the medical provider or card issuer cannot repossess your car.
- In some states, the creditor must first give you notice of the right to catch up on delinquent payments. (See **Curing a Default** below.)
- A self-help repossession cannot breach the peace.
- Self-help repossession is generally illegal on certain American Indian reservations. In Louisiana, self-help repossession is illegal unless the creditor is a licensed financial institution or bank that has a state or U.S. charter and the repossession agent has a state license. In Wisconsin, the consumer can object

to self-help repossession if the consumer does so within 15 days of receiving notice of a pending repossession. Self-help repossession is legal in Maryland only if the credit agreement allows it.

- A creditor cannot use self-help to repossess a car owned by active duty military personnel if the debt was incurred *before* the individual entered active duty. Children, spouses, and other dependents of active duty military personnel are similarly protected, but only if they apply to a court for an order prohibiting repossession.

After the creditor repossesses your car, the creditor will then sell it, typically for much less than it is worth. If so, you may find yourself being sued for the amount of money that the creditor claims remains to be paid on the loan after deducting the proceeds of the sale. This can be thousands of dollars.

This chapter provides advice on how to avoid repossession and what to do if a car is repossessed. Manufactured home repossessions are discussed in Chapter 16.

STRATEGIES TO PREVENT REPOSSESSION

Keeping Current on Car Payments. Do not pay credit card debts, medical bills, or other low priority debts ahead of car payments. If you skip payments on low priority debts, you will not be in immediate danger of losing your property. Skip one or two car payments and you risk losing your car. If you find it necessary to miss payments on low priority debts, try to get caught up on your back-payments as soon as possible.

Keep Your Car's Damage Insurance Current. If your damage insurance lapses, the creditor is likely to add replacement insurance to your car payments that is much more expensive and offers much less protection than insurance you could purchase yourself. You will have even more trouble keeping up your now higher cost car payments.

Consider Cancelling Other Insurance and Add-ons. Often, as part of a car sale, the dealer has sold you add-on products—a service contract, credit life insurance, credit accident and health (or disability) insurance, credit unemployment insurance, GAP insurance, theft protection, tire protection, key fob replacement, or an auto club membership. These add-ons are often overpriced or even worth very little. Find out whether you can cancel these add-ons and get a rebate of the unused part of their cost. The rebate may help you make one or more of your payments on the car and may make future payments lower.

Negotiate with the Creditor. Some creditors may be willing to allow you to skip a payment or make a payment late. If you get an agreement, confirm it in writing. Make sure the agreement is one that you can comply with. For example, if the creditor allows you to make a payment ten days late, make sure before you agree to this that you really can make the payment then.

Curing a Default. The following states give consumers a right to cure—a second chance to make up late car payments before repossession: California, Colorado, Connecticut, the District of Columbia, Iowa, Kansas, Maine, Massachusetts, Missouri, Nebraska, New Hampshire, Puerto Rico, Rhode Island, South Carolina, South Dakota, Virginia, West Virginia, and Wisconsin. Pay attention to the notice you will get telling you how many days you have to pay the amount past-due to avoid repossession. Rights to cure auto *leases* are available in Connecticut, the District of Columbia, Illinois, Iowa, Kansas, Maine, New Hampshire, New Jersey, New York, Rhode Island, West Virginia, and Wisconsin.

Sell the Car. If you cannot afford your car loan payments, insurance, and maintenance costs, you are generally better off selling the car than having it repossessed. Selling the car yourself before it is repossessed will bring in a much higher price than a repossession sale would, you will not have to pay the creditor for the creditor's repossession, storage, and sales expenses, and you can obtain a larger rebate on any service contract, automobile insurance, or credit insurance that you cancel along with the sale. Your credit rating will also be higher than if the car is repossessed.

Because the creditor has a lien on your car, you can only sell it with clear title if you use the sale proceeds to pay the creditor the full outstanding balance. If you cannot sell the car for as much as is owed on the loan, you will have to pay the creditor the difference, unless you convince the creditor to take less.

Avoid anyone who offers to "broker" a sale or lease of your car to another consumer. In many states car brokerage is illegal. A scammer may take money from both you and the new "purchaser," but not complete the paperwork for a real transfer in ownership or forward payments to your lessor or creditor. Instead, you will lose the use of your car but still owe the creditor or lessor the full amount.

Return the Car to the Creditor, but Make Sure You Get a Fair Deal. Done incorrectly, voluntarily turning the car in to the creditor will not help you much. You will still owe the creditor if the repossession sales proceeds are less than what you owe and you will have waived your claims and defenses. Voluntarily turning the car in might make sense if you obtain a *written agreement* from the creditor that you do not owe anything else on the loan. Also try to have the creditor state in the agreement that it will not report the default to a credit reporting bureau.

The situation is similar when you turn in a leased car. It is a common mistake to believe that you will have no further obligation after you turn the car in early. You will have no further obligation (except excess mileage or unusual wear) if you turn the car in at the *scheduled* termination of the lease. Your liability at *early* termination may be thousands of dollars. Before turning in a leased car early, negotiate to reduce or eliminate your early termination liability. Make sure to get this agreement in writing.

Thwarting a Self-Help Repossession. Self-help repossession can take place on the street or even in your driveway. But a repossessor cannot legally break into a locked garage. Repossessors also cannot seize a car they cannot find, but most states make it a criminal offense to conceal collateral (such as your car) or to move it out of state. It is also becoming more and more difficult to hide a car because of technological advancements in tracking cars.

Most courts say that if you or a family member is present during the repossession and objects, the repossession should not continue. But your objection should *not* involve force. Politely and firmly tell the repossessor not to take the car. Do not be swayed by any legal advice offered by the repossessor.

Never resort to force. Never meet force with force. If the repossessor uses force or threats, or otherwise breaches the peace, call the police. Do not take matters into your own hands. After the fact, consult an attorney. There are significant legal remedies available to challenge an illegal repossession.

Never resist government officials in the performance of their duties, but make sure the person is not just impersonating a government official. Government officials should only operate pursuant to written court orders and should not assist self-help repossessions. Ask for the official's identity and the reason why the official is there. Inspect any documents the official waives around claiming to be a court order.

When you are delinquent on a car loan, it is risky to bring your car in for repairs to the dealer or anyone else the creditor would know. Do not drive the car to the creditor's place of business to discuss a work-out agreement. You may have to walk home if you fail to reach a satisfactory arrangement.

File for Bankruptcy Protection. Once you file for either a chapter 7 or 13 bankruptcy, no one can take any action against your property, including repossessors. Although a lender may later ask the bankruptcy court for permission to take the car, there can be no repossession before obtaining that permission. A chapter 13 bankruptcy also can help you keep the car in the long run because you can spread out your payments (both past-due and new payments) over three to five years. Keeping the car will be more difficult if you file under chapter 7, because at some point you will have to pay the creditor either the lesser of the car's value or the total amount that remains owed on the car loan.

Minimize the Loss of Personal Property Inside the Car. Property left in a car has a way of disappearing after the car is seized. If you anticipate a repossession, remove your personal property such as tools, GPS devices, media players, clothes, and sporting equipment from your car. Remove any important records from the glove compartment. There are some items, however, such as children's car seats and a spare tire, that should be left in the car while you use it. Make a list of these items and photograph them so that you will be in a better position to claim them if the car is repossessed.

WHAT TO DO *AFTER* YOUR CAR IS REPOSSESSED

Get Back Personal Property Left in the Car. Creditors cannot keep your personal property that was left in your car after it has been repossessed. The lender can only keep the car itself. As soon as possible, demand both by phone and in writing any property left in the car specifying each item. Make the request *quickly* before the property disappears.

In Some States You Can Reinstate the Contract and Get the Car Back. The following states allow a consumer to reinstate the contract after repossession in at least some circumstances: California, Connecticut, the District of Columbia, Illinois, Maryland, Mississippi, New York, Ohio, Rhode Island (although the phrasing of the law is not completely clear), and Wisconsin. Reinstating the contract allows you to recover the repossessed car by paying only the back-due payments, not the full amount of the debt. You may also have to pay the costs of the repossession and any storage charges, plus possibly one or two payments in advance. You must act quickly. In most states where it is allowed, you have only a few weeks to reinstate after repossession.

You Can Redeem the Car. In every state, after a repossession, you can redeem the car. This means that you can get the car back by paying the full remaining amount due plus expenses (redemption does not apply to leases). The creditor must notify you of the date of the car's sale or a date after which the car will be sold and the creditor must include a telephone number to call to find out how much you have to pay to redeem the car. You can redeem the car up until the very moment before the car is sold.

If you are having trouble keeping up with monthly payments, you are unlikely to be able to pay off the whole debt at once. If a car is important to you and worth more than the debt, consider borrowing from friends, relatives, or elsewhere. Don't mortgage your house to get your car back because defaulting on that loan may result in your losing your home.

Try to Negotiate with the Creditor. If your car has just been repossessed, you might be able to negotiate to get the car back. You are in a particularly strong position if you have significant claims or defenses relating to the car, its credit terms, or its repossession. If a car has minimal resale value, the creditor should also prefer a workout agreement to a worthless asset.

Get the Car Back by Filing Bankruptcy. You can get your car back by filing bankruptcy, even after it has been repossessed, as long as you do so before the creditor sells it. Once you get the car back, if you want to keep it for the long-term, you must make payment arrangements, which as explained below, will vary depending on whether you file a chapter 7 or 13 bankruptcy.

In a chapter 7 bankruptcy, you must pay the creditor the lesser of the full remaining balance of the debt or the car's value. Some creditors let you make this payment in installments, but other creditors will require you to pay the full amount in one lump sum.

In a chapter 13 bankruptcy, you have several ways of keeping the car. Probably the best one is to set up a plan to pay off the car loan in monthly installments over a period as long as five years. The interest rate charged in a chapter 13 plan can, in some instances, be lower than what you are paying on the car loan. You may even reduce the amount owed to the current value of the car, if the car's value is less than the amount you owe, particularly if you bought the car over 910 days before your bankruptcy filing.

When the Repossession Was Wrongful. You can file a lawsuit to get the car back and receive damages if the car was taken improperly, but this will require the help of an attorney.

CREDITORS' COLLECTION EFFORTS *AFTER* THE REPOSSESSION SALE—THE DEFICIENCY ACTION

After repossession, the creditor will sell your car and apply the sale price (after deducting all repossession and sale expenses) against the amount you owe. If the net sales proceeds are more than the amount you owe, the creditor must pay you the "surplus." Far more commonly, however, the net sale proceeds will be less than the amount you owe. When the net sale proceeds is less than the amount you owe, it is called a "deficiency." If there is a remaining amount due, creditors will then come after you for the deficiency. When a lessor repossesses a leased vehicle, the result is the same. The car is sold and the lessor seeks a further amount called "an early termination charge."

Once your car has been repossessed, your deficiency obligation is no longer backed up by any collateral, and should be treated as a low priority debt just like a hospital bill or a credit card debt. You should not pay it ahead of more pressing obligations, such as rent or utility bills. With a repossession already indicated on your credit record, an unpaid deficiency amount will not do much more to hurt your credit score.

Many defenses may be available to you if a creditor attempts to collect this deficiency through a lawsuit. The flip side of creditors being able to seize and sell your car without court supervision is that they have to strictly follow certain rules, and they often do not. Your legal rights are strong where the creditor or lessor trips up and you may be able to eliminate the amount demanded, or even end up with a positive recovery for yourself. But you will need help from a lawyer to effectively defend a lawsuit seeking a deficiency or early termination charge. Here are some defenses to look for (see National Consumer Law Center, *Repossessions* (9th ed. 2017), *updated at* www.nclc.org/library for more detail):

1. ***Claims concerning the car or the credit terms.*** Was the car a lemon, or did the dealer misrepresent the car's quality or the credit terms?
2. ***Is the car collateral on the loan?*** Sometimes the creditor trips up on a technical requirement to make the car collateral for the debt. Does one spouse own the car and the other spouse is obligated on the loan? Is the car collateral for an earlier loan but not listed as collateral in a refinancing of the original car loan? If the creditor has not taken the car as collateral, it cannot repossess the car, even if you defaulted on a loan used to purchase the car.
3. ***Were you in "default" when the car was seized?*** If a creditor routinely accepts your late payments, the creditor may be prohibited from seizing the car just because a payment is late. It may have to notify you first that it will no longer accept late payments. You may not be in default if you gave the creditor notice you were withholding payments because the car was a lemon. Did the creditor repossess before your right to cure period had expired?
4. ***Did the car's repossession breach the peace?*** When a seizure is wrongful, the creditor generally should not keep the car or collect a deficiency. The creditor may owe you money instead.

5. ***Improper repossession sale or miscalculation of the deficiency.*** If the creditor does not sell your car, but instead keeps it, the creditor cannot seek a deficiency. If the creditor sells the car, it must strictly follow correct procedures as to notices and the sale. Failure to follow the procedures exactly often can eliminate the deficiency.

   You must be notified that the creditor will sell your car, describing the car, the nature of the sale, the time and place of a public auction or the date after which the car will be sold privately, and other important information. The sale cannot be too rushed and it cannot be overly delayed. *Every* aspect of the sale, including the advertising, the manner, the time, the place, and the terms must be "commercially reasonable." Look out for low price sales to insiders.

   Check to see if the creditor correctly calculated the amount of its claimed deficiency. If the creditor asks you to pay a deficiency after the car has been sold, in most states the creditor must send you a summary of its calculations, along with an address or phone number where you can get additional information.

6. **Auto leases.** Your defenses will be different if the car you leased is repossessed. The amount the creditor (also known as "the lessor") claims you owe must follow the complex formula stated in the lease and must also be reasonable. The terms of the lease also must be properly disclosed and not misrepresented.

15

Utility Terminations

TOPICS COVERED IN THIS CHAPTER

Utility providers have a powerful method of forcing you to pay your utility bills—they can shut off your service. But you often have various ways to avoid such termination even when you cannot pay your utility bills and you also may have rights to get your service turned back on. Just as importantly, you should consider ways to reduce the cost of future utility bills. Your ability to catch up on past payments may depend on reducing future utility costs, and avoiding termination now may be only temporary if utility costs are permanently unaffordable.

YOUR RIGHTS WHEN THE UTILITY THREATENS TO TERMINATE YOUR SERVICE

Utilities Must Follow Rules Before Terminating Your Service. You have rights when companies threaten to terminate your utility service, particularly the larger utilities usually regulated by your state public utility or public service commission. Your rights vary a lot by state, so you should ask the consumer division of your state utility commission what rights you have.

If the utility does not follow the termination rules, you should be able to stop the termination or restore service, at least temporarily, and may even be able to sue for damages. Report it to your public utility commission, either the consumer division or the commission's division dealing with the particular type of service involved, such as gas or electricity. The commission has a lot of clout with the utility.

If that does not work, you may have to go to an attorney or a local community action program or your state attorney general office. Some states have a utility consumer advocate or rate counsel who may be able to help.

Notice. Prior to termination of your utility service, you must be given notice that the service is subject to termination and notice of your rights to prevent termination. Usually written notice is required, but some states also require face-to-face notice.

Utility Can Terminate Service Only for Serious Delinquencies. States typically permit disconnection for non-payment, but often do not allow disconnections if you only owe a very small amount or if you have not been delinquent for very long. If you dispute that you owe a bill, in most states the utility cannot terminate service until the dispute is resolved. If you dispute part of the bill, you may have to pay the undisputed amount to preserve your rights. When you pay your bill, it is a good idea to note that the payment only covers the undisputed charges.

Limit on the Times or Days When Shut-Offs Can Occur. Many states allow shut-offs only during regular working hours on weekdays. Some states prohibit shut-offs on holidays and even the day before a holiday or weekend.

Right to a Hearing. Before or after termination, you may have a right to appeal the termination to both the utility and to the public utility commission. In many states, informal appeals can be made by telephone prior to termination and, often, utility service will be maintained or reconnected during the appeals process.

A utility commission's consumer division responds to phone calls, letters, and visits by residential customers. Many of these complaints are resolved informally by consultation between the consumer division and the utility. Consumer divisions also hold hearings on complaints that cannot be resolved informally.

You do not need a lawyer at the hearing, but it can help to have someone experienced with utility issues come with you. Bring all relevant documents, such as past bills or, if you are asserting protection from termination due to illness, a physician's letter or affidavit.

Right to a Deferred Payment Plan. Before utility service is shut off, most states require that you be informed about the ability for you to prevent shut-off and instead to pay your overdue bills through a reasonable installment plan, often over six months or less.

The utility will want you to keep current on future utility bills as they arise and also pay something each month toward the back-due bills. If this is more than you can afford, be aggressive in negotiating with the utility's representative. Agreeing to payments you cannot afford will just lead to utility termination. In some states, utilities are not required to enter into a second payment plan with you if you did not keep up with your first payment plan.

Instead, explain your financial circumstances and push for a plan you can pay. The utility may agree to this as long as you make regular payments each month. Payment plans need not have the same payment each month. For example, seasonal workers may want to pay less toward arrears in the winter and more in the summer, or vice versa. If a company refuses to agree to a payment plan that you can afford, help can perhaps be obtained from the consumer division of the utility commission, although the level of assistance varies quite a lot from state to state.

Shut-Off Limits Due to Weather and Vulnerable Occupants. In many northern states, heat-related utilities cannot be shut off between November 1 and March 31st (or some similar period). In other states terminations are forbidden during extreme weather (hot or cold), but can move forward when temperatures return to normal.

Some states have protections against shut-offs for households with older or disabled residents, or households with infants. Generally, financial hardship must be shown and in some states you also have to show efforts to obtain state energy assistance.

Even where states prohibit disconnections for certain reasons, your bill will still be charged and you will eventually have to pay or service will be shut off. Thus you should pay something, if you can, even during months your service is not subject to shut off.

No Termination If There Is Serious Illness or a Very Young Child. In many states, there can be no shut offs for households whose members face a serious illness, are threatened with serious illness, depend upon life support systems, or whose members include a pregnant woman or very young children. An illness may have to be certified by a doctor.

Tenant Protections Where Landlord Fails to Pay the Utility Bill. When a landlord who is responsible for providing utility service does not pay the utility company, tenants are at risk of shut off. In some states, tenants must receive a special shut-off notice if the landlord is delinquent, and may be able to stop the termination by making small (or even no) payments to the utility.

Where Landlord Tries to Shut Off Your Utility Service. It is illegal in almost every state for a landlord to cut off your electricity, heat, or water as a way of making you move or pay your rent. Landlords must go through the courts to evict tenants. If the landlord tries to shut off your utilities, you should go to court to obtain relief.

Bankruptcy Can Prevent or Restore a Termination. Although it is rarely a good idea to file bankruptcy solely because of your utility bills, you may have other financial problems which lead you to consider bankruptcy. The mere filing of your bankruptcy will automatically stop any shut off and require the utility to restore service for at least twenty days. The utility can only terminate service after that twenty-day period if you fail to pay bills arising *after* the bankruptcy is filed.

If you successfully complete your bankruptcy case, you never have to pay any of the amount due at the time you filed for bankruptcy. The utility, though, can also require that you provide adequate assurance that *future* bills will be paid, such as providing a new security deposit.

Finding Emergency Assistance to Help You Pay Your Delinquent Bills. Before a disconnection, utility companies often must provide you with information about energy assistance programs that can help pay your bills. Here are some sources of emergency assistance that may provide you with funds to prevent a utility termination:

- *"LIHEAP," the Low-Income Home Energy Assistance Program.* Contact your local community action program or locate the LIHEAP agency in your area at www.acf.hhs.gov/ocs/liheap-state-and-territory-contact-listing.
- *Emergency assistance for families with children.* If you have children and you are about to lose essential utility services (water, heat in the winter months, etc.), contact your state public utility commission, state or county departments of health, welfare and housing agencies to see if special emergency funds may be available to help you. This type of assistance varies significantly from state to state, and may not be available in your state.
- *State emergency assistance.* Some states have special funds to help prevent utility terminations. Many counties have "homeless prevention" funds which can be used to prevent utility terminations. Contact your local community action program or the county department of social services.
- *Utility fuel funds.* Many utilities have a special fund to help people pay their utility bills. Contact both the utility which is threatening to shut off your service and any other utility from which you receive service to see if they have a fund that can assist you.
- *Salvation Army, local churches, and other places of worship.* The Salvation Army and other local religious and charitable organizations often have money that is available to help needy people in the community with emergency bills such as utilities. Check with the utility company, the public utility commission, or the department of social services. Many churches, synagogues, and mosques that have these funds do not limit them to their own members.

HOW TO GET YOUR UTILITY SERVICE TURNED BACK ON

If your service has been shut off, it may be difficult to get it restored, and it may even be difficult to obtain new utility service from the same company if you move to a new residence. The utility will typically demand that you pay the old bill plus late charges, a reconnection fee, and often a deposit. Of course, obtaining utility service at a new address is not an issue where the landlord supplies the utility service at the new address or the utility service is in someone else's name responsible for payments.

Here are some things to try when, because of unpaid bills, a utility refuses to restore service or denies you service at a new location.

Dealing with an Old Bill. If an old bill is several years past-due, it is possible that the utility cannot legally require you to pay it before providing you with new service. Also in some states the utility cannot require you to pay the old bill before they will give you service at a new address. Check with the utility commission or a local attorney. Filing of a bankruptcy immediately entitles you to restore service or to obtain service at a new address.

You can also ask the utility to allow you to pay off the old bill in installments over a period of months. If you are ready and willing to pay for future service as it is provided, and to pay for the old service over time, the utility should not have reasonable grounds to deny you this new service. Many states have specific rules addressing how much you'll have to pay to get new service.

Late Charges. You not only have to pay the old bill, but also late charges related to that bill, in states that allow utilities to impose late charges. If late charges are very high, contact the consumer services division of your state public utility commission to challenge the amount or negotiate with the local utility about the amount. The utility may be more lenient in waiving old late charges if you present the reason you were having financial difficulties at the time.

Reconnection Fee. Try the same type of arguments and negotiation with reconnection fees as late charges. Some states prohibit or limit reconnection charges.

Deposits. Before establishing new or renewed service, the utility may ask you for a deposit, usually equal to the average bill for one to three months. If you believe that a deposit is too high, complain to the public utility commission's consumer division. If you cannot afford the deposit, you can also request assistance from one of the sources of emergency assistance listed earlier in this chapter. When you have established a good payment record, request that the utility return the deposit to you with interest. Instead of a deposit, some utilities accept the signature of someone else, who agrees to be responsible for some or all of any payments you fail to make.

WAYS TO REDUCE YOUR UTILITY BILLS

Even if you can avoid utility shut-offs, in the long run you will be in trouble if you cannot afford your utility bills going forward. Thus it is essential to reduce the cost of future bills as much as possible.

Changing Your Communications Services (Telephone, Internet, and TV). Today, the rapidly evolving communications marketplace provides more options for paring back services to meet your basic communications needs.

Voice Service: Are you paying for both landline and wireless telephone service? Can you cancel one of these telephone services? Is your voice service part of a bundle? If so, after reading the sections below, examine the services included in the bundle to make sure that it is still the best value for you.

Wireless Service: Are you paying for additional voice and data services that you don't need? If you have a telephone plan with a monthly bill, study your bills to get a handle on how much voice and data you are actually using and whether you should switch to a lower cost plan. Also check to see if you are free to switch companies or if you are under contract to stay with your current provider. Another issue to explore is whether you can use your phone with a different provider.

Prepaid service may be an attractive alternative. There is no contract or early termination fee, there may be the option of purchasing a cheaper refurbished phone or using one you already own, and you pay upfront for a set amount of service and continue to pre-pay as you go. You will not run the risk of a larger than expected bill, although you can still spend down your account faster than you intended, requiring you to reload funds into the account.

Internet and Cable TV Service: Can you let go of the cable TV (pay-TV) service and rely on streaming shows over the internet or by using a digital TV antenna? In a fast changing market, cable TV providers are responding by offering smaller, cheaper packages. Contact your cable company to see if you can save money, but try to avoid teaser rates.

Weatherization and Energy and Water Efficiency. Many utilities have programs that provide free or low cost weatherization or energy efficiency services, either available to all households or prioritizing older or low-income persons or homes with disabled persons and/or children. In the best programs, the utility conducts a full energy audit and provides extensive weatherization services.

Other programs simply provide hints on how you can reduce usage, or only supply energy efficient light bulbs, insulation for hot water tanks, "low flow" efficient faucets, or other energy efficiency products. Call your local energy and water providers to find out what programs they have available.

A number of government programs provide weatherization assistance for owner-occupied housing and rental units. One of these is the federal Weatherization Assistance Program (WAP) where qualifying households may receive at no cost up to several thousand dollars in weatherization benefits. Many states have their own weatherization programs and cities have Community Development Block Grant money which is sometimes used to help low-income households weatherize their homes. Although there may be a waiting list for all of these programs, the benefits are often so great that it is worthwhile to add your name.

Free weatherization is a definite win for the customer receiving the benefit. However, unless there is an almost immediate payoff in terms of energy savings, you should not invest much of your own money in weatherization efforts at a time you are having trouble paying your bills, where any money might be better spent paying the overdue utility bills. Nevertheless, some relatively inexpensive procedures reduce energy and water bills by a surprising amount.

On a windy day check for air leaks around your windows and doors. You can use a lit stick of incense to detect leaks around windows and doors by moving the stick around the frame and watching to see if there is any wind blowing the smoke. If you are a tenant, try to get the landlord to fix these leaks properly. If the landlord does not fix the problems, or you own your own home, try a number of homespun fix-ups:

- Use caulk, or weather stripping for air leaks around windows. In the winter you can seal windows with heavy-duty clear plastic sheets or clear plastic film. In a pinch you could use clear plastic tape to seal the cracks.
- For leaks around doors, leave a rolled up towel next to the bottom of the door. If necessary, use weather stripping or tack up a blanket or large towel to stop leaks around the top and sides of doors.
- If there are holes in the walls, try to plug them up by stapling plastic sheeting over the holes and caulking the edges of the plastic. You will be surprised how much warmer a house or apartment can be without the heat loss from cracks between openings and walls.
- If you have a fireplace that is not in use, make sure the flue is tightly closed. As the home warms up, you can consider turning down the heat.

Turn off lights and your heating or cooling systems when you are not at home. Also close the door for any rooms you are not using, and don't try to heat or cool unused, unoccupied rooms. Try turning down the temperature on your hot water heater a notch, and when on vacation, turn the temperature to a lower vacation setting.

Leaky toilets and faucets waste a surprising amount of money. Your water utility may provide free toilet leak detection kits or you can purchase inexpensive leak detection dye tablets at the hardware store. Many water companies have programs that assist homeowners with low cost plumbing problems. Putting an inexpensive displacement bag (a special strong plastic bag for your toilet tank that you can buy at a hardware store) or a heavy plastic bottle in an old toilet tank will cut down on the amount of water consumed each time you flush.

Discounted Utility Rates. Often utilities have special programs which allow certain customers to reduce how much they pay in utility bills. Programs differ by state.

Discounted Rates for Financially Distressed Households. Many utilities have special programs for low-income households, households with older persons, or households with persons with disabilities that reduce bills by a set amount each month or based on the size of the bill. Check with your utility to see what is available and how to enroll.

PIPPs or Energy Assurance Programs. Utilities in Illinois, Ohio, and a few other states have plans by which families pay a certain percentage of their income for utility service if that amount is less than what they would otherwise pay. This results in lower bills. Typically, consistent payment of the lower amount is rewarded by gradual forgiveness of old, unpaid bills. The best way to determine if a utility has such a program is to contact the utility or the public utility commission's consumer division in your state.

Telephone Discounts. Lifeline is a federal program that helps eligible low-income households pay for wireline or wireless voice or broadband internet service from participating companies. Eligible households obtain monthly discounts for voice and/or broadband service and many states provide an additional discount. The most popular Lifeline product is a prepaid wireless voice and data bundle that has no deposits, no early termination fees, and minutes paid for by the Lifeline program are added to the phone account each month. Consumers can purchase additional minutes as necessary. Consumers can find companies that participate in the federal Lifeline program in their area at https://data.usac.org/publicreports/CompaniesNearMe/Download/Report. Consumers should contact their state's public utility commission's consumer division or the local telephone company for details about state Lifeline services.

Discounted Internet Service Offerings. Keep an eye out for discounted internet packages that often stem from merger deals. Companies such as Comcast offer a discounted internet service for low-income families with school-aged children. For example at the time this book was published, Comcast had a program called Internet Essentials that cost $9.95/month and helped subsidize the cost of a computer; AT&T "Access" had a $5/month and $10/month internet service for low-income households as a condition of its merger with DirecTV. There are restrictions that apply. For example, consumers cannot have prior debt with the company.

Reducing Your Bill Through Government and Other Assistance. If you have a low income and high utility bills, you are probably eligible for one or more source of assistance with your utility bills. The Federal Low Income Home Energy Assistance Program (LIHEAP), run by each state, helps low-income families pay their winter heating bills and in some states their summer cooling expenses. Benefits are also provided to renters and some public and subsidized housing tenants whose heat is included in their rent.

The size of a family's LIHEAP benefits generally depends on the family's income and the number of household members, and may also depend on housing type, fuel type, fuel prices, weather conditions, or actual energy consumption. To apply, contact your local community action program, a county department of social services office, or other local agency administering the program.

In many states, the Salvation Army or other charitable organizations operate a "fuel fund" which helps people pay their bills if they make a little too much money to qualify for LIHEAP or if LIHEAP funds have run out. Contact your state utility commission or the agency that distributes LIHEAP funds in your area.

Level Payment Plans; Dealing with Quarterly and Bi-Monthly Bills; Changing Your Due Dates. Several strategies can make it easier to pay your utility bills each month even though they do not decrease your yearly costs. If you have difficulty meeting your heating bills in the coldest winter months or your air conditioning bills in the hottest summer months, a level payment plan will help. Each month you pay the same amount—one-twelfth of your expected annual bill. Since the utility company is estimating your usage over the next twelve months, you may receive either a "catch up" bill or credit every six or twelve months, since actual usage will vary from the estimate.

In some areas, utility services are billed quarterly or every other month, which may be more difficult for you to manage than monthly bills. Contact your utility company to explain the difficulty and ask them to bill you on a monthly basis or to accept monthly payments. Make sure there are no "service charges" or "finance charges" or this type of payment plan may not be the best solution for you.

If your main source of income arrives on the fifth of the month, but your utility bill is due to be paid on the fourth, it will be more difficult to pay your utility bill on time than if it was due on the fourteenth, causing additional interest or late charges. Often utility companies will change their billing cycle for you if you explain the situation.

16

What Every Homeowner Should Know About Mortgage Payments

TOPICS COVERED IN THIS CHAPTER

First Considerations

Surprising Facts About Partial Mortgage Payments

How to Determine the Status of Your Mortgage Loan

Disputing the Amount Due

Escrow, Taxes, and Insurance

Reduced Mortgage Rates for Active Duty Military

FIRST CONSIDERATIONS

Mortgage problems tend to have a snowballing effect if not resolved quickly. Small issues grow into big problems that can eventually lead to foreclosure—always act sooner rather than later.

If you are having trouble resolving mortgage-related problems on your own, try a nonprofit housing counselor or attorney. The Department of Housing and Urban Development (HUD) certifies housing counseling agencies and you can locate such an agency by calling HUD at 800-569-4287 (TDD 800-877-8339) or by going to www.hud.gov. If a housing counselor cannot help, the counselor may refer you to a local attorney or legal services program. Do not wait too long to get assistance. An experienced advocate in your corner may help you fix the trouble before it grows.

Your Mortgage Servicer Plays the Key Role. To resolve an issue with your mortgage, do not contact the lender owning your mortgage loan. Always contact your mortgage servicer who has been hired by whoever owns your mortgage loan. The servicer receives your mortgage payments, applies them to your mortgage balance, and deals with other day-to-day activities on your account. If you have any questions about your mortgage—always contact your mortgage servicer.

Occasionally the owner of your mortgage, the servicer, and the original lender are the same entity, but more often they are three different companies. For example, Acme Mortgage Company may have given you a loan, and then sold your loan to Best Bank that has hired ABC Servicing Company as its mortgage servicer.

You may have several different servicers during the life of your loan. Your servicer changes if the owner of your mortgage loan decides to hire a new servicer, or if the owner sells your loan to someone who uses a different servicer. Whenever your mortgage loan is sold to a new owner, you will get notice of the contact information for both the new owner and your new servicer. You also can request in writing that the servicer tell you the name and contact information for the owner of your mortgage loan.

Your Rights When Your Servicer Changes. Federal law requires that you get notice whenever your servicer changes, including the effective date of transfer and the new servicer's contact information, including a toll-free number to call with questions. You also get notice as to the date when you should start sending payments to the new servicer instead of the old one.

You can keep sending on-time payments to the old servicer for up to 60 days after that date, and the new servicer must treat it as a timely payment, and cannot charge a late fee, claim your account is in default, or report the payment as late on your credit report. This applies even if the old servicer does not forward the payment in a timely way to the new servicer.

SURPRISING FACTS ABOUT PARTIAL MORTGAGE PAYMENTS

Try not to make a mortgage payment for less than the amount due (a partial payment). The servicer typically does *not* apply a partial payment to your mortgage. Instead the servicer may return your partial payment check back to you uncashed. If so, you should set the money aside and *not* use it to pay other bills, so you can use it later to help with your mortgage payments. In the worst case scenario, if foreclosure becomes inevitable, you will have some money saved for moving expenses.

Other servicers keep your partial payment in a "suspense account" until you pay the remaining amount due for that one monthly payment and instead assess you a late fee. As a result, it is easy to get confused as to how much you owe. To avoid problems, check your most recent mortgage statement for the monthly payment amount, since it can change over time. Also check your statement each month to be sure last month's payment was applied correctly. If a partial payment is put in a suspense account, the statement must explain what you must do for the payment to be applied.

HOW TO DETERMINE THE STATUS OF YOUR MORTGAGE LOAN

You receive monthly statements from your mortgage servicer or a coupon book with similar information. The statements include the amount due for the billing period; an explanation of the total amount due on the account including fees; a breakdown of how your last payment was applied; transaction activity; partial payment information; and contact and account information.

If you are more than forty-five days behind on your mortgage payments, the monthly mortgage statement also includes: the date when the account became delinquent; a notification of possible risks, such as foreclosure, and of the expenses that may be charged if the account is not brought current; an account history for the previous six months or the period since the last time the account was current; a notice indicating any loss mitigation program to which you have agreed, if applicable; a notice of whether the servicer has started foreclosure; the total payment amount needed to bring the account current; and a list of homeownership counselors and counseling organizations that you can contact.

DISPUTING THE AMOUNT DUE

You can dispute the amount the servicer says is due in a monthly statement. For example, your servicer may have failed to or incorrectly credited your payment, neglected to make payments out of your escrow account and instead forced you to pay for extra insurance, charged unnecessary or duplicative fees, or improperly refused to accept a payment. Contact the servicer right away.

Dealing with your mortgage servicer can sometimes be frustrating. Many mortgage servicers are large companies that handle tens of thousands or even hundreds of thousands of mortgages. You may speak to a different person each time you call, and you may get conflicting or confusing information from one person to the next. Make a note in a notebook each time you talk to someone at the mortgage servicing company, including the date, time, name of the person you spoke with, and what you talked about.

Provide any documentation that the servicer requests and keep copies for yourself. Make a note in your notebook of what you provided, when you provided it, and how you sent it to the servicer (email, fax, mail, overnight mail service). If the servicer does not provide you with the information you requested or if you dispute how the servicer is handling your account, you may send the servicer a more formal request, called a "notice of error" or "request for information," to ensure that they respond in a timely manner and correct any errors.

Sending Your Servicer a Notice of Error or Request for Information. Your servicer must respond to a written request for information or investigate any claims of error concerning your account, including your escrow account. Your writing must identify your account, such as an account number, along with your name and the address of the property. Include the reasons you believe the account is in error. Be clear and as specific as possible about any question you have or information you are requesting. Your letter can both dispute an error and ask for more information.

Your request should not be written on a payment coupon or included with your payment, but should be in a separate letter to your servicer. Make a copy and send the letter return receipt requested, so that you have a record of when the servicer receives it.

You must send the notice to the address the servicer has identified as appropriate for such a request, which often is different than the address for mailing payments. Otherwise, the servicer may not respond or you may lose the legal right to force your servicer to correct the error. The servicer may have sent you a separate letter listing the address or it may be listed on a transfer of servicing statement, an annual escrow statement, or a monthly billing statement. You can also check the servicer's website or call the servicer's customer service center. Be sure to send your notice to the correct address as your servicer may have many different addresses listed on its website and statements.

Here is an example of such a letter to the servicer:

SAMPLE "REQUEST FOR INFORMATION/NOTICE OF ERROR"

Ken and Susan Consumer
12 Budding Bloom Lane
Elizabeth, New Jersey

January 23, 2019

Last Dollar Mortgage Co.
398 Rockefeller Drive
St. Albans, WV 25177
Attention: Borrower Inquiry Department
RE: Account #123234

Dear Last Dollar Mortgage Co.:

We dispute the amount that you claim is owed on our monthly Mortgage Statement and request that you send us information about the fees, costs, and escrow charges on our loan. Please treat this letter as a "notice of error" and a "request for information" under the Real Estate Settlement and Procedures Act (section 2605(e)).

Specifically, we are requesting the following information:

- A payment history or schedule that can be easily read and understood listing the dates and amounts of all payments and transactions credited or debited to our account, including any escrow account and any suspense account, and showing how they have been applied or credited or, if not applied, showing how they have been treated;
- A breakdown of the amount of claimed arrears or delinquencies on our account, including an itemization of all fees and charges you claim are currently due;
- The current balance in any suspense account and the reason why such funds were deposited in the account;
- The payment dates, purpose of payment, and recipient of all foreclosure fees and costs that have been charged to our account or have been advanced on our behalf since [*insert date Last Dollar Mortgage took over the servicing*];
- The payment dates, purpose of payment, and recipient of all escrow items charged to our account in the last twenty-four months;
- A breakdown of our current escrow payment showing how it was calculated and the reasons for any increase or decrease in the last twenty-four months (include a copy of any annual escrow statements prepared within the last twenty-four months); and
- Any notes created by your personnel reflecting communications with us about our mortgage account.

Also, on October 1, 2018, we sent our October payment to First Dollar Mortgage Co., which had been servicing our mortgage before it was transferred to you. Our October payment was never credited to our account. Please correct this error.

Thank you for taking the time to acknowledge and answer this request as required by the Real Estate Settlement Procedures Act (section 2605(e)).

Very truly yours,

Ken and Susan Consumer
[certified mail]

The servicer must acknowledge receipt of your request within five business days of receipt, and must respond within thirty business days (forty-five days if it notifies you of the extension). The response cannot simply state that it was right or that it has no information. Federal law requires that the servicer conduct a "reasonable investigation" based on your request. Its written response should show that it did this investigation. For sixty days after you send a notice of error about a payment dispute, the servicer cannot give any information to credit reporting agencies that a payment related to your inquiry is overdue.

Request Validation of the Debt. The first time an attorney for the lender or for the servicer sends you a letter demanding payment, that letter should include a notice of your right to dispute the mortgage debt. Sometimes the notice of your right to dispute will arrive separately within five days after the attorney first communicates with you about the debt. If you then dispute the debt in writing within the next thirty days, the attorney must stop collection efforts while your dispute is investigated.

Setting Up a "Tender" Defense. If you dispute the amount you are delinquent on your mortgage loan, you may want to offer the undisputed amount that is delinquent, while not paying the amount you dispute. This is called a "tender." The letter should also state that the amount is offered in "full satisfaction of the dispute." That way, if you are right about what is owed, you are not delinquent and the servicer should not be able to foreclose. On the other hand, if you also withhold the amounts that are not in disputed, the servicer can claim it has the right to foreclose.

Most often, your tender will be returned and then you may have the defense that the money was offered and refused, depending upon your state law. Keep your letter and the servicer's response as proof. You should set the money aside, if possible in a bank account, while the dispute is being resolved. You can add the claim of tender to your defenses in the legal process, if the matter reaches foreclosure.

ESCROW, TAXES, AND INSURANCE

Your Rights Concerning Your Escrow Account. If your monthly mortgage payment includes an amount to cover property insurance and taxes on your home, you have a mortgage with an "escrow" or "impound" account. Your servicer is supposed to pay the insurance and tax bills for you when they are due.

Under federal law your servicer must give you an initial statement when your escrow account is first set up and periodic statements at least once per year after that. These statements must include the amount of your current escrow payment, the amount your escrow payment will be for the next year, the total amount you paid into the escrow account during the past year, and the total amount paid out of the escrow account during the past year for taxes, insurance premiums, and other escrow bills. However, the servicer is not required to send this statement if you are more than thirty days behind in payments.

If your annual escrow account statement shows that there is a balance of $50 or more from the previous year, you are entitled to a refund. If your statement shows that your account has a balance smaller than expected (a "shortage") or a negative balance (a "deficiency") your servicer will include this amount in your next annual escrow statement so that it is paid back in future escrow payments over the next year. If you want to spread out repayment of this shortage or deficiency for more months than the servicer is offering you, ask the servicer. If that does not work, ask for the supervisor in the escrow or collection department. On the other hand, as long as you pay what the servicer requests for escrow, the servicer must pay your property tax and insurance even if there is not enough money in your escrow account.

Servicers should pay from your escrow your taxes, property insurance, and other escrow bills on time, before the deadline for avoiding penalties such as interest or late fees. You should not have to pay for interest and late fees, and should ask the servicer for a refund if these are included in your escrow account statement. If the bill for interest or some other penalty is sent to you instead, send this bill to your servicer (keeping a copy) and insist that they pay it with their funds.

Avoid Force-Placed Insurance. If you do not have an escrow account and the servicer believes you do not have homeowner's insurance covering your home, it will purchase over-priced insurance providing you only limited protection, and then charge you for it or add it to your monthly payments. This is called "force-placed insurance" and you should avoid this at all costs.

If your own insurance company or servicer notifies you that you do not have homeowner's insurance, take this seriously and act immediately. If you do have insurance, provide the servicer with proof—the policy number, the name of your insurance company or agent, and written proof you have the insurance. If you don't have insurance, obtain your own insurance as soon as possible, and provide the servicer with proof and request that they cancel the insurance that they purchased for you.

If your insurance is being canceled for non-payment and there is an escrow account on your mortgage, the servicer must pay your existing insurance policy rather than purchase force-placed insurance, even if there is not enough money in the escrow account to pay your policy. The servicer will then require that you repay any money it advanced to pay your policy, usually by adding the amount to your future escrow payments.

Private Mortgage Insurance. Most mortgage borrowers are required to purchase private mortgage insurance (PMI) protecting the lender against a mortgage loan default. This cost is included in your monthly payments. PMI is expensive and only protects the lender. Cancelling PMI brings down your mortgage payments and has no down-side for you. If you have PMI, the servicer must cancel it on your request if your remaining mortgage loan balance is less than 80% of your home's purchase price. Also try to ask the servicer to cancel PMI whenever your home is worth a lot more than your mortgage balance.

Credit Life and Disability Insurance. Credit life, disability, and unemployment insurance coverage pays off some of your mortgage loan if you pass on, become disabled, or unemployed. This insurance is overpriced, expensive, and offers limited protection. Consider cancelling it, particularly when you are having trouble paying your mortgage. Look at your loan documents and monthly statement to see if it is listed there.

REDUCED MORTGAGE RATES FOR ACTIVE DUTY MILITARY

When a homeowner entered into a mortgage loan *prior* to become active duty military, federal law requires that the homeowner while on active duty and for one year thereafter shall not pay an interest rate exceeding 6%. This includes any fees or other charges payable on the loan (late charges, for example). Any interest that you have been paying over 6% is eliminated while you are on active duty and for another year—the excess interest is not just put off until later.

If you are paying more than 6%, you not only can get your rate reduced, but the lender has to give you a credit for any interest charged to you above that rate while you were on active duty. One year after you leave active duty, the rate can be increased to the old rate.

To take advantage of this law, you must provide the lender or other creditor with written notice including a copy of the orders calling you to military service and any orders extending active duty. This must be done no later than 180 days after the date of the termination of military service. The interest rate reduction is then retroactive to the date active duty began.

17

When You Are Having Trouble Making Mortgage Payments

TOPICS COVERED IN THIS CHAPTER

This chapter explains ways to temporarily or even permanently reduce your mortgage payments if you are having trouble keeping up with your payments. The next chapter describes your rights when your home is actually in foreclosure. The last two chapters describe the bankruptcy option, which offers additional rights to save your home. Sometimes bankruptcy may be a better option because it lets you deal with all your debt problems at the same time.

Another option, not discussed in this book, is applying for special funds that nonprofits, a city, or state may offer to help those facing foreclosure. Contact a nonprofit housing counselor or other specialist to locate any such options, but be careful to avoid scammers that design their rip-offs to look like assistance offered by a nonprofit. Never sign away rights to your home in order to get help.

This chapter instead provides advice on getting help from your mortgage servicer for what is called "loss mitigation." Foreclosures are costly for mortgage lenders and they prefer to find an alternative by giving their servicers loss mitigation guidelines. A servicer must consider these guidelines before it can conduct a foreclosure sale.

THE HELP OFFERED DEPENDS ON THE LENDER INVOLVED

Different lenders have different loss mitigation guidelines. Fortunately, just a few entities own, insure, or guarantee almost all residential mortgage loans in the United States: Fannie Mae, Freddie Mac, the Federal Housing Administration (FHA), the Department of Veterans Affairs (VA), and the U.S. Department of Agriculture's Rural Housing Service (RHS). You must identify who owns or insures your mortgage in order to know your options for modifying your mortgage payments. To determine who owns your loan, use these tips:

- Fannie Mae: Go to www.knowyouroptions.com/loanlookup.
- Freddie Mac: Go to https://ww3.freddiemac.com/loanlookup.
- FHA: Because some lenders use FHA forms for all their mortgages, do not assume you have an FHA mortgage just because your loan documents say FHA or HUD. Look at your monthly statements for an itemized charge for FHA insurance. Or look for a box checked off "FHA insured" on your settlement statement.
- VA-insured: Loans and billing statements identify VA insurance.
- RHS guaranteed loan: Closing documents will reference to RHS insurance coverage. Older loans may refer to FmHA insurance or guarantees.
- RHS direct loans: Closing documents should mention the "Section 502 Single-Family Housing Program" and the loan will be serviced by a national servicing center in St. Louis identifying itself as a servicer of RHS direct loans.
- For all loans: Send a request for information letter to your servicer (see Chapter 16).

In unusual situations, someone other than the above entities will own your mortgage loan, and then it may be more difficult to learn your loss mitigation options. Try asking for options similar to those available for Fannie Mae and Freddie Mac loans, since these set the industry standard.

The HAMP Program Has Expired for New Applications. The Home Affordable Modification Program (HAMP), a major federal effort to reduce foreclosures during the Great Recession, and related programs expired at the end of 2016. This chapter instead describes loan modification programs in place today. (Note though that FHA calls its current loan modification program FHA-HAMP.)

OPTIONS FOR FANNIE MAE AND FREDDIE MAC LOANS

Fannie Mae and Freddie Mac are large government-chartered corporations that own or guarantee over one-half of the home mortgages in the country. Fannie Mae and Freddie Mac have similar loss mitigation guidelines, divided between short-term options for temporary problems and long-term options for significant changes in your financial circumstances. When you ask for loss mitigation help for a Fannie or Freddie loan, your servicer must review your request by considering a series of specific options in a required order. If you do not qualify for the first one on the list, your servicer must go on to the second, continuing until you qualify for some form of relief.

To request loss mitigation from either Fannie or Freddie, complete and submit Form 710—Mortgage Assistance Application to your servicer. Indicate you are experiencing hardship, either a loss of income or increase in expenses. You need not be in default, if default is "imminent" due to a change in your financial circumstances.

Options for Temporary Hardships. Under Fannie and Freddie guidelines, if your servicer considers your hardship to be temporary, it should offer you a repayment or forbearance plan. A temporary hardship might be a short-term drop in income (such as a loss of your job) or a one-time major expense. You may not agree with a servicer's assessment that your hardship is only temporary, such as when your loss of income is long-term due to a divorce or medical condition. Press this point because, as described below, you have more options where a hardship is long-term.

Repayment plans are applicable when your temporary hardship is now over, but you are so far behind on your mortgage payments that you cannot get caught up right away. Fannie and Freddie will offer you a repayment plan where for up to a year you make each month your regular mortgage payments and a portion of your back-due payments. The repayment plan must be realistic, so that you can make the increased payments over the repayment plan period. In judging what you can afford, remember that your temporary financial difficulties will also have left you with other overdue obligations, such as utility bills or urgent needs for your children that have been postponed.

Forbearance plans, on the other hand, apply when you are currently experiencing a temporary hardship. A forbearance plan allows for reduced or suspended payments for up to six months, and even longer if you are unemployed. At the end of the forbearance period, the servicer must evaluate you for a long-term solution. What that option will be will depend on your financial circumstances at the time. It could be a repayment plan, a permanent reduction in payments, or an option involving your loss of ownership of the home.

Home Retention Options for Long-Term Hardships—The Flex Modification. The Flex Modification is Fannie and Freddie's primary loss mitigation option for borrowers who want to keep their homes but are facing a long-term hardship (such as your disability, the death of your spouse, or divorce). Your servicer can offer you a "Flex Mod" in response to your loss mitigation application, or your servicer can offer this option unsolicited, based on its unilateral determination that you qualify.

The Flex Mod Based on the Servicer's Unilateral Evaluation. Fannie and Freddie require that their servicers review all borrowers for eligibility for a Flex Mod when a borrower is between 90 and 105 days behind in payments (they can also do this review a second time later). The servicer performs this evaluation based solely on information from its own records, including a property valuation, your current interest rate, the amount of your arrearage, and the unpaid balance that you owe. The servicer does not need income or any other information directly from you to decide on your eligibility. Instead, it applies a formula to the information it already has.

If the result shows you are eligible, the servicer will offer you a trial modification plan that will lower your payments. After you make three-to-four required monthly trial payments, you sign a permanent Flex Modification agreement and your loan is modified so that your mortgage payments are reduced.

The Flex Mod Based on Your Loss Mitigation Application. You can also apply directly to your servicer for a Flex Modification using the Form 710 application. To qualify, the servicer must find that your hardship is not temporary and that you are at least 60 days in default or meet the "imminent default" standard if you are less than 60 days behind. You can apply for a Flex Mod as long as a foreclosure sale has not yet occurred. If you submit your initial complete application at least 37 days before a scheduled foreclosure sale, the foreclosure must be delayed.

The Flex Modification Terms. With one exception which will be discussed below, the terms of a Flex Mod is the same whether you receive a unilateral offer from your servicer or apply for the modification yourself. The Flex Mod formula favors borrowers with little or no equity in their homes, and particularly borrowers who are underwater (meaning they owe more on the mortgage than the home is worth). The formula can also provide a significant benefit for borrowers whose interest rate is well above the current market interest rate. The servicer must offer you the modification if the modification reduces your monthly payment.

The flex modification involves four changes to your loan terms. First the servicer adds your current arrearage to your unpaid principal balance, so that you repay your arrearage gradually each month over the full term of the loan. Second, as long as your equity in the home is less than 20% of the home's current market value, the servicer reduces your interest rate to a current national market rate. Third, the servicer extends the repayment term of your loan to forty years from the date of the modification, thus reducing your monthly payments.

And fourth, you are charged interest only on part of the principal balance, called principal forbearance; the remainder of your loan principal is a zero interest loan. The smaller the portion of your balance that is subject to interest charges, the lower your monthly payment. You still owe the part of the principal that has zero percent interest and you must repay it eventually; also, this portion of the loan is still secured by your home. First, the servicer sets aside the amount of your outstanding principal on the loan that exceeds your home's current market value. For that part of your principal, you pay zero percent interest.

After modifying your loan using the four steps described above, the servicer determines if the resulting payment of interest and principal reduces your payments by at least 20%. If not, the servicer may further reduce the interest-bearing principal to an amount equal to only 80% of the property's current market value, further reducing your monthly payment. Nevertheless, no more than 30% of your principal can be charged zero interest.

The Special Flex Mod Terms for Borrowers Who Submit an Application. In a Flex Modification calculation available only for those who initiate the application process before the loan is 90 days overdue, the servicer targets a new payment (for principal, interest, and escrow) that is not more than 40% of the borrower's gross household income. This is over and above any reduction created by the Flex Mod evaluation described immediately above.

Options That Involve Giving Up Your Home. If your servicer finds you are not eligible for other Fannie or Freddie loan modification options, it must then evaluate you for options that involve giving up your home. You may also want to consider these scenarios even though you qualify for an option that instead reduces or delays your mortgage payments.

No one likes to give up their home, but there are options which involve giving up your home that are better for you if a foreclosure is otherwise inevitable. This is a hard decision, as it involves emotional as well as family and financial considerations. But sometimes not saving your home is the wisest financial move you can make, particularly if your house is worth substantially less than the combined amount of your mortgages.

On the other hand, moving may involve leaving your neighborhood, result in your children having to change schools, or require you and your partner to make a difficult commute. You will have to consider the costs and benefits of renting as well.

Fannie and Freddie may propose a "short sale" that offers you benefits if your home is worth less than the mortgage balance. In this scenario, you would sell your home yourself to a third party, usually through a realtor. Fannie or Freddie accepts the sale proceeds to satisfy your mortgage, even if the proceeds are less than the amount owed. Realtors, particularly those who have experience dealing with a particular servicer, may help convince the servicer to agree to a short sale. As a last resort, the servicer will consider a "deed in lieu of foreclosure" transaction, where you voluntarily transfer title to your property to the servicer in exchange for a release from your liability on the mortgage debt.

Servicers are authorized to provide relocation assistance up to $3,000 in connection with these options. In the "deed in lieu" scenario, there is also a short-term lease option available which can ease the move from the home.

Short sales and deeds in lieu are almost always poor choices if your home is worth significantly more than your outstanding mortgage balances. If you have to lose your home, it is far better to sell it on your own because you get to keep the amount by which the sale price exceeds the total of first and second mortgages on the home. But you have to act quickly before the home is sold in foreclosure. If you ask, the servicer is likely to give you a short delay in a foreclosure to let you sell the home yourself, but only if you already have made substantial progress toward a sale, such as a signed "purchase and sale" agreement.

If you have favorable mortgage terms, it might be attractive for the buyer of your home to assume your mortgage, that is take over your mortgage payments. A mortgage is assumable if the original loan documents say it is or, in most states, if the documents are silent on the issue. Other mortgages contain a "due-on-sale" clause, preventing assumption in most situations. But even then lenders cannot block certain transfers from parent to child or from one spouse to another. Lenders also may voluntarily agree to an assumption even when the mortgage contains a due-on-sale clause.

You should apply for a short sale or deed in lieu of foreclosure by completing and sending the servicer the same Form 710 loss mitigation application, which prevents a foreclosure sale while your request is being considered. For both short sales and deeds in lieu the documentation requirements are less strict the further behind in payments you are. If your financial documentation shows that you have the ability to contribute funds to reduce the amount owed, the servicer can require that you make some contribution to reduce the debt before a short sale or deed in lieu can be approved. Be sure to get the terms of a short sale or a deed in lieu in writing, including any release from liability that the servicer agrees to give you.

Second mortgages and other liens against your property may create barriers to a short sale or a deed in lieu, because the new owner will not have clear title. However, Fannie and Freddie guidelines allow the servicer to advance you funds to get rid of small junior liens if this facilitates the transfer of the property.

Tax Consequences of Short Sales and Deeds in Lieu. Many short sales and "deeds in lieu of foreclosure" cancel part of your debt, which has tax implications since forgiveness of debt can be treated as taxable income in the year the forgiveness took place. Nevertheless, you will typically not owe any additional taxes. There are several common situations where the IRS will not count the discharged debt as income. Because tax issues are complicated, get help from a qualified tax professional.

Some lenders will still send an IRS Form 1099-C both to you and to the IRS any time they agree to forgive your debt. Do not ignore this Form 1099-C, but instead file IRS Form 982 with the IRS, attaching an explanation, if applicable, why the discharged debt should not count as income. You also will have to file the longer Form 1040 tax return.

OPTIONS FOR FHA-INSURED MORTGAGES

When you get behind on an FHA loan, you may be sent a useful pamphlet "How to Avoid Foreclosure." This pamphlet is also available at www.hud.gov/offices/adm/hudclips/forms/files/pa426h.pdf. FHA's comprehensive handbook covering its loss mitigation guidelines, FHA Single Family Housing Policy Handbook (HUD Handbook 4000.1), is available at http://portal.hud.gov/hudportal/HUD?src=/program_offices/housing/sfh/handbook_4000-1.

HUD-funded foreclosure prevention counseling can be obtained from your HUD regional office or you can call 800-569-4287 (TDD 800-877-8339) or go on www.hud.gov to find HUD-approved counselors. Check a counseling agency's website to see if it provides foreclosure prevention counseling.

If you experience difficulties with a servicer who is not following FHA guidelines, you can seek help through the FHA National Servicing Center (NSC). Mail Department of Housing and Urban Development, National Servicing Center, 301 N.W. 6th St., Suite 200, Oklahoma City, OK 73201 or call 888-297-8685. Be sure to send your servicer a copy of any letter you send to the NSC.

Servicer Initial Obligations When You Are Delinquent. Servicers will send you notice of your default of an FHA mortgage which explains what you need to do to get your loan reinstated. Servicers must also make reasonable efforts to arrange a face-to-face interview with you before three full monthly installments are overdue. The servicer may not initiate foreclosure until it has considered whether you qualify for one of the loss mitigation options discussed below.

Before You Get to the FHA-HAMP Program. While FHA-HAMP can reduce your monthly loan payment, some borrowers are not eligible for FHA-HAMP—they only qualify for a repayment plan or a forbearance agreement, which do not permanently change the basic terms of their loans. In a repayment plan, each month you make your normal monthly payment plus pay a portion of your delinquent payments on top of that. The plan gives you the opportunity to get caught up on your back-due payments over a period of months. A forbearance agreement does not excuse you from eventually making all your payments, but does allow you for a period of months to reduce or skip your payments.

There are three basic situations where you will only be offered a repayment plan or a forbearance agreement instead of the FHA-HAMP program:

1. ***If you have not experienced a verified loss of income or increase in living expenses,*** the servicer must offer you a short-term repayment plan or forbearance agreement. If the plan is going to extend for longer than three months, it must be in writing; shorter plans can be provided orally. The plans cannot extend longer than six months, unless HUD authorizes the extension.
2. ***You do not have "continuous income"*** that is reasonably likely to continue through at least the next twelve months. Continuous income includes employment income, pensions, Social Security, disability, veterans' benefits, and child support payments. FHA's option for borrowers without continuous income is a special forbearance plan that reduces or suspends your payments for a fixed time or until you begin to receive continuous income, up to a maximum of one year. At the end of the forbearance period the servicer must evaluate you for the full range of FHA loss mitigation options.
3. ***If you have too much income,*** you can be forced into a repayment agreement of up to six months. This happens if you have sufficient net income left after you pay your normal monthly living expenses and your recurring monthly debt, so that you can handle a repayment agreement that will bring you current within six months. In addition, if your current total mortgage payments take up less than 31% of your gross income, you must also be considered for a repayment plan of up to six months.

Who Qualifies for the FHA-HAMP Program. Unless you are excluded by one of the threshold tests described above, your servicer must evaluate you for FHA-HAMP which can permanently reduce your monthly payments. FHA-HAMP uses a complicated formula set out below to determine your loan modification, based on your income and loan payment. Once this loan modification is determined, you will be on a three-month trial plan on reduced payments. If that goes well, you will receive a permanent modification with lower mortgage payments.

To qualify for the FHA-HAMP program, the property must be owner-occupied. The borrowers must be in default or at imminent risk of default. Borrowers who have received a chapter 7 bankruptcy discharge and did not reaffirm their mortgage debt are eligible for FHA-HAMP, as are borrowers currently in bankruptcy. A default on an FHA-HAMP trial modification does not preclude later eligibility for a new modification, so long as the borrower can demonstrate changed circumstances justifying the new application. Borrowers are limited to one permanent FHA-HAMP modification in a two-year period.

Calculating Your FHA-HAMP Loan Modification. The first step in determining your FHA-HAMP loan modification is to calculate a monthly payment that FHA thinks you can afford, called the "target payment amount." Select the greater of 80% of your current monthly payment (including escrow) with 25% of your gross monthly income. The target payment is the lesser of that resulting number and 31% of your gross monthly income.

The next step initially calculates a proposed modification. The total amount of outstanding unpaid interest, advances, and legitimate foreclosure fees and costs are added to the existing principal balance to form a new modified principal balance. This new balance is amortized over a 360-month term running from the modification date. A new fixed interest rate is set at a current market rate. These calculations generate a new monthly payment, which is added to the current monthly escrow payment to produce an estimated total monthly modified payment.

If this initial modification calculation produces a number at or below the "target payment amount," the servicer should offer you a modification with those fixed terms. If it produces a number higher than the "target payment amount," then FHA determines that you need more help. Your servicer must then reduce the principal balance to which the new interest rate and 360-month term is applied to reach a lower monthly payment for you. With one exception discussed below, the principal balance is reduced enough so that your payment gets down to the target monthly payment. FHA calls the amount of the principal balance that is reduced a "partial claim."

A partial claim does not eliminate your obligation to pay the amount reduced from your principal balance, but instead is an interest-free loan, secured by a secondary lien on your home. You do not have to pay this loan off until you pay off your FHA first mortgage or stop living in the home. The FHA-HAMP program can provide you with as large a partial claim as you will need to bring your payments down to a "target payment," but the total number of partial claims FHA will offer you during your mortgage is limited to 30% of the unpaid principal balance owed at the time of default.

If the cap is reached, your payment is lowered as far as possible until the partial claim cap is reached, as long as your total modified monthly payment is lower than 40% of your gross monthly income. If your payment would be higher than 40% of your gross income, you should be considered for special forbearance or an option involving loss of your home.

Short Sales and Deeds in Lieu of Foreclosure. FHA provides for a short sale, letting you sell your home and use the proceeds to satisfy your mortgage even if the proceeds are less than the amount you owe on the loan. The FHA limits approvals of short sales based on the ratio of the property's value to the outstanding debt and on the ratio between the short sale purchase price and the property's value. To qualify for an FHA short sale you must document financial hardship. No documentation is needed if you occupy the property, are ninety days or more delinquent, and have a credit score below 620.

You must be able to sell your home within four months of your approval. This period may be extended for two more months if you have a signed purchase and sale agreement or if your lender qualifies under certain program rules. The sale proceeds must pay off any liens that are junior to the FHA mortgage. The FHA will provide you with an incentive payment of up to $3,000 when you complete the short sale.

FHA offers a "deed in lieu of foreclosure" option that lets you transfer your home voluntarily to the FHA in exchange for a release from all your obligations under the mortgage. You must submit verification of hardship, and a complete application with calculation of your cash reserves. You can avoid this documentation requirement if you occupy the property, are ninety days or more delinquent, and have a credit score below 620. The FHA will generally not accept a "deed in lieu" if you have a tenant. Instead you must first attempt to sell your home through a short sale.

The FHA pays you $2,000 for completing a deed in lieu. However, if there are any other liens on the property, the payment may be used to help pay off those liens. The deed in lieu option will not be approved unless all junior liens can be paid off with the transfer.

A short sale and a deed in lieu of foreclosure can have tax implications. For more on both these tax implications and for other useful information about short sales and deeds in lieu, refer to the discussion above in this chapter concerning Fannie Mae and Freddie Mac short sales and deeds in lieu.

OPTIONS FOR VA MORTGAGES

For mortgage loans guaranteed by the Department of Veterans Affairs (VA), the VA expects the servicer to exhaust all possible alternatives before pursuing foreclosure. (In some cases, the VA actually takes over the loan and then you work with the VA instead of the servicer.) If the servicer fails to exhaust the alternatives discussed below, contact one of the eight VA regional centers. The contact information for the center serving your state is found at www.benefits.va.gov/HOMELOANS/contact_rlc_info.asp.

The major loss mitigation options for VA-guaranteed loans are describe below. For more information, see VA Servicer Handbook M26-4, available at www.benefits.va.gov/WARMS/M26_4.asp.

Repayment Plans. A repayment plan is a written agreement between you and your servicer to reinstate a loan that is at least two months in default. For a period of at least three months (you can request a longer period) you pay the normal monthly payment and an agreed upon portion of the arrearage. Repayment plans may be renegotiated at any time.

Special Forbearance. Special forbearance is a written agreement between you and the servicer setting out terms for reinstating a loan that is at least two months in default. The servicer agrees to suspend all payments or accept reduced payments typically for three-to-four months, but the forbearance can be approved for longer periods. You agree to pay the total delinquency at the end of the forbearance period or agree to some other repayment option at that time.

Modifications. The servicer may modify a VA-insured loan without the agency's prior approval. The loan must be in default or, with VA approval, at imminent risk of default. The cause for the default must have been addressed so that it is not expected to re-occur. You must be considered a good credit risk, but a past default is not determinative for this factor, and you must have made at least twelve payments on the loan.

If you meet these conditions you can qualify for a "standard VA modification," where your servicer adds unpaid interest, taxes, insurance, certain assessments (such as for water and sewer charges) to the new principal balance. Legal fees and foreclosure costs may also be added to the modified balance, if they do not exceed the VA's fee schedule. Late fees and processing costs may not be added. The new principal balance is then amortized over a longer period of time and with a different interest rate, thus lowering your mortgage payments.

The standard modification may result in a decrease or up to a one percent increase in the interest rate, and the new rate must be fixed. The modification may extend the loan term to the shorter of 360 months from the date of the modification or 120 months from the original loan maturity date (unless the original loan term was less than 360 months, in which case the loan term may be extended to 480 months from the loan origination date).

Without VA approval, a loan cannot be modified more than once within three years and not more than three times during the life of the loan. A modification that does not meet the standard guidelines discussed above may still be approved if the VA determines that the modification is in the best interest of the veteran and the agency.

A "VA Affordable Modification" is another option that targets a total monthly payment not greater than 31% of your gross monthly income. After your arrears are added to your principal balance, the interest rate may be reduced to a fixed level based on current market rates, the term may be extended, and payments may be further reduced through principal forbearance. You must submit a complete loss mitigation application to be considered for this option.

Finally, the VA allows servicers at their discretion to offer a trial plan for a "Streamline Modification" without a complete application. The offer should provide for a reduction in the principal and interest payment of at least 10%. The borrower accepts the offer by beginning trial plan payments, and, after making three monthly payments, signs a permanent modification agreement.

Assumptions. If a workout is unsuccessful, your servicer may hold off a foreclosure for a reasonable amount of time to permit you to sell or transfer of the property to someone else. It may be attractive for the new owner to "assume," that is take over, your mortgage payments. The VA must approve the assumption and the new owner must pay a fee of one-half of 1% of the loan balance as of the date of transfer. There is also a processing charge that cannot exceed $300 and the cost of a credit report, unless state law sets a lower amount. The VA in appropriate circumstances can even reduce the loan balance for the new owner to the amount the new owner paid for the home.

Compromise Sales and Deeds in Lieu of Foreclosure. A "compromise sale" is what the VA calls a short sale. For both the compromise sale and deed in lieu of foreclosure, the servicer does not have to review your financial information if you are more than 60 days past-due (being past-due is also referred to as being "in arrears"). For both options, you lose your home, but your mortgage loan debt is fully satisfied. The VA authorizes servicers to advance you up to $1,500 for moving expenses.

In a compromise sale, you sell the home yourself. In the "deed in lieu" scenario, you turn the home's title over to the servicer. The VA must approve any deed in lieu, although it strongly encourages servicers to accept deeds in lieu if no alternative allows retention of the home and there is little likelihood of a short sale. The deed in lieu will usually not be accepted if there are any junior liens on the property. For more advice on short sales and deeds in lieu, see this chapter's discussion concerning Fannie Mae and Freddie Mac short sales and deeds in lieu.

OPTIONS FOR THE RURAL HOUSING SERVICE (RHS) GUARANTEED LOAN PROGRAM

The Rural Housing Service (RHS), a division of the U.S. Department of Agriculture and formerly known as FmHA, runs two home loan programs. This section describes options for the program that guaranties loans made by private lenders. For more detail, see chapter 18 of RHS Handbook HB-1-3555, available at www.rd.usda.gov/files/hb-1-3555.pdf. The next section describes options for the RHS program that makes government loans directly to borrowers.

Special Forbearance. An RHS special forbearance is an agreement between you and the servicer to temporarily reduce or suspend payments for one or more months, followed by a repayment plan which may be combined with a loan modification. There is no time limit on the repayment plan, so long as, during the term of the plan, the amount past-due (also referred to as "accumulated arrears") do not exceed an amount equal to twelve monthly mortgage payments. To be eligible for a forbearance plan you must have experienced a loss of income or increase in expenses and your payment must be at least thirty days past-due ("in arrears").

Modification. RHS offers two modification options that permanently change one or more loan term. These options, described below, are available if you have experienced a permanent drop in income or increase in expenses, have regular income to support reduced payments, and are in default or at imminent risk of default.

The Standard Modification. This option allows your servicer to add onto your principal balance delinquent interest, escrow advances, and foreclosure fees and costs (except for late fees and administrative costs). It then sets a fixed interest rate that can even be below the current market rate, and extends the repayment term up to thirty years from the date of the modification. No trial period is required. If the loan has been modified within the last two years, the RHS's approval is required to authorize a second modification.

The "Special Loan Servicing" Modification. This option allows for a more flexible restructuring of the loan by extending the term up to forty years, reducing the interest rate to the current market rate or below, and setting aside a portion of your principle balanced called a "mortgage recovery advance." The advance amount, which is a non-interest bearing lien on the property, cannot exceed an amount equal to twelve months of principal and interest due under the mortgage plus foreclosure fees and costs. Subject to this limit, the servicer must apply enough of an advance so that the modified total monthly payment (including escrow) is no more than 31% of your current monthly gross income. After the modification, the ratio of the total debt payments to your monthly income can be no more than 55%. If you are in default you must complete a three-month trial plan before the modification becomes permanent. You can receive only one permanent Special Loan Servicing Modification over the life of your loan.

Preforeclosure Sale and Deed in Lieu of Foreclosure. A pre-foreclosure sale is the RHS's term for a short sale. It allows you to cancel the mortgage debt with the proceeds of a market sale, even if the sale proceeds are less than the amount owed. You must submit an application and be approved for this option. The sale price must fall within a certain range based on the property's market value and the sale must be completed within a designated time frame. Get written confirmation that you do not owe anything on the loan even if the sale proceeds are less than the outstanding debt.

A deed in lieu of foreclosure lets you voluntarily transfer the property in exchange for a release from all your obligations under the mortgage. The agreement must be in writing and should clearly state that you have no further obligation on the mortgage loan after turning over the deed. Other loss mitigation options should be considered first, including a pre-foreclosure sale. More information about short sales and "deeds in lieu" is found earlier in this chapter's section on Fannie Mae and Freddie Mac short sales and deeds in lieu.

THE RHS DIRECT LOAN PROGRAM

RHS administers a direct loan program where the U.S. Department of Agriculture extends the loan and remains the owner of the loan at all times, including during foreclosure. You deal with the single Customer Service Center (formerly the "Centralized Servicing Center") in St. Louis, Missouri, 800-793-8861. It is easier to get assistance if you have your account number handy.

RHS offers a number of special servicing programs designed to assist you, but only when your mortgage payments are at least two months overdue. Apply for these special servicing options quickly, because foreclosure can start just a month later.

Payment Assistance. You may be eligible for payment subsidies, referred to as "interest credit" or "payment assistance." The subsidies are set yearly and reduce the amount of interest you have to pay. If your income drops during the year, you can lower your payments by documenting this promptly with the Customer Service Center. Much but not all your payment subsidies are added back on to the principal balance owed if you sell the property, so that the amount you owe may not even go down over time.

Payment Moratorium. A payment moratorium is available when circumstances beyond your control mean that you are temporarily unable to continue making full payments without substantially impairing your standard of living. Courts are divided as to whether you can apply for a payment moratorium after RHS has decided to foreclose.

Under a payment moratorium your monthly payments may be reduced or suspended, based on need, for up to two years. Eligibility for the moratorium program is reviewed at least once every six months and you should be provided with sixty days' notice before the moratorium is terminated.

When the moratorium is terminated, your monthly payments are recalculated based on the balance at that time. If you are unable to afford the payments after they are recalculated, some or all of the interest that came due during moratorium may be canceled.

Delinquency Workout Agreement. A "delinquency workout agreement" allows you, over a period of no more than two years, to get caught up on delinquent payments by paying a portion of the delinquent amount in addition to your scheduled mortgage payment.

Protective Advance. A "protective advance" is an RHS advance of money to pay your taxes or insurance and then recalculates the loan balance and payments. The RHS may demand the advance's repayment within one year or amortize the advanced amounts over the loan's remaining life.

Loan Modification. Sometimes repayment plans are not feasible because your finances have suffered a long-term setback and will not recover. In such a situation the RHS can add onto your principal balance the unpaid interest and escrow advances (but not foreclosure costs, late fees, and other administrative expenses). Because the length of the repayment term of RHS direct loans cannot be extended for any substantial additional time, these modifications almost invariably increase your monthly payment.

Short Sale and Deed in Lieu of Foreclosure. A short sale allows you to satisfy the full debt owed to the government with the proceeds of a sale, even if the sale proceeds are less than the amount of the debt. RHS must approve short sales and the price must meet RHS requirements related to the value of the property and size of the total debt. RHS may set time limits for the completion of the sale. The short sale is overseen by a local RHS office and not by the centralized Customer Service Center.

If you apply for debt forgiveness and the application is approved, a deed in lieu of foreclosure allows you to transfer the home voluntarily to the government in return for a release of all liability for the debt. The RHS typically looks at this as the last option, when a short sale cannot be arranged.

In a short sale and in a "deed-in-lieu," follow the correct procedures to make sure you are not liable for the remaining debt after the sale proceeds are deducted, particularly when your RHS subsidies are added back onto the debt when you sell the home or provide a deed in lieu. Otherwise the federal government aggressively pursues these remaining balances. Submit an application with current financial information to RHS. If approved, you will receive written confirmation of the release of liability from the full debt. More information about short sales and deeds in lieu is found earlier in this chapter's section on Fannie Mae and Freddie Mac short sales and deeds in lieu.

Appeals. You can appeal certain RHS decisions, such as a denial of a moratorium application or the commencement of foreclosure. You lose the right to appeal if you do not act within the required time (usually 30 days from notice of the decision). Appeal options include mediation or a formal hearing before a USDA hearing officer.

THE LOSS MITIGATION APPLICATION PROCESS

Start Loss Mitigation Discussions As Early As Possible. Starting early avoids the difficulty of negotiating at the last minute with a potential foreclosure sale date pending and also avoids potential foreclosure fees and costs, which can be substantial. It is better to begin negotiations before the lender has turned the matter over to a foreclosure lawyer. You also appear more responsible if you try to prevent the problem from getting out of hand.

In some cases you can even apply for relief *before* you default on your mortgage when a default is reasonably foreseeable—for example, after you lost your job or your adjustable rate mortgage is about to reset to unaffordable monthly payments. Some servicers are reluctant to consider loan mitigation if you are not in default, but they may have the authority to do that if your default is imminent.

When a foreclosure is pending, careful attention must be given to preventing the sale as part of your request for a modification. A foreclosure sale cuts off your ability to modify the mortgage loan and also ends your ownership in your home. You should also request a modification prior to filing for bankruptcy. Once bankruptcy is filed, some servicers may (incorrectly) act as though their options for assisting you are more limited, when they in fact are not.

The Importance of Getting Help. Find a nonprofit counselor or lawyer with experience with mortgage workouts to help you through the process. In many cases, counselors will have access to programs and lender personnel that you cannot reach directly yourself.

Find a nearby HUD-approved counseling agency by calling 800-569-4287 (TDD 800-877-8339) or by checking www.hud.gov/offices/hsg/sfh/hcc/hcs.cfm. Many cities and states also have programs to assist homeowners in default. Contact your local government housing office or a community group that addresses housing and homeownership to see if they can refer you to a counselor. If you received pre-purchase education about homeownership, contact the organization that provided your classes to find out if they also provide foreclosure prevention assistance or can refer you to an organization that does. It also can't hurt to ask the servicer if it has a program for homeowner assistance in your community.

If someone unsolicited offers to help, make sure you are dealing with a legitimate nonprofit agency with experience in default and delinquency counseling. Too often, someone who advertises or approaches you about mortgage counseling is really just a con artist who will get you into more trouble.

Your Loss Mitigation Application. In applying for loss mitigation, do not contact the owner of your mortgage loan, but instead, contact your mortgage servicer. The servicer should have workout specialists who will tell you what documents you need to provide, take your application, and provide information on the application process.

Some servicers will ask you to speak only to their attorney once the legal process of foreclosure has begun. Although some attorneys will readily participate in workout discussions or give you permission to speak with the servicer directly, others will need to be pushed. Unresponsive attorneys should be reported to the servicer or to the mortgage owner if necessary.

Federal rules require that your servicer assist you in completing the application. As long as a foreclosure sale is not scheduled within 45 days, your servicer must acknowledge in writing within 5 days that it received your application and must describe any missing documents you still need to send.

As long as the servicer has received your complete loss mitigation application at least 37 days before a scheduled foreclosure sale, it must within 30 days evaluate you for all available loss mitigation options and tell you which ones you are eligible for. You do not have to ask for a specific option, although there is nothing wrong with doing so. The servicer's letter must give specific reasons for any denial of a loan modification. As long as the servicer receives your complete application at least 90 days before a scheduled foreclosure sale, you can appeal the denial of a loan modification.

These rules only apply to your initial application to a given servicer. You can always submit multiple applications to the same servicer, however the servicer has more discretion as to the nature and speed of its responses for any subsequent applications.

Pay Attention to Any Pending Foreclosure Sale. It is not unusual for mortgage servicers to continue with a foreclosure while you request loss mitigation options. Often the servicer's loss mitigation department and the servicer's lawyers conducting a foreclosure sale do not communicate. But if you submit your first complete loss mitigation application at least 37 days before a scheduled foreclosure sale, federal rules require the servicer to delay the sale, review the application, and give you a written decision before allowing a sale.

If this rule does not protect you, always request a delay of a foreclosure sale long enough to complete the loss mitigation review. Unless the servicer agrees in writing to suspend the foreclosure proceeding, assume that the foreclosure process will continue. If the foreclosure sale is a court-supervised process, make sure you notify the court of your agreement with the servicer to delay the foreclosure. Always verify that the sale is actually canceled.

Loss Mitigation Fees, Foreclosure Fees, and Late Charges. While modification fees are not permitted under some loss mitigation programs, servicers otherwise may charge a fee for handling workout options. Some servicers want this fee at the beginning of the workout process regardless of the application's outcome. Request a waiver or a fee reduction to make the workout affordable. Late charges will almost always be waived.

The servicer's out-of-pocket costs to modify your mortgage, such as appraisal fees and credit report charges, probably will not be waived. The servicer will also expect reimbursement from you for foreclosure fees and costs if the servicer has already begun to incur such fees. Examine all fees to make sure that they are reasonable. You can also request an agreement to pay some or all of the fees in installments or to have the fee lumped together with the loan balance.

Where you are charged attorney fees for a foreclosure and the foreclosure does not take place due to your loss mitigation agreement, ask for them to be credited back to your account. Refunds or credits for fees paid to auctioneers, sheriffs or court officials, or for legal advertisements should also be made depending upon when the foreclosure sale is canceled. To the extent foreclosure fees and costs are valid, they need to be paid or otherwise accounted for in the loss mitigation process.

Documenting a Workout Agreement. Even if there is a delay in signing the final forms for the workout, make sure you have a writing spelling out the agreement's basic terms and that any foreclosure proceeding is postponed or stayed. Never sign a release or similar agreement asking you to give up all your legal claims against the lender until after the actual workout agreement is finalized. Make sure the lender signs the agreement and it is recorded, if necessary, with the mortgage in the property registry.

If Your Loss Mitigation Review Is Not Going Well. If you aren't receiving sufficient cooperation from a servicer in reaching a loss mitigation resolution, ask to speak to a supervisor. You also can appeal a denial, and the servicer's supervisory staff not involved in the original decision must review your appeal and notify you in writing of their decision. You can also complain directly to the mortgage's owner or insurer. Fannie Mae, Freddie Mac, and some other owners have "loss-mitigation" departments that will intervene, if pushed, to address a proposed workout.

You can also send the servicer a "notice of error" or a "request for information," as described in Chapter 16. This may get your servicer to focus appropriately on your loss mitigation review. You can also register a complaint about a mortgage servicer directly with the Consumer Financial Protection Bureau that may attempt at least an informal resolution at www.consumerfinance.gov/complaint.

Your efforts in all of these steps may be more effective with the help of a housing counselor or attorney. Even if you tried to obtain a workout on your own, it may be time to seek help if the negotiation with the lender is not working out well.

18

Defending Your Home from Foreclosure

TOPICS COVERED IN THIS CHAPTER

Your Rights in the Mortgage Foreclosure Process

Getting Legal Advice to Stop a Foreclosure; Advice to Avoid

Delaying the Foreclosure Process

A Chapter 13 Bankruptcy May Stop a Foreclosure Permanently

State Temporary Bans on Foreclosure; Conference and Mediation Programs

Your Options After the Foreclosure Sale

Special Protections Against Foreclosure for FHA, VA, and RHS Mortgages

Special Protections for Active Duty Military

Foreclosure of Land Instalment Sales

Foreclosure Protections Where Mortgage Resulted from a Home Improvement Scam

Foreclosures of Manufactured (Mobile) Homes

Foreclosure for Unpaid Condominium Fees

The prior two chapters provide advice when you are having trouble involving your mortgage payments and your rights to engage in loss mitigation and loan modifications. However, a foreclosure sale may be so close at hand that a workout agreement or loan modification is not possible, or the lender may not agree to an acceptable arrangement. In these situations, you should consider the options laid out in this chapter.

You are not powerless when you face with a foreclosure sale, but you need to be realistic in defining your objectives. You often have a good chance of achieving one of the following two objectives:

1. If you have the financial resources, you can keep your home by paying back delinquent payments and legitimate fees or costs. It also is possible to prevent foreclosure by "redeeming" your home.
2. If you do not have the financial resources, you can delay the foreclosure sale to give you enough time to find a long-term solution to the underlying problem that caused you to fall behind on your mortgage payments.

This chapter also has special advice for nine particular types of foreclosures:

- If your mortgage is backed by three different government agencies—FHA, VA, or RHS;
- If you or your spouse are now on active duty in the military;
- If you have a land installment sale contract;
- If your mortgage resulted from a home improvement scam;
- If your mortgage is for a manufactured home;
- If your manufactured home is facing eviction from a manufacture home park; and
- If your condominium faces foreclosure for unpaid condominium fees.

The next chapter examines yet another type of threatened foreclosure, one based on unpaid property taxes to the city or town. In addition, Chapter 21 sets out your rights if a creditor other than your mortgage lender is trying to seize your home for an unpaid court judgment.

YOUR RIGHTS IN THE MORTGAGE FORECLOSURE PROCESS

Preliminary Notices. To protect your rights, you need to be informed about what is happening—the worst thing you can do is ignore everything. If you are behind on your mortgage payments, stay on top of things: carefully read the notices you receive, keep track of deadlines, and contact the servicer or foreclosure attorney at regular intervals.

In every state, you are entitled to notice of a pending foreclosure on your home. But do not rely on the fact that you will get this notice—either because of servicer negligence or problems with mail delivery. Always pick up any certified or registered mail, even if returned to the post office. Keep all the notices that you receive from the servicer, lender, or foreclosure attorney in one place, like a folder or notebook. Also document all related phone calls with the date, time, name of person that you spoke with, and the substance of your conversation.

Notice of Default. You will almost always get a "notice of default" or "notice of delinquency" from the loan servicer that says that you have fallen behind on your payments. It may look like any other collection letter. It tells you how many payments you are behind and the payment amount to catch up and get out of default, often called "the arrears." It will also give you a deadline to make this payment to avoid foreclosure.

Typically, your payment of the total amount of the arrears will stop any foreclosure. Partial payments are often rejected unless they are made as part of a workout agreement or loan modification.

If you cannot pay the total arrears, review the prior chapter about seeking a workout agreement or loan modification. Otherwise, do not delay, but review immediately your other rights to deal with the foreclosure. The deeper you get into the foreclosure process, the harder it will be to stop it. A big advantage to paying off an arrearage when you get the initial notice is that you will not yet be responsible for major foreclosure fees and costs that come due after the case is referred to an attorney for foreclosure.

Notice of Acceleration. After notice of default, or sometimes combined with the notice of default, you typically receive a notice of acceleration. It says that now you don't just owe the past-due installments, but you owe the full mortgage balance, payable either immediately or by a certain date. Receipt of a notice of acceleration indicates that the foreclosure process is moving quickly and that you must act immediately to deal with the pending foreclosure.

The Right to Reinstate. Many states and mortgage contracts allow you a second chance even after the servicer demands the full balance on the loan, by "reinstating" the mortgage. Usually, this means getting caught up on your missed payments together with foreclosure fees and costs. Many mortgage contracts give you this "right to reinstate" up until five days before the foreclosure sale, and some servicers accept payment right up to the sale date. Your servicer may require that the payment be by certified or bank check and sent to the law firm handling the foreclosure.

Occasionally, servicers claim you did not meet your obligations in some other way, such as failing to keep the property insured. These defaults can also be "cured" by taking care of the problem.

Even where you do not have a legal right to reinstate your mortgage, servicers often will agree to reinstate voluntarily, although others will not. When the servicer will not allow reinstatement, you can often force the lender to allow a reinstatement by taking the matter to court. Most judges will not want to put your family on the street when you have money to pay the arrears, and even in states where judges do not have this power, offering to pay in front of a judge sometimes embarrasses the lender into accepting the payment.

Using Bankruptcy to Cure the Default. Even where the servicer will not accept payment of your arrears to reinstate the mortgage, if you file for bankruptcy before a foreclosure sale is completed, you then have a right to cure any default by paying the amount overdue. In a chapter 7 bankruptcy, you have to pay the arrearage immediately if you want to avoid foreclosure. If you file under chapter 13, you can make those payments in installments over a period of years.

The Right to Redeem. You also can "redeem" your home up to the time of a foreclosure sale (and in a few states for a limited number of days after the foreclosure sale). To redeem, you must pay the servicer the whole mortgage balance in one payment plus the lender's foreclosure fees and costs. Some states allow a second type of redemption where, after the foreclosure sale, you pay the person who bought your home at the foreclosure sale the amount that person paid to purchase the home plus the person's related costs. Unless you can obtain a new loan to do so, either type of redemption is clearly impractical for you if you are having trouble even making your monthly payments.

How Long Does Foreclosure Take? A foreclosure can take from three months to a year or more. Much depends on your state, the servicer, and your own actions. Check local practice and stay on top of all foreclosure-related notices. But no matter how long the foreclosure takes, your own delay in developing a plan always will make matters worse for you.

How a Lender Gets Permission to Foreclose. Foreclosure procedures are established by state law and by local practice. In some states, the lender first files suit in a court, usually in the county where your home is located. You receive a summons or a similar notice usually brought to the house by a sheriff, constable, marshal, or process server. This notice gives you a period of time to respond to the foreclosure lawsuit and to raise your defenses. Your answer must be in writing and filed with the court. If you do not respond at all, a default judgment will be entered against you. If you file a response the court may only enter a judgment against you if it finds your defenses have no merit. A court judgment for the lender gives the lender permission to sell your home unless you can work out an agreement or take some other action (such as bankruptcy) to prevent the sale.

Other states use "non-judicial foreclosures." Servicers are allowed to hold a foreclosure sale without a court or other official permission to go forward. They advertise the home for sale, using a legal notice in a newspaper. The servicer sends you a notice of the time and place for the sale. If you want to challenge this type of foreclosure, you must either file for bankruptcy or file a lawsuit and ask the court to stop the sale. With a lawsuit, you may have to file a bond protecting the lender.

The Foreclosure Sale. Servicers must send you notice of the date and time your home will be sold. In some states, this notice is combined with the notice of acceleration, discussed above. The sale date is a key date because that is when you lose your rights as the owner to obtain a workout or to use the bankruptcy process to prevent foreclosure.

Generally, a foreclosure sale is a poorly advertised and poorly attended auction, either at your home or at a local courthouse or government building. Where a court ordered the foreclosure, the auctioneer will be a sheriff or court official. Otherwise, it will be conducted by someone hired by the servicer. Often only the foreclosing lender attends, who bids no more than the balance of the debt. You can bid at the auction, but you will have to make an immediate down-payment and pay the balance within a short period of time. After a foreclosure sale you will receive notices about eviction. In most states the servicer must go through a separate court procedure to get permission to evict you. Only a government official can carry out an eviction. The eviction consists of a supervised change of locks and removal of your personal property from the house.

The Mortgage Deficiency or Surplus. Once a foreclosure sale is completed, pay careful attention to all notices you receive. These may include notices of who bought the property and how much they paid. Always ask on your own who bought the property and the sale price because sometimes this information is not sent to you.

If the sale does not bring in enough to pay off the amount due on the loan, in many, but not all states, you will remain responsible for the balance, called a "deficiency"—the remainder due on the loan plus costs, minus the amount the lender was paid from the sale proceeds. You may also receive notices about the deficiency, including collection letters and court papers. In some states your deficiency can be limited if you act to protect your legal rights by responding to these notices or court papers. If you do have to pay a deficiency, this will be an unsecured debt like credit card or medical debt and it is thus low priority debt, until the lender sues you for that debt. Because deficiency claims are unsecured debts, they can be discharged in bankruptcy.

An exception is if your loan is insured, guaranteed, or made by the VA or the Rural Housing Service (RHS). When these agencies seek a deficiency, they can seize your federal tax refund. Also they can seize a portion of your Social Security and certain other federal benefits, although the first $750 a month is protected from seizure. But, even though the debt is owed to the federal government, you can also discharge it in bankruptcy.

On the other hand, if the sale brings in enough to pay off the amount due including all foreclosure costs, you are entitled to any amount by which the sale price exceeds that, called a "surplus." Although consumers are rarely owed a surplus, if your home sells for more than the outstanding balance, contact the servicer or its foreclosure attorney. If they say you are entitled to a surplus, be sure to give them your new address when you move, so they can send you a check.

If the servicer does not tell you whether you are entitled to a surplus, send a Qualified Written Request to the servicer, as described in Chapter 16. If fees and costs eat up your surplus, and they seem unreasonable, dispute them or even challenge them in court.

GETTING LEGAL ADVICE TO STOP A FORECLOSURE; ADVICE TO AVOID

When threatened with foreclosure, immediately seek legal help. It is better to get this help too soon rather than too late. Free help may be available at a neighborhood legal services office (go to www.lawhelp to find a legal services office) or a bar association panel of pro bono attorneys. A small number of lawyers in your area may handle foreclosure defense cases for a fee and many lawyers will help you file a bankruptcy. Exercise care in hiring a lawyer. The highest priced lawyer may not be the best. Find someone you feel comfortable with, at a price you can afford. Also try to get a referral for the lawyer from someone you trust. More information about finding a lawyer can be found in Chapter 1.

Another good source of help is nonprofit foreclosure prevention counseling (sometimes called "default counseling"). Contact a local nonprofit housing organization to find out where this service is offered in your community or call 800-569-4287 (TDD 800-877-8339) or visit www.hud.gov to find a HUD-approved housing counseling agency near you.

Scams to Avoid. Some businesses offer help to people facing foreclosure in order to rip them off. A pending foreclosure of your home is public information and scam artists will find that information and then contact you. Scammers may ask for thousands of dollars, saying they are offering you a loan or have arranged a payment plan or loan modification. In reality they will do nothing. Even worse, these scammers may (even without you realizing it) have you sign your deed over to them, with a bogus option to buy it back.

If someone seeks you out to save your home, odds are the offer is bogus and will only get you deeper into debt and prevent you from taking the steps that will save your home or improve your situation. Requests for high fees or for money to pay the mortgage are another sign of a scam. An offer of a new mortgage as a way out of foreclosure will be on terrible terms and will just make your situation impossible to resolve. If you do sign a new mortgage under pressure of foreclosure, you have three business days to cancel.

DELAYING THE FORECLOSURE PROCESS

Foreclosure can move very quickly, but you can exercise your legal rights to slow down the process. Delay gives you time to put in place a long-term solution, such as to refinance your mortgage, sell your home privately, arrange a workout agreement or loan modification, or save up money to get you caught up on your payments. You cannot properly delay foreclosure just because you need more time. The actions you take must be based on some underlying legal claim or defense that is raised in good faith.

Procedural Defenses May Delay the Process. Foreclosures are rarely contested by homeowners, and lenders' attorneys may be sloppy in their procedures and sometimes do not comply with pre-foreclosure requirements. Lender errors can be to your benefit when you are contesting foreclosure, forcing the lender to start over or at least to comply with procedural requirements.

You are likely to need the help of a lawyer or other professional to determine lender compliance with required procedures. Examples are failure to give you proper notice, failure to give you a fair chance to correct the default, failure to properly advertise the sale, failure to introduce the original documents in the foreclosure proceeding, failure to sue all the proper parties, failure to bring the foreclosure proceeding in the name of the real mortgage owner, or discouraging bids at the foreclosure sale. There may also be procedural requirements that involve considering you for loss mitigation options. Under certain state laws you may be able to defend against a foreclosure if the servicer seriously violated these procedures.

In states where foreclosure actions are brought in court, raise defenses in that action. In states where lenders use the nonjudicial foreclosure process, you have to bring a legal case of your own, asking the court to stop the foreclosure.

Servicer's Past Acceptance of Late or Partial Payments As Grounds for Foreclosure Delay. Courts may refuse to allow foreclosure if the servicer surprises you by suddenly calling the whole loan due when the servicer has been lenient in the past in accepting late or partial payments. It instead must warn you that late or partial payments are no longer acceptable before it calls the whole loan due and attempts a foreclosure. If the servicer accepts a payment after the foreclosure has started, you can argue that there is no longer a default, and the servicer must restart the foreclosure process. This may involve giving a new notice of acceleration.

Asking the Court for More Time. A judge may give you a delay if foreclosure will cause serious hardship. The hardship should be documented and involve more than just the loss of your home, such as that a family member has a serious illness. The hardship must be temporary as well; if permanent, the judge may feel that now is as good a time as any to allow the foreclosure.

If you have a great deal of equity in your home, a judge may allow you a short period of time to sell the home without foreclosure, allowing you to get the best possible price and recover your home equity. Even if you are unable to make payments during this time, the lender is not hurt because there is enough value in the property to eventually pay the lender's full claim.

A Chapter 7 Bankruptcy May Create a Temporary Delay. A chapter 7 bankruptcy case cannot address a foreclosure in the long-term but filing the bankruptcy typically delays the foreclosure at least 60 days, as long as you have not recently filed another bankruptcy case. While the bankruptcy is pending, the lender cannot continue foreclosure without permission of the court.

You cannot file a chapter 7 bankruptcy solely to delay foreclosure. You must have some other legitimate purpose for filing bankruptcy. For most homeowners in financial distress, this is hardly a problem because there are lots of other debts outstanding.

A CHAPTER 13 BANKRUPTCY MAY STOP A FORECLOSURE PERMANENTLY

Unlike a chapter 7 bankruptcy that only delays a foreclosure, a chapter 13 bankruptcy filing may eliminate the threat of foreclosure by letting you slowly get caught up on past-due payments over a period of years, while at the same time, you must continue to make your regular monthly payment. Do not file the chapter 13 bankruptcy too soon, and instead pursue options to modify your payments discussed in the prior chapter. But you definitely do not want to wait too long and certainly should file the chapter 13 bankruptcy before the foreclosure sale.

You also need to leave yourself enough time to participate in required credit counseling with an approved credit counseling agency before filing bankruptcy. Fortunately you can do this over the internet or by telephone. See Chapter 25 for more information about this requirement.

Curing Delinquent Payments and Reinstating the Mortgage. Chapter 13 bankruptcy works best where you fell behind in your mortgage payments because of a temporary financial setback and you have resolved the problem that caused your setback. Filing the chapter 13 bankruptcy (the same as in chapter 7) automatically stops the foreclosure—at least temporarily. In addition you can pay back your delinquent payments in installments over a period of three to five years, but you must also make your regular monthly payments as they come due. You may have to pay interest on the back-due amount, a commission to the bankruptcy trustee for handling your payments, and certain fees the servicer has already charged, if they are legitimate.

For example, assume you are six months behind on $800 monthly mortgage payments so that you owe $4,800 and also assume the servicer has charged $600 in various fees. In a five-year chapter 13 case, you cure by making future $800 payments as they come due and catching up on the past-due $5,400 in sixty monthly payments of $90 each, plus interest and the trustee's commission, so you pay $890 a month plus interest and the commission.

As long as there has not been a foreclosure sale, you can cure delinquent payments in a chapter 13 bankruptcy even if the servicer has already demanded you pay at once the full loan amount or even if a court has ordered a foreclosure sale. The bankruptcy process also gives you an opportunity to raise defenses to the lenders' claim, including defenses that fees are excessive. These defenses can be raised as part of the determination as to how much you have to pay under your chapter 13 bankruptcy plan. Chapter 13 bankruptcy may also permit you to get rid of other liens and mortgages on your property. These bankruptcy options are discussed in Chapter 25.

Sale of a Home in a Chapter 13 Bankruptcy. If you can no longer afford your future mortgage payments, you will not benefit from bankruptcy's ability to cure past delinquencies. You can, however, use the bankruptcy process to sell the home on your own in an orderly fashion, thereby keeping your equity and avoiding the problems of a foreclosure sale. This is likely to work only if the home's sale price is enough pay both the mortgage lender and at least something to your other creditors.

Request that the court approve your realtor. When a sale is arranged, many title insurance companies require that you obtain an order from the bankruptcy court approving the sale and allowing the property to be sold free of liens.

STATE TEMPORARY BANS ON FORECLOSURE; CONFERENCE AND MEDIATION PROGRAMS

Several states and local court systems have created programs that offer settlement conferences and mediations for foreclosures. These programs are designed to encourage the servicer to agree to alternatives to foreclosure. Even though how these programs work will vary, they all give you the opportunity to discuss your situation with a live person as opposed to leaving messages in the servicer's voicemail system. Often the programs refer you to housing counselors and other advocates who can help you through the process.

Carefully review any notices you receive about mediation programs. Sometimes a mediation session is scheduled automatically when a servicer starts a foreclosure. In other programs, you have to request mediation and you may have only a limited time to make the request.

State and local governments also have at various times authorized stays of foreclosures limited to the duration of a particular economic crisis or natural disaster. Check for any restrictions on foreclosures in your state. State bans are only temporary, but they may give you an opportunity to get back on your feet.

YOUR OPTIONS AFTER THE FORECLOSURE SALE

Redemption and Setting Aside the Sale. Some states, for a very limited number of days after the foreclosure sale, allow you to "redeem" the home back from the lender—in other words, they allow you to pay off the full mortgage and related fees and charges. This way, you end up with clear title to the property. Another option in some states is to redeem your home from the person purchasing it at the foreclosure sale, paying that person the total purchase price plus interest and allowable costs. State law may provide you only a very limited number of days after a foreclosure sale to redeem in this manner, but other states give you up to a year to redeem from the purchaser. Even if you do not have a right to redeem after the sale, you may be able to buy the home back from the purchaser, particularly if the buyer was your mortgage lender.

In some areas there are local nonprofit agencies that help borrowers with financing to purchase their homes back after foreclosures. Another option is to find another purchaser for your home willing to pay more than the redemption amount. You still lose your home, but you get to keep the difference between what you sell the home for and the redemption amount. Those funds may be very helpful in your search for new housing. Redemption has strict time deadlines and strict procedures, so it is best to try to have an attorney to assist you in redeeming the home.

You can also ask a court to set aside the foreclosure sale because proper procedures were not followed or because the price was unconscionably low. This is a long shot and you must act quickly, almost always with an attorney's help.

Rights As a Tenant in Your Own House. After the foreclosures sale, you are a tenant at will in your own home, now owned by someone else. To evict you, the new owner must comply with your state's landlord-tenant eviction law. This usually means filing a lawsuit in court. You can save the new owner from dealing with the difficulty and time involved in an eviction processes by vacating voluntarily if the new owner gives you cash to help in the move and to find new housing. This option is called "cash for keys." You can also offer the new owner that you will pay rent if you are allowed to stay in the home. Even a short extension can help you find a new place to live.

SPECIAL PROTECTIONS AGAINST FORECLOSURE FOR FHA, VA, AND RHS MORTGAGES

FHA Loans. Lenders cannot begin legal foreclosure proceedings on an FHA-insured loan if your only default is an inability to pay an escrow shortage in a lump sum. They also cannot foreclose for missed payments until at least three monthly payments are overdue. After the President declares a disaster affecting your home, the lender may not start or continue a foreclosure on your home for 90 days.

You also may be able to delay a foreclosure if the servicer has failed to comply with servicer requirements for an FHA-insured mortgage loan. Key requirements are that the servicer must:

- Consider whether you qualify for FHA loss mitigation options *before* initiating a foreclosure.
- Give you notice of your default by the end of the second month of your delinquency, explaining what you must do to get reinstated.
- Make reasonable efforts to arrange face-to-face or telephone interviews with you before three full monthly installments are overdue.

If you have an FHA mortgage and are threatened with foreclosure, and you do not have an attorney, you should at least contact a HUD-approved counselor. To find a HUD-approved counselor, call 800-569-4287 (TDD 800-877-8339) or check www.hud.gov/offices/hsg/sfh/hcc/hcs.cfm. Sometimes a counselor can convince a lender to give you a second chance. Alternatively you can call HUD for help at 877-622-8525. Stay on the line until a HUD field officer picks up.

VA Mortgages. If you have a VA mortgage, the lender cannot foreclose unless you fail to make three full monthly payments. The lender must give the VA thirty days' warning of its intent to foreclose and must make all reasonable efforts at forbearance before actually foreclosing on the property. The lender must consider temporary suspension of payments, extension of the loan, and acceptance of partial payments. If the lender still intends to foreclose, you can stop the foreclosure by paying all overdue payments, all late charges, and any of the lender's foreclosure expenses to date.

The lender's failure to meet its obligations in this area can be a defense to foreclosure. For example, send a letter to the lender asking it to consider foreclosure avoidance strategies. The lender's failure to respond appropriately is evidence of its failure to meet its responsibilities. Another option is to contact the regional VA office serving your state, explain the reasons for your default, and ask about the best plan for getting your mortgage payments back on track.

RHS Mortgages. For private loans guaranteed by the Rural Housing Service (RHS), the lender must follow RHS guidelines when they foreclose. For example, you can assert a defense to foreclosure that the lender failed to consider RHS loss mitigation options before foreclosing.

Other loans come directly from the RHS. Before it forecloses, RHS must notify you about loss mitigation options, consider you for them if you ask, and implement the options you qualify for. RHS's failure to perform any of these obligations can be raised as a defense to foreclosure. You can also appeal the RHS's loss mitigation decisions with the Department of Agriculture (RHS's parent agency), and a foreclosure should not proceed until an appeal has been resolved.

SPECIAL PROTECTIONS FOR ACTIVE DUTY MILITARY

If you are on active duty in the military or left within the past nine months, or you are the spouse or dependent of someone on active duty, you have special protections from foreclosure under the Servicemembers Civil Relief Act. This Act applies to all types of mortgage loans, but *only applies* if you entered into the loan *before* your current period of active duty.

Even if you are in a state that allows nonjudicial foreclosures, the lender must obtain a court order or your written permission to foreclose on your home. You can also ask make a written request with the court for a ninety day (or even longer) delay in any court foreclosure case brought against you. The request must explain why your military duties affect your ability to appear in court, give the date when you will be able to appear, and include a statement by your commanding officer that your military duties prevent you from appearing in court and that leave is not authorized.

Make sure you get in writing that the case against you has been delayed. The court also can lower your mortgage payments or add your back payments to your loan balance if your military service affects your ability to make your payments.

FORECLOSURE OF LAND INSTALMENT SALES

Your foreclosure rights are very different if you have a special type of home mortgage called an "installment land contact," "land sale contract," "contract for deed," or "bond for deed." This chapter calls them "land installment sales." In a land installment sale scenario, you do not take title to your home until you have made all the monthly payments that are due, often for more than 10 or even more than 20 years. You pay property taxes and are responsible for repairs, but you do not yet have title to your home.

Land installment sales have far fewer protections from foreclosure than do other types of home mortgages because state foreclosure laws often do not apply. You may not have the right to certain notices, and may not have the right to reinstate or cure delinquent payments or to redeem your home.

In fact, if you miss a payment, the lender may try to evict you under your state's rules for landlords and tenants, which offer you less protection than state laws dealing with foreclosures. Fortunately, this is not always the case—for example, in Illinois, Maryland, Ohio, Oklahoma, and Texas, your rights are closer to those that apply in a normal home foreclosure.

Some (but not all) bankruptcy courts treat land installment sales like mortgage loans, so that a chapter 13 bankruptcy plan can cure back-payments over a three-year to five-year period. When bankruptcy courts do not treat land installment sales like mortgages, you still have important rights in bankruptcy to keep your home.

FORECLOSURE PROTECTIONS WHERE MORTGAGE RESULTED FROM A HOME IMPROVEMENT SCAM

You have special rights if your foreclosure results from a home improvement loan and the contractor deceived you or performed shoddy work, and the contractor was the one who initiated the loan or referred you to the lender. In this scenario, you can argue in court that you do not have to pay the loan because of the contractor's performance.

The loan agreement may even say that you can raise the seller's conduct as a defense on the loan. Because you do not owe on the loan, they cannot foreclose. On the other hand, small errors or minor problems with the work probably will not be enough to be a foreclosure defense.

You will have to raise this issue either in the judicial foreclosure action or in your own court action where the lender seeks to foreclose without a judge's order. You may fare best where you get the help of an attorney. Ask the attorney to refer to NCLC's *Federal Deception Law* Chapter 4, *updated at* www.nclc.org/library.

FORECLOSURES OF MANUFACTURED (MOBILE) HOMES

The law often is unclear as to whether a manufactured home is considered real estate. If the manufactured home is treated as real estate, the foreclosure rules are similar to any other home. If the manufactured home is treated as personal property, the foreclosure rules then are similar to car repossessions discussed in Chapter 14, above. The answer will vary from state to state and often will depend on where the home was when the loan documents were signed. Was it on the dealer's lot or was it attached semi-permanently to your own land or at a manufactured home park? Is there a title to the home or are the ownership documents recorded in the local land records?

You should consider seeking a loan modification (as discussed in the prior chapter) if you are behind on payments, whether your manufactured home is classified as real estate or as personal property. Similarly, no matter how your state law treats manufactured homes, filing bankruptcy can stop its seizure and provide options for curing the default. In addition, manufactured home loan documents often state that you have the right to "cure" your delinquent payments. You can stop the seizure if within 30 days of the notice date you pay past-due amounts, late charges, and related fees.

If your manufactured home is treated as personal property, a lender may send a representative to repossess your manufactured home; more likely, however, your lender will take you to court and try to have the court order a sheriff to seize your manufactured home. Like other court actions, you should get legal help as soon as possible to defend against the lender's claims.

Manufactured Home Evictions from Parks. If you rent park space for your manufactured home, failure to make your lot rent payments can result in your eviction. Typically, the park owner must first file a legal action to evict you. In some states, this legal action will be similar to other landlord and tenant actions, as discussed in Chapter 20. Other states have special legislation dealing with manufactured home park evictions, and these may even allow a park owner to seize your home.

You will need to check with a specialist who is knowledgeable about these issues in your state, such as a lawyer, manufactured home park tenants' association, or manufactured home owners' association. You should deal with your lot rent as a priority debt just as high as your manufactured home loan payment.

FORECLOSURE FOR UNPAID CONDOMINIUM FEES

If you do not pay your condominium fees, in many states the condo association has a priority lien on your home, meaning that it can foreclose on your unit to collect the amount due. Such a lien can also complicate your ability to obtain a loan modification from your mortgage lender, unless you first get caught up on your condo fees. Other times the condo association may just sue you in court for the fees.

Communicate with the condo association's trustees or property manager if you cannot pay your condominium fees. Let them know the reason and see what kind of payment plan you can work out. As the other owners are your neighbors, they may be willing to work out an agreement that helps you through difficult times.

19

Property Taxes and Tax Sales

TOPICS COVERED IN THIS CHAPTER

Reducing Property Tax Debt

Managing Seriously Delinquent Property Tax Debt

Contesting a Tax Sale

Setting Aside a Completed Tax Sale

Redemption Following the Tax Sale

Most mortgage lenders require you to pay into an escrow account, and the lender, through its servicer, then pays your property taxes and insurance from that escrow account. Even if there is not enough in your escrow account, the servicer will typically pay your property taxes. You could eventually face foreclosure on your mortgage loan if you do not pay what you owe into your escrow account. Your servicer will usually do the same even if you do not have an escrow account—in that case, you face foreclosure if you do not repay the servicer for the taxes it has paid for you.

On the other hand, if you own your home free and clear of a mortgage, then you are responsible for paying the property taxes on your home. Failure to do so could eventually lead to a "tax taking" of your home and the eventual loss of your ownership of your home. This chapter examines ways to reduce the size of your property taxes and also how to respond to a potential tax sale of your home.

REDUCING PROPERTY TAX DEBT

Challenging the Assessment. Your property taxes are based on the assessed value of your property, and you can reduce your property tax by successfully challenging your home's assessment. You can challenge that the assessed value is too high. More commonly, homeowners claim that their home is assessed for more than comparably valued homes in the neighborhood. How much other homes are assessed for and what their characteristics are is a matter of public record, and may even be available online. Otherwise, your local assessor's office will have the assessment information.

You do not need to hire an expert to value your home or that of other similar homes in your community, although that can certainly help. You can testify yourself and you can also represent yourself without a lawyer. You initially challenge an assessment not in a court, but before a local tax board, agency, or company hired by the tax assessor that will have looser procedures and requirements than a court. If you lose your challenge, you typically have the right to go to court to appeal the ruling.

Often you only have a short period of time after a new assessment or a tax bill to challenge the assessment. Be sure to meet all deadlines. Some states require you also to make full payment on the tax bill or at least the amount you are not contesting while the assessment is being challenged. Although it may seem that you are not gaining anything if first you have to pay the full amount before challenging that amount, this is not the case. If you win, not only will you receive a refund of the excess amount you paid, but your tax bills will be smaller for years into the future.

Abatement, Exemption, and Deferral Programs. Every state has a program to lower or delay property taxes for at least some homeowners, often called abatement, exemption, or deferral programs. Typically, you will not be offered these programs unless you ask for them. A surprising number of homeowners are eligible for these programs, but never request them. It definitely pays to check if you qualify.

Each state's program is different, but states may provide relief for disability, low income, or personal status (such as veteran, disabled veteran, firefighter, or police officer). Every state has some kind of relief for older homeowners. Often if the spouse qualifying for relief passes away, the other spouse can continue receiving the relief. If you do not qualify for any of the categories of relief available in your state, some states let tax assessors grant hardship exemptions for age, infirmity, or indigence. In some states general information about the programs can be found on tax bills.

To request relief you submit an application with proof of your eligibility. Often this must be done shortly after you receive a tax bill, or you will have to wait until the next bill to apply. One frustrating thing about seeking this relief is that, while you are legally entitled to it, some assessor's offices are not familiar with the programs or discourage people from applying.

But your home may be at stake, so be persistent. If necessary, find out on your own about your state's programs and educate the assessor's office about them.

You may be able to get help with this at your local legal aid office. If need be, go to court to press your rights, after documenting as much as possible what happened at the assessor's office.

The amount of relief available will depend on the state program and the nature of your application. In some states, the tax amount is reduced to a more affordable level; in other states it is reduced by a fixed percentage. Some states freeze the property's assessment for older homeowners so that the assessment does not increase after a certain trigger date. Other programs do not permanently reduce your tax bill, but defer when you have to pay all or part of the tax to sometime in the future, such as when you sell the house. Some states also let older or indigent homeowners perform community service instead of paying taxes.

MANAGING SERIOUSLY DELINQUENT PROPERTY TAX DEBT

Deferred Payment Plans. If you are behind on several property tax payments, you will also owe penalties and interest. Some (but not all) taxing authorities permit you catch up on what you owe in installments to avoid a tax sale of your home. You will have to pay something toward your overdue balance while at the same time keeping up with new tax bills. This may prevent you from being charged more penalties if you stay current on the payment plan.

Compromising on Outstanding Tax Bills. The taxing authority may have the power to reduce your delinquent taxes or to waive penalties and interest. This is another avenue to consider, but be aware that this is not available in some states. You often have to pay the "compromised amount" in one lump sum.

Contacting Your Mortgage Servicer. If you still have a mortgage loan on your home (even a home equity line of credit), a good approach is to contact your servicer for help. Even though the servicer has not required you to pay into an escrow account, the servicer still has a strong self-interest to avoid a tax sale. The tax sale is likely to bring in far less than the amount owed for taxes and the mortgage, and the taxing authority has priority over your mortgage servicer to receive the proceeds first. If the servicer takes no action to help you, it stands to lose a lot of money. The servicer can help by paying the back-taxes for you and then have you repay that amount over time as part of a repayment plan or through an escrow account it sets up on your mortgage.

A Chapter 13 Bankruptcy. A chapter 13 bankruptcy filing will invoke the "automatic stay" which prevents any tax sale process from continuing. After the automatic stay is in place, you can set up a plan whereby you pay the delinquent amount in installments over 36 or even as many as 60 months. There are other advantages and costs of a chapter 13 bankruptcy filing, as discussed in Chapters 24 and 25, below.

Special Rights of Military Personnel. Active duty military personnel have special protections against tax sales where the home is owned and occupied by the servicemember or the servicemember's dependents. These protections apply even if a co-owner owes the taxes.

Any tax sale must first be approved by a court and the court can "stay" (a "stay" is legalese for "stop") a tax sale for up to 180 days after the servicemember's period of active duty ends. Interest on unpaid taxes is limited to 6%, no penalties can be assessed, and, if there is a tax sale, the servicemember can redeem the sale up to 180 days after leaving active duty. (Redeeming the sale is discussed below.)

CONTESTING A TAX SALE

Once your property tax bill is seriously delinquent, the taxing authority will begin a process to sell your home to repay the tax debt. Your best chance to prevent or delay the sale is to act quickly. Your rights also are very different depending on whether or not your state requires an order from a judge before the tax sale takes place. Whether it does or not, a bankruptcy filing can stop the process. Other than that, you do not have strong options to prevent the tax sale. Nevertheless, the last section in this chapter will explain your rights to keep the home even after a tax sale through redemption.

If Your State Requires a Court Order to Sell the Home. If the taxing authority has to go to court to proceed with a tax sale of your home, you should participate in the court case and raise all available defenses. Were all notice requirements followed? Were all the property owners named in the lawsuit? You will probably need a lawyer to identify possible defenses.

If Your State Allows a Tax Sale Without a Court Order. In most states the taxing authority can proceed with a tax sale just by notifying you and the sale does not involve a judge. In that case, you will have to file your own lawsuit to stop the tax sale. Unfortunately, there are few grounds in such a lawsuit to stop the sale. Generally it is too late to challenge the assessed value of the property if you did not raise that in a timely way with the tax agency after receiving the tax bill. You will certainly need the help of a lawyer if you are going to try this avenue, but even with a lawyer, it is a long shot.

SETTING ASIDE A COMPLETED TAX SALE

Once a tax sale has been completed, typically either you manage to redeem the home, as described in the next section, or you lose the home. A third possibility is to find grounds to go to court to set aside the completed tax sale. The grounds to do this are very limited and to even try, you will need a lawyer to investigate why the sale was illegal. Was notice improper? Was the tax sale conducted improperly? Were the taxes no longer due? Was there fraud? Did the purchaser have the authority to purchase? Did the taxing authority mislead the homeowner? Typically low sale price is not grounds to set the tax sale aside.

REDEMPTION FOLLOWING THE TAX SALE

In most states, even after the tax sale has been completed, you still have a chance to save your home through a process called "redemption." You have a specified period of time to do this, and this deadline is strictly enforced, so it is critical that you determine and act within the deadline for your state.

Often you have as long as a year to redeem. But time periods vary, and the redemption will be much simpler and often for less money if you act quickly after the tax sale.

To redeem, you have to pay the entire unpaid taxes, penalties, interest, and the costs and expenses incurred by the purchaser at the tax sale. Typically someone facing a tax sale does not have the cash to make this large lump sum payment. On the other hand, many homeowners facing a tax sale do not have a mortgage on their home—usually if there is a mortgage, the servicer would have paid the property taxes to avoid the sale, and then there would not be a problem of unpaid property taxes.

Having a home free of a mortgage may make it possible to borrow the redemption amount with a new mortgage or with a reverse mortgage. But avoid any lender who seeks you out. Scammers search lists of tax sale properties and contact desperate homeowners with rip-off deals that will just make matters worse for you. If your home equity is a lot more than the redemption amount, you should be able to obtain a legitimate mortgage loan and avoid predatory lenders. Shop around for the best deal. See also the discussion at Chapter 5.

Another option is to ask the purchaser at the tax sale if you can pay the redemption amount in installments. But be careful of the terms. Some speculators purchase at tax sales to take advantage of the homeowner's desire to redeem. They offer homeowners fraudulent sale-leaseback schemes or high rate loans.

You can also file a chapter 13 bankruptcy and pay the redemption amount in installments on terms you propose and that are approved by the court. Contact a bankruptcy attorney to see whether you have three or even five years to spread out the redemption amount, or whether the amount must be fully paid before the redemption period expires. Also ask the bankruptcy attorney if there are other advantages to redeeming through a chapter 13 bankruptcy.

20

Evictions and Getting Out of a Lease

TOPICS COVERED IN THIS CHAPTER

Getting Out of a Lease

Responding to a Landlord's Eviction Attempts

This chapter provides advice on the best way to deal with two different problems: (1) you want to move to less expensive housing, but the landlord wants you to pay for breaking the lease; or (2) you want to stay in the residence, but your landlord is seeking to evict you.

GETTING OUT OF A LEASE

If you can no longer afford your lease, a good option is to move to housing you can afford. This is better than being evicted and being forced under severe time pressure to find another residence. If you move before your lease is up, you may be liable for part or all of the remaining months of rent on the lease, but being able to switch housing on your own schedule may be worth it.

If you instead wait to be evicted, the speed of the eviction process may force you to make unwanted choices, to pay extra expenses, and to accept a less than satisfactory alternative living arrangement. Being evicted may make it harder for you to rent elsewhere in the future, and may impair your credit rating.

The section describes how you can tell how much you will owe if you break your lease and steps you can take to reduce any such charges.

Read the Lease. The essential first step to determining your liability if you break your lease is to read your lease:

- If the lease says either party can terminate the lease after a specified notice, you can give that notice, wait the specified number of days, and then leave.

- Determine if you are now in a month-to-month or week-to-week lease. The lease might have always been that or at some point (such as after the first year) the lease become month-to-month or week-to-week. If your lease is now month-to-month or week-to-week, the lease and your state's law will let you end the lease after providing a short notice to the landlord.
- If a lease is for a longer term (such as a one-year lease) and you leave during the middle of the term, you will have liability. As long as the landlord makes a good faith effort to find a new tenant, you will typically remain obligated to pay rent for the remaining time or until the landlord finds a new tenant during the remaining time on your lease. However, many leases instead contain a "liquidated damages" provision to govern early lease termination, in which you pay a specified amount (such as two months' rent or a percentage of the remaining rent). These liquidated damages provisions are enforceable so long as they are reasonable.
- You may wish to find someone else to take over the lease from you (often called "assuming the lease") so that you will no longer be responsible for the remaining months. Your lease may contain rules or procedures for lease assumption. Typically the landlord will screen and must approve the new tenant. It is important to familiarize yourself with these rules and procedures before negotiating a lease assumption with a prospective new tenant.
- Another option is "subletting" your residence. You keep your lease, but you rent out the space to another tenant or tenants. You remain the tenant as far as your landlord is concerned, and you in effect become the landlord to the new tenants. Subletting lets you recover some or all of the rent you need to pay your landlord for the time you are not occupying the unit. But subletting also carries risks. You remain liable for property damage a subtenant may cause, you may need to ensure that repairs are made and take enforcement action if a subtenant violates the lease, and you still remain liable to the landlord even if a subtenant fails to pay rent. Many leases prohibit subletting and such prohibitions are generally enforceable. Be sure to review your lease first if you are considering a sublet.
- If you want to wait until the lease is up, make sure to understand what, if any, notice is required to ensure the lease terminates. Some leases contain automatic renewal clauses or provisions that convert the lease into a month-to-month tenancy unless timely written notice is given.

Legal Limits on Your Liability. Although your maximum liability is usually the remaining months' rent on the lease, there are a number of reasons why what you legally will owe will be different:

- The law in some states limits your maximum liability when you break the lease.
- The lease itself may indicate the maximum amount you are liable.
- You will not owe rent to the extent the landlord finds a new tenant to pay the rent. Thus it is to your advantage to give the landlord as much advance notice as possible so it can find a new tenant. Also make sure the landlord is marketing the unit in good faith, and check a few times to see if there are tenants already moved in.
- In addition to liability based on the remaining months in the lease, you will also be liable for damage to the apartment, which may eat up much if not more than your security deposit. To reduce this cost, clean the premises, leave it in good condition, and even take photos or a video showing if it is in good condition or the limited nature of any damage. Having the apartment "move-in ready" will also speed up when a new tenant can move in, offsetting the rent you owe.
- If you signed a lease first and then become active duty military, you will only owe one more month's rent after you break your lease if you are given orders for a permanent change of station or to deploy for ninety days or more. Notify the landlord and enclose a copy of your military orders.

You may have also have additional rights to abandon your rental if the residence does not meet local housing, health, fire, and building ordinances, heat or hot water is unavailable, appliances are not safe or in working order, or the unit contains insect or rodent infestation. Although you may be able to move without paying future rent, it is usually best to find attorney representation to press this right. There are significant differences between states as to your rights and how you go about abandoning a rental because of the unit's condition.

Reducing Your Liability by Talking to the Landlord. It is always worth the effort to talk to your landlord about your options. How far you get will depend on the landlord, the landlord's view of future rental market conditions, and how many rental units are vacant in the area at the moment. If the landlord is concerned that it will be difficult to find a new tenant for your unit, you may be able to negotiate a reduction or delayed payment of rent, allowing you to stay in the apartment for the remainder of the lease.

On the other hand, if the landlord thinks it can easily find a new tenant for your unit who will pay a higher rent, the landlord might let you break the lease without owing for the remaining months on the lease. You can even try to get the landlord to agree not to charge you for back-rent if you move out by a certain date. Landlords will often do this to get you out of the apartment more quickly and avoid expensive court costs. The landlord also may let you move out early with no liability for the remaining months if you have arranged for responsible tenants to assume the lease. Be sure to get in writing any deal you make with the landlord!

Not all landlords will sue you if you leave without paying all of what you owe for the remainder of the lease. Nevertheless, particularly if the landlord is a larger property management firm, your non-payment may be reported to a "tenant screening agency" that keeps track of tenants' payments. Then you may find it difficult to find alternative housing in your own name if potential new landlords check with a tenant screening agency and discover the delinquency.

If you are taken to court for breaking the lease, you may have to pay what you owe plus attorney fees, if such fees are allowed by the lease agreement and state law. It is in your best interest to let the landlord know that if you are sued that you don't have non-exempt assets to pay the court judgment (in other words, you are collection-proof) and the lawsuit may be a futile exercise. Filing bankruptcy may also eliminate what you owe the landlord.

RESPONDING TO A LANDLORD'S EVICTION ATTEMPTS

Although some defenses to eviction are available, landlords can nearly always remove you eventually for non-payment of rent. Often your best option when faced with an eviction is to buy yourself enough time to find alternate housing that is both affordable and adequate, with minimal disruption to your life.

Be wary of attorneys or other professionals who claim that they can keep you in an apartment indefinitely. These services are often rip-offs. Some will take your money and never file any papers on your behalf. Others will file inadequate defenses or improper bankruptcy petitions.

If You Are Sued for Eviction, You Have the Right to a Fair Trial. While the legal steps for an eviction vary from state to state, you have the right to a court hearing before you are evicted. Lockouts, utility shut-offs, dumping your possessions on the street, and other eviction-related harassment are illegal in all states, even when you are behind on your rent. When landlords take these actions, seek legal assistance because you have rights to get back into the apartment and be compensated for your damages. Your legal case will be stronger if you let the landlord know in writing that just because you are locked out or the utility is shut off, you still want to stay in the apartment.

Most court eviction actions take place very quickly, perhaps in as little as two weeks. In some states, the process can take considerably longer, particularly if there is a reason that you should not be evicted. Appeals are also possible if you lose.

If you lose an eviction case, the court will usually order that you move out immediately. If you do not move out, court officials or the sheriff will come to put you and all your belongings out. This may happen only days after the court ruling (even on holidays and weekends), but can take weeks, depending on the state.

The Notice to Quit. In most states, the first step in an eviction is a notice from the landlord telling you that you must pay your rent or move within a short time, often called a "notice to quit" or a "notice to vacate." This notice is not a court order to vacate, but instead is your landlord telling you to leave. Before you must leave, you have certain legal rights. Until a court orders you to leave, it is also illegal for a landlord to change your locks, put your things out on the street, or to call the police to force you to move out. Instead, landlords must go to court after the time allowed in the notice has expired. (In a few states, this notice is not required and the landlord may go directly to court.)

Generally, the notice will give you a specified number of days in which to vacate the premises. In many states, the notice must also give you the right to stay in the apartment by paying all owed back-rent within a specified number of days. In other states, there is not that right, and the landlord can ask the court to evict you no matter how much you offer to pay.

Sometimes the landlord will also claim other violations of the lease, such as excessive noise, damage to the premises, or keeping a pet forbidden by the lease. These violations can usually be cured by taking care of the underlying problem within the allotted time. Certain types of lease violations—usually serious violations like engaging criminal activity on the premises—cannot be cured and the tenant becomes legally obligated to vacate within the (usually very short) notice period.

Negotiating with the Landlord. After receiving a notice to move out, talk to the landlord. If you are having trouble paying your monthly rent in a lump sum, some landlords agree to accept weekly or biweekly installments. Landlords sometimes also agree to lower the rent, at least temporarily. You might get an agreement to lower the rent for a few months with your promise to move out in a few months. A court case is expensive for the landlord, and it will often give you extra time to move out if you agree to do so. You may be in the best position to evaluate how amendable the landlord will be to a delay or modified rent payments.

Rent Assistance. Various sources of temporary rent assistance can also buy you some time. Emergency rental assistance may be available through the local public assistance office or community action agency. Church groups and private charitable organizations are other potential sources of financial assistance to pay back-rent or give you a loan for your moving expenses and money for a new security deposit.

Tenants who do not already receive a government housing subsidy can apply for various kinds of government housing assistance, including special rental assistance, state or nonprofit housing programs, Section 8 subsidized housing, and traditional public housing. Waiting lists are quite long. Urgent circumstances, such as homelessness, illness, or small children, sometimes move applicants higher on waiting lists. The first place to contact for more information is your local or regional housing authority and your local legal services office.

Additional Rights of Public Housing Tenants. Public housing tenants have a right to a grievance hearing with the local housing authority before the housing authority can initiate an eviction action. This is an opportunity to ask for more time or to resolve the reason for the eviction.

The First Steps in an Eviction Action. Eviction actions have different legal names in different places, such as "forcible entry" or "unlawful detainer." This book uses the term "eviction action." The landlord will send you a complaint and a summons to appear in court—generally by a process server or a local official. The court hearing often is within as few as five days after you are served the summons. You must act promptly.

If you disagree with a landlord's complaint, or if you have any defenses, immediately contact the court and file an answer or counterclaim, either with the help of an attorney or on your own. Many landlord-tenant cases are held in less formal housing courts or state district courts, so that it is easier for you to file your own answers or counterclaims without using a lawyer or sophisticated legal terminology.

Attending the Eviction Hearing. Typically you should attend the eviction hearing—whether or not you have already moved out. Even if you believe you have no defenses, attend the hearing to make sure you know what is going on, such as that the landlord does not misstate the amount of rent you owe or ask that you be put out by a quicker than normal process. You can also ask the judge to give you additional time before moving if there are such special circumstances as illness of a family member, small children, or older tenants in the family, or unavailability of emergency shelter. The judge will be more likely to grant additional time if you are able to offer at least partial rent or have made efforts to find other housing.

Raising Defenses. At the eviction hearing, be prepared to present your defenses, including relevant documents and witnesses, if any. When you receive the summons, also check with the court clerk whether you have to raise these defenses in a written answer before the hearing. Your defenses will be jeopardized if you do not appear at the hearing.

Legal advice may be necessary to understand your best defenses. In many communities, eviction clinics or legal pamphlets on tenants' rights are offered by the local legal services office, the bar association, or the court clerk.

If your defense involves the procedure by which the landlord instituted the eviction hearing, your defense will be most compelling to a court if the landlord's error caused you confusion, mislead you about your rights, or caused you concrete harm. Did the landlord's notice confuse you about how much rent was needed to stay in the unit or the date by when to pay it? Did the court summons give you less time to prepare than the law requires? Did the landlord fail to let you know that you could stay in the unit if you paid back-rent (if that is the law in your state)?

A defense to eviction is if the landlord's purpose in evicting you is to retaliate against your organizing with other tenants in the building or complaining about conditions to government officials or the landlord. This defense often is not available under state law if you are also behind in your rent payments.

In most states, another defense is that the property is not in livable condition or properly maintained, such as that the apartment has been cited for housing code violations. Ask the housing inspector how to get a proper copy of the code violation report to bring to court with you. For other problems, you might take pictures or videos. For lack of adequate heat, you might have a disinterested witness testify. Many states require that you give prior notice to the landlord of the bad conditions before using the conditions as a defense—put the notice in writing, send it with a return receipt, keep a copy, and bring everything into the court hearing.

Appeals. If the court orders an eviction, you have the right to appeal the case to a higher court. This may buy you more time to move in a more orderly fashion. The threat of an appeal may also allow you to negotiate more time with the landlord. You should only consider an appeal if you honestly believe you have a case. Frivolous appeals can result in fines or other sanctions against you.

An appeal may require that you pay certain filing fees or other court charges. Sometimes these fees can be waived if you can show you cannot afford to pay them. However, regardless of your income, you will probably have to post a bond to cover the rent while your case is on appeal. Usually this can be accomplished by paying future rent into escrow as it comes due.

Steps to Take After the Court's Eviction Order. Even before the court orders you evicted, start making plans to move. After the order, you should quickly finalize your plan for new housing to avoid being forced out into the street. In some states, but not all, you will get notice of an actual date you will be forced out of your housing. Typically you will only have a very short period of time. Consult the sheriff, a court clerk, or your local legal services office about how long you are likely to have.

If you have not vacated by the time specified in a court eviction order (unless the landlord in writing gives you more time), a sheriff or a similar official may move your belongings onto the sidewalk or, if you are fortunate, place them in storage. You will then have to pay moving and storage costs before you can get the property back.

The Landlord's Suit for Back-Rent. After you move or are evicted (or even as part of the eviction action), landlords will sometimes sue for back-rent or property damage and the landlord's attorney fees. This should be treated like any other lawsuit to collect a debt, as discussed earlier in Chapter 4. In the lawsuit, you should raise, if applicable, substandard housing conditions, miscalculation of the amount owed, illegal attempts by landlords to seize your property, a landlord's attempt to lock you out or a shut-off of utility service, or any improper debt harassment.

Special Eviction Defenses for Military Families. If you or your spouse is on active duty with the military, the court must postpone an eviction case upon your request if your ability to pay the agreed rent is materially affected by your being on active duty. The court can also revise the lease to allow you to take in a paying subtenant, revise the due dates for the rent, or make other orders that will preserve your tenancy.

Using the Bankruptcy Process to Stop Evictions. Your rights are limited if you wait to file bankruptcy after a court has ordered your eviction. If instead you file a chapter 13 bankruptcy *before* the court's eviction order, you may be able to stay in the residence by paying the rent arrearage under a payment plan that could extend for several months or even years. But you will have to make payments both for current and the back-due rent.

Even then, this right is limited. You must have a "long-term lease." "Long-term leases" are include leases for federally assisted housing programs, manufactured home parks lots, leases for some rent controlled apartments, or where a state law prohibits landlords from refusing to renew residential leases unless there is a serious ground for termination. But filing a bankruptcy petition does not in itself give you a long-term lease. Even with a long-term lease, you must also have a right under your state's laws at the time you file the bankruptcy to stay in the residence if you make all back-due payments—even though the chapter 13 bankruptcy gives you extra time to make those back payments.

If instead you file a chapter 7 bankruptcy before a court has ordered an eviction, the bankruptcy will delay your eviction, usually for three to five months while the bankruptcy case is pending. This is usually shortened if the landlord goes to the bother of asking the bankruptcy judge to do so. After the delay, the landlord can proceed with the eviction, but you will not owe back-rent.

If you are in public housing or a similar rental where a government agency is the landlord, the law gets more complicated. A chapter 7 bankruptcy filing should keep you in your unit without paying back-rent as long as you continue to make new rent payments as they become due. But back-rent will still be due if fraudulently incurred, such as where you intentionally misrepresented your income to the landlord.

21

Civil Court Judgment Debt

TOPICS COVERED IN THIS CHAPTER

CIVIL COURT JUDGMENT DEBT—WHAT IT IS AND WHAT IT MEANS

Civil court judgment debt is debt that a court has ruled that you owe. The creditor has sued you and the judge has ruled in the creditor's favor. If you do not respond to the lawsuit, the creditor wins by default, which is the same as the judge ruling for the creditor. Once the judge has ruled that you owe a certain amount, this amount is the judgment debt.

Even if a debt was originally a low priority debt, it becomes high priority once a judge rules that you owe a certain amount. Once a debt becomes judgment debt, it can quickly lead to loss of wages, benefits, bank accounts, personal property, and even your home. In extreme cases, it can even result in your incarceration. You have rights to limit these consequences, but to do so, you must understand these rights and raise them aggressively when a creditor tries to take these steps.

Although you should have received notice of a lawsuit against you and notice of any ruling from the court that you owe a debt, surprisingly often consumers never know that a judgment was entered against them. The first they learn about the court ruling is when their wages are garnished, their bank accounts frozen, or their property seized. Always pay close attention to any legal documents sent to you so that you can head off the worst. Chapter 4 has tips to defend a lawsuit against you.

On the other hand, a creditor cannot seize your wages, bank account, or property unless and until it brings a law suit and a court enters a judgment against you. There are two exceptions to this.

1. Secured creditors, such as your auto or mortgage lender, can seize their collateral if you get behind on your payments to them. *See* Chapters 14 and 18.
2. The government can garnish your wages and seize tax refunds to repay student loans or other debt owed to the government. *See* Chapter 13.

But for credit card, medical, and other unsecured debt owed to private creditors, your wages, bank account and property are not at risk until a court issues a judgment against you.

Even if a court does enter judgment against you, there are still legal limits on how much or if any of your wages, government benefits, and money in your bank account can be seized. There are also limits on whether property can be sold to pay off your debts. For many people, these limits mean that there is nothing that a creditor or court can do to make you pay a court judgment. This is called being "judgment-proof" or "collection-proof."

To be collection-proof, your income must be low enough that it is fully protected from garnishment, that all of the money in your bank account (if you have one) consists of government benefits or is otherwise protected from seizure, and that your personal property and home are all exempt from seizure. In that case, you do not have to worry about the judgment debt until your financial situation substantially improves. When your financial situation does improve, however, the creditor may be able to collect on its debt at that point.

If you are not collection-proof, then you must pay careful attention to the implications of a court judgment against you. This outlines how to protect your wages and property from seizure to pay your court judgment debt and other steps you should take when your wages and property are at risk.

GARNISHMENT OF YOUR WAGES

When there is a court judgment against you, the creditor has the right to "garnish" your wages. This means that the creditor can get a court order requiring your employer to deduct a portion of your wages from your paycheck and send it to the court to be applied to the judgment debt. With the exception of a student loan debt or a debt owed the government, garnishment can take place only *after* the creditor obtains a court judgment against you.

After obtaining a court judgment, the creditor must file a request for garnishment with the court clerk, sheriff, or another local official depending on state practice. A notice is then issued to the "garnishee" (your employer), directing it to turn over a portion of your paycheck at a specified time. You must be given notice of the garnishment and you can request a hearing to prove that state or federal law protects your money from garnishment. In some states, you have the right to ask the court to reduce the amount of the garnishment because of hardship or because you have recently received public assistance.

A portion of your wages is protected from seizure. Federal law protects most of your wages from garnishment, and, if your wages are very low, your paycheck is entirely protected. "Wages" that are protected include commissions, vacation pay, sick pay, disability benefit payments, and pension and retirement payments. The first $217.50 from weekly take-home pay, after taxes and Social Security are deducted, cannot be garnished at all. This amount will go up if the current federal minimum wage of $7.25 per hour goes up.

If your take-home pay is between $217.50 and $290 a week, then only the amount over $217.50 can be garnished. If your take-home pay is more than $290 a week, then 25% of your wages can be garnished. For example, if your weekly take-home pay is $250, then $32.50 a week ($250 minus $217.50) can be garnished. If your take-home pay is $600 a week, $150 a week (25% of your pay) can be garnished. A higher amount can be garnished if the debt is for child support or alimony. If your wages are garnished, your employer will be given instructions about how to make these calculations. You do not have to do anything to trigger the protected amounts, but you may want to double-check your employer's calculations.

Importantly, this is the *federal* limit on garnishment. *State* law may limit garnishment even more or even prohibit wage garnishment. However, neither the federal nor state limits on wage garnishment may apply once your paycheck has been deposited into your bank account.

Federal law also protects you from being fired because you are being garnished for a debt. This protection does not apply, however, if your wages are being garnished for more than one debt.

If you are an independent contractor. Some workers are classified by their employers as independent contractors. (Your employer is probably treating you as an independent contractor if it is not deducting your Social Security contribution from your pay check.) Most courts rule that federal limits on wage garnishment do *not* apply to payments you receive as an independent contractor. In theory, a creditor could get an order seizing all of the payments to you as an independent contractor to repay a judgment debt. However, this will be complicated for the creditor and many creditors won't even try to do so. In addition, some states protect independent contractor payments the same as wages.

GOVERNMENT BENEFITS COMPLETELY PROTECTED FROM GARNISHMENT

Many types of federal and state benefits are *completely* protected from garnishment. Examples are Social Security, Supplemental Security Income (SSI), and veteran's benefits (except to pay certain child support obligations). These benefits are protected no matter how much you receive. States also usually exempt TANF (Temporary Assistance for Needy Families) and unemployment compensation benefits from garnishment as well. But once you put these benefits into your bank account, different rules apply.

FREEZES AND SEIZURES OF YOUR BANK ACCOUNT

A creditor can get a court order seizing money from any of your bank accounts to repay a judgment debt. Certain federal benefits, such as Social Security, SSI, and VA benefits, that are deposited in your bank account are protected (with exceptions for child support and debts owed to the federal government).

Federal law requires your bank to protect certain benefits that are direct-deposited into your account within the last two months. The bank is prohibited from turning over any Social Security, SSI, or VA benefits deposited within the last two months. The bank must send you a notice telling you what it is doing, but you do not have to take any steps to protect these benefits.

Social Security, SSI, or VA benefits deposited into the account *more than* two months beforehand are also protected—but the protection is *not* automatic. You will usually have to fill out papers and possibly go to court if you need to protect more than the last two months of benefits.

An easy way to protect all your Social Security, SSI, or VA benefits is to have them loaded onto a Direct Express prepaid card, instead of sent to a bank account. Those funds will then be automatically protected, no matter when they were received. You can sign up for the Direct Express card by calling 1-800-333-1795 or by visiting www.USDirectExpress.com.

As discussed below, other protections for your bank accounts require you to fill out papers and possibly go to court. For example, states usually protect workers' compensation, unemployment compensation, and state employee retirement benefits from seizure, and some even allow you to protect wages deposited into your bank account. Some states have laws that protect a set amount in a bank account, such as $200 or $1,000, regardless of the source of the funds.

When a creditor obtains an order to seize your bank account, the bank typically will freeze the funds in your account, giving you a short period of time to claim that the funds are protected from seizure. The burden is on you to show that the funds are protected.

Usually you will find out that your funds have been frozen when you try to withdraw money, write a check, or use your debit card. Social Security, SSI, or veterans benefits directly deposited into your account during the last two months *cannot* be frozen. But other benefits can be frozen, and you must act quickly to show that at least some of the frozen funds are protected by law and should be unfrozen.

If some of your money on deposit is protected from seizure but some isn't, it may be helpful to set up two accounts, one of which receives *just* protected funds. That way, it's easier to prove that all the money in that account is protected. Spend the money in the unprotected account first.

PROTECTING YOUR CAR AND PERSONAL POSSESSIONS FROM SEIZURE

In theory, after a creditor gets a court judgment, it can ask a sheriff to seize your car, household goods, or other personal property and then creditor would sell the property to repay the debt, often called "judgment execution." In practice, most states limit this kind of seizure so much that a creditor has no financial incentive to have this property seized and sold. You have more to fear from wage garnishment or seizure of your bank account than from loss of personal property.

In many states, exemption laws protect your car and other personal property from seizure to pay a court judgment. (Exemption laws do not apply to secured creditors. For example, an auto lender can repossess your car if you do not keep up on your car payments. *See* Chapter 14.)

Exemptions laws vary considerably by state. Some laws specify that a specific dollar amount of all your personal property is exempt from seizure, such as $8,000. You can choose which items of your personal property you want to keep, as long as what you keep has a value of $8,000 or less. Others specifically exempt an item of personal property, such as a car, if its value is under a certain amount.

The value of your car or personal property typically is not determined based on what the property is worth, but how much "equity" you have in the property. Your equity is how much the property is worth now minus any amount you still owe on a loan that takes that property as collateral. For example, if your car is worth $10,000, but you owe $7,000 on your car loan, your equity in the car is only $3,000. A $3,000 property exemption would fully protect your $10,000 car from seizure to repay a judgment debt. Remember, however, that if you do not keep up on your payments for the $7,000 car loan, the auto lender can still repossess the car.

States may list certain types of personal property that are totally exempt from seizure, no matter how much money they are worth, such as tools and supplies required for your occupation, clothing, a bible, and certain household goods.

Some creditors or their attorneys or collection agents may try to force you to turn over property that by law is exempt from seizure, pointing to small print in the contract that says you agreed to waive rights under state exemption laws. Do not give in—these contract provisions are illegal and unenforceable.

If the creditor asks a sheriff to seize personal property that is exempt, file a notice of exempt property or take similar steps specified by your state law. In many states, you will need to file papers with the sheriff or a public official by a certain deadline in order to get the benefit of an exemption. The sheriff also cannot seize property in your possession which does not belong to you. To stop its seizure, the property's rightful owner may have to file a declaration of ownership with the appropriate office.

If the sheriff is able to properly seize your property, it will then be sold at public auction, and the part of the proceeds that are not exempt will go to the creditor to help pay off the judgment. These auctions are usually poorly attended and bring low bids. For this reason, creditors rarely seize used household goods, which will have minimal resale value. If property is sold at auction, you or your friends can attend the auction and re-purchase the possessions at a bargain price. After a sale, if the sale proceeds are not enough to pay the judgment in full, the creditor may keep trying to collect the remainder.

Court judgments remain on the books for many years. Even if a creditor does not try to seize and sell your property after obtaining a judgment, it still may try to do so years later.

Because state exemption laws are complex, you may want to get professional help to understand which items of your personal property are subject to seizure. Look also for a guide to exemption laws for your state, which may be available from the local bar association, a legal services office, or a nonprofit consumer credit counseling agency. Make sure the guide is up-to-date.

PROTECTING YOUR HOME FROM SEIZURE

Your home is at risk of foreclosure if you do not keep up on mortgage payments. Your home is also at risk of being sold if you owe a judgment debt, but that risk is much smaller. When a creditor obtains a court judgment on a debt, even just credit card or medical debt, the creditor can then put a lien on your home for the amount of the debt. With a lien in place, the creditor can then force a sale of your home or the creditor can simply hold onto its lien and wait for you to sell the home before trying to collect on the lien.

In some states, if husband and wife own a home jointly, the home cannot be seized to pay the debts that only one spouse owes. On the other hand, if both spouses are obligated on the debt, the judgment creditor can force a sale.

Most states have a homestead exemption that protects your home from being sold to pay a judgment debt as long as your equity in the home is less than a certain amount. While some states protect $100,000 or more, many states protect less. And few states completely prohibit a creditor from forcing the sale of your home to pay a judgment debt, no matter how much the home is worth.

A homestead exemption can protect your home from seizure based on a judgment debt. However, a homestead exemption does not protect you if you are in default on a first or second mortgage, on a home equity line of credit, or on any other debt if your home is collateral for that debt. In addition, in some states, to benefit from a homestead exemption, you must file a declaration of homestead with your registry of deeds office. In a few states, the declaration must be filed before the credit is granted. If you live in a state where a declaration is required, you should always file it as early as possible. In other states, the protection is automatic.

The homestead exemption is a powerful protection. The exemption's dollar amount applies not to your home's value, but instead to the equity in your home—home equity is your home's present value minus the amount you owe on your first and second mortgages as well as any home equity lines of credit or other loans if your home is collateral for the loan.

Example:

Mr. J lives in a state with a homestead exemption of $75,000.

His home is worth $200,000.

He has $100,000 in principal still due on his first mortgage.

And Mr. J has $25,000 owed on a home equity loan.

The total secured debt on his property = $125,000.

In this case Mr. J's equity in his home is $200,000 - $125,000 = $75,000.

Since the homestead exemption is $75,000, his home is fully protected. A creditor cannot force the home to be sold to pay a judgment debt.

If Mr. J's home increases in value to $220,000, and if the total secured debt on his property stays the same, then his equity increases to $220,000 - $125,000 = $95,000. The homestead exemption of $75,000 no longer protects all of Mr. J's equity. The creditor can force a sale.

The first $100,000 from the sale goes to pay off the first mortgage holder. The next $25,000 pays off the home equity loan. Mr. J. keeps $75,000, the amount of the homestead exemption. After these deductions from the sale price, the judgment creditor gets whatever is left up to the amount of the debt. If there are still any sale proceeds left over, those go to Mr. J.

Even though the home is worth $220,000, the creditor under such facts will probably *not* try to sell the home to satisfy its lien. If the forced sale of the home only brings in $210,000 and selling expenses are $10,000, then there will be nothing left for the judgment creditor. The judgment creditor instead may wait until Mr. J sells the property, since the judgment creditor's lien stays on the home for many years. When Mr. J sells his home, anything Mr. J clears over $75,000 (after paying off the first mortgage and home equity line of credit) goes to pay off the judgment creditor's lien, up to the amount of the debt.

One possible way of getting rid of judgment liens is to file for bankruptcy. To the extent the property is exempt when you file for bankruptcy, the lien can be permanently removed. Bankruptcy is discussed in Chapters 24 and 25.

THE DEBTOR'S EXAMINATION AND DEBTOR'S PRISONS

There are no debtor's prisons in the United States, but you can still be imprisoned if you do not show up for a debtor's examination. After obtaining a court judgment, a creditor can ask a judge to order you to appear in court or in the office of the creditor's attorney to answer questions about your income and assets to help the creditor find income or property that the creditor may seize. In some states this procedure is called a debtor's examination, but the procedure goes by other names in other states. Some creditors routinely request a debtor's examination. Others never do.

A debtor's examination is a court-ordered appearance. Failure to show up can result in arrest, citation for contempt, and a jail sentence. A notice to appear for a court examination should *never* be ignored. Always appear or ask the court in writing for a postponement. Courts usually grant a postponement if the creditor agrees to the request or if you have a good reason.

In responding to a notice of a debtor's examination, review your assets *well before the examination.* Determine if all your property is protected by law and if all your income is exempt from garnishment. If so, immediately tell the creditor's attorney listed on the notice. This may be sufficient to get the creditor to drop the request for an examination since it will just be a waste of everyone's time. But make sure to get this in writing—do not rely on an oral promise that the examination will be dropped.

If there is an examination, be careful how you answer questions since your answers are made under oath and often are recorded by a court reporter. Lying under oath is perjury, which is a crime punishable by jail. On the other hand, do not volunteer information until you are asked for it. If the examination reveals that you have assets or income not protected by law, the creditor can obtain court orders allowing it to seize those assets or income.

In some states, judges also have the authority to order debtors to make payments on the judgment debt. If you do not pay, the judge can hold you in contempt of court and put you in jail. But even in these states, you must be given an opportunity to prove that you do not have the financial ability to make the payments.

EXEMPTION PLANNING

If you have property that can be seized to pay a judgment debt, consider "exemption planning" that maximizes the protection of your state's exemption laws by converting property that can be seized (for example, cash) into property that cannot be seized (for example, household goods or your home).

For example, Mrs. Q has $10,000 in equity in her home and $10,000 in a bank account. Her state has a $20,000 homestead exemption and lets her exempt $3,000 in cash. Her home is thus completely exempt from seizure by a judgment creditor, but $7,000 in her bank account is at risk of seizure.

Instead of losing $7,000 to the creditor, Mrs. Q can prepay the mortgage by $7,000. Her equity in the home increases from $10,000 to $17,000, but her home is still protected by the $20,000 homestead exemption. Her remaining $3,000 in cash is fully protected by the state's $3,000 cash exemption.

Courts often—but not always—rule that exemption planning is valid. Exemption planning is different than an improper transfer of property where you try to give away property to a friend or relative or sell it for a less than it is worth to someone who will later return it. Creditors can have these bogus transfers cancelled as "fraudulent transfers" or "fraudulent conveyances."

WORKOUT AGREEMENTS TO PROTECT WAGES AND PROPERTY

If your wages, bank account, personal property, or home is at risk from judgment debt, you can approach the creditor or whomever is collecting the debt about a "workout" agreement, even after a court judgment is entered against you. Offer to pay all or a portion of the amount due, over a period of months or even years. The amount you offer to pay should be directly related to what the collector can seize. Do not offer to pay $3,000 over twelve months when the only items the creditor could seize have a market value of $500.

Always get a workout agreement in writing. The written agreement should excuse you from attending any debtor's examination that has been scheduled and should contain a promise not to use wage garnishment or seizure of your property as long as you continue to make payments. Also ask for an agreement to waive the remainder of the debt if part is paid. Some creditors accept partial payment if they know they can't get payment in full. For the creditor, some payment is better than none.

BANKRUPTCY IS THE MOST POWERFUL WAY TO PROTECT WAGES AND PROPERTY

The most powerful way to prevent loss of wages or property from a judgment debt is to file for bankruptcy. The bankruptcy will immediately stop any seizure and may allow you to keep your property permanently. Bankruptcy rights are examined in Chapters 24 and 25.

22

Debts Related to Criminal Law

TOPICS COVERED IN THIS CHAPTER

An important and increasingly widespread category of consumer debt is fines, fees, surcharges, and other costs assessed by courts, state agencies, or even private parties as a result of a consumer's law violation—everything from a traffic ticket to a fee for using a government-appointed lawyer to the premium on a commercial bail bond. Non-payment of these criminal justice debts can have serious consequences, and you should never ignore them, but instead understand your rights and deal with these debts in a careful and reasoned manner.

This chapter helps you identify your criminal justice debts, explains why such debts require immediate and careful attention, and then provides advice on dealing with these debts. The chapter explains your defenses to incarceration for non-payment, provides advice on how to keep your driver's license when it was suspended for non-payment of criminal justice debt, and describes your ability to obtain a payment plan or otherwise reduce or delay payment. Finally the chapter sets out your rights in responding to a collection action—that a debt is too old, that state law protects your income or assets from seizure, and what a bankruptcy filing can and cannot do to deal with criminal justice debt. More than for most other debts, the advice of an attorney is recommended and the chapter has tips on finding an attorney.

IDENTIFYING THE TYPE OF CRIMINAL JUSTICE DEBT YOU HAVE

When you are being dunned for a debt, it is important to determine if it is criminal justice debt, and if so, the type of debt and to whom the debt is owed. This will often determine how you respond to that debt. If you think it might possibly be criminal justice debt, contact your lawyer in the criminal proceeding to ask them to send information about how much you owe, to whom, for what, and what your options for payment are. If you don't have a lawyer, ask the court clerk or the company or government office that is demanding payment.

Types of Government and Court Debt:

- *Fines:* Monetary fines are imposed by courts as penalties for committing an infraction, misdemeanor, or felony.
- *Fees:* User fees or costs are imposed to help government recover the costs of prosecuting, incarcerating, or supervising criminal defendants, or to otherwise pay the costs of the legal system. Examples include jury fees, expert witness costs, costs of extradition, costs of incarceration, and appointed defense counsel costs. Unlike fines, fees and costs are not intended to be punitive and the amount charged may be based on the cost of providing the service or based on a preset schedule.
- *Surcharges:* Surcharges are a flat fee or percentage added to a fine to fund a particular government function, rather than being tied to the cost involved in prosecuting the defendant.
- *Interest, collection costs, payment plan costs, and penalties:* If you do not immediately pay your fine, fee, or surcharge, the amount may grow with interest, collection costs, late payment penalties, and costs associated with a payment plan.
- *Restitution:* A defendant pays restitution to compensate crime victims for losses suffered as a result of the defendant's actions. Usually it is sent to the victim, but in some states it goes to a government agency.

Debts Owed to Private Companies. Surprisingly, many criminal justice debts are now owed to private companies rather than to the state. These private companies may offer and charge you for bail bonds, prison phone and video-calling services, debit release cards, probation, court-ordered rehabilitation programs, and GPS monitoring. Your rights may be different dealing with debts owed to a private company than to the government.

Who Is Now Seeking to Collect the Debt? Often the government, court, or private party that imposed the debt on you is the person who is now trying to collect on the debt. Other times, private debt collection agencies are even hired to collect debts owed the government.

WHY YOU MUST PAY SPECIAL ATTENTION TO CRIMINAL JUSTICE DEBT

In some states, not paying criminal justice debts can result in your imprisonment. Outstanding criminal justice debt can lead to your arrest on debt-related warrants and your detention in jail while awaiting a hearing to explain the reasons for your failing to pay. Your payment also may be a condition of your sentence or probation, and your probation is extended until the debt is paid. Many "clean slate" programs that expunge criminal records require participants to have fully paid off their fines and fees.

If you have outstanding criminal justice debt, you may be required to appear at regular court review hearings, which can be disruptive of your other obligations. The government can also seize your tax refunds and bank accounts and part of your wages, offset your public benefits, and even seize your property. Government agencies can also hire debt collectors and report your debt to a credit bureau.

Unpaid criminal justice debt also can get larger over time, due to mandatory interest, penalties for late payment or non-payment, or other collection costs that accrue from the date of judgment or missed payment. In some states, interest may even accrue when you are in prison or jail.

For these reasons, pay close attention to criminal justice debt. Both governments and private companies have the unique ability—beyond what is available to most other creditors—to enforce collection of criminal justice debt through the criminal legal system. These are high priority debts, which should be prioritized ahead of credit card, medical, and many other debts.

Carefully read any mail from courts or government agencies. Show up to court appointments, or contact the court as soon as you can if you can't make that date. If going to court interferes with a job or otherwise is a hardship, ask about ways to make reports or payments to the court online or over the phone rather than in person. If you cannot pay criminal justice debts, explain to the court or government agency why you cannot pay. Talk to an attorney about ways to cancel or reduce your debt.

The Risks of Using a Bail Bondsman. If you cannot pay your bail, a bail bondsman may pay your bail, and charge you a premium of around 10% of the bail. You permanently lose this 10% even if you show up in court and even if you win the case. You also agree that you and anyone who guarantees your bail must repay the bondsman if you fail to appear and the bail is forfeited.

If the bail is forfeited, you or your guarantors who put up property as collateral for the loan may lose that property if the amount is not paid immediately. You and your guarantors are also likely to be subject to harsh and deceptive collection attempts, including threats to send arrestees back to jail without a legal basis to do so, forcing bail bond cosigners to turn over property that was used as collateral in cases where the arrestee complied with the terms of the bail, and threatening or apprehending individuals in order to coerce them to make premium payments. Bail bondsmen may seek to collect undisclosed or illegal fees and may engage in deception about the terms of the bail agreement and your legal options. Do not always believe what a bail bondsman tells you.

DEFENDING AGAINST INCARCERATION FOR NON-PAYMENT OF CRIMINAL JUSTICE DEBT

If you face incarceration for non-payment of criminal justice debt, you should seek legal counsel and press your constitutional rights. The government should not imprison you because you cannot afford to pay a debt. The U.S. Supreme Court has ruled that it is unconstitutional to imprison you for debt without a meaningful consideration of your ability to pay or the availability of alternative punishments.

Nevertheless, not all courts in practice consider your ability to pay and some do so only in a cursory or inadequate manner. This is where having a lawyer can help. You can ask the court to appoint a free attorney for you, or contact your local public defender office, legal services office, or bar association for help finding an attorney.

If you do not have an attorney, you should tell the court that you are unable to pay the court debt and should not be punished for that reason. Be prepared to explain why you cannot afford the debt, and to provide evidence of your inability to pay, such as proof of your income, necessary expenses for yourself and your family, receipt of public benefits, outstanding debts, and reasons you have been unable to work or to earn more, such as disability, incarceration, childcare obligations, or unsuccessful efforts to get a new job.

The more information and details you document the better. Documenting your financial circumstances is *not* an assessment of character. In most cases, honestly conveying financial hardship will help you and will not result in more jail time due to your inability to pay.

KEEPING OR REINSTATING YOUR DRIVER'S LICENSE

Forty-three states and the District of Columbia suspend millions of drivers' licenses for non-payment of traffic violations as well as other criminal justice debts—even if you cannot afford to pay the fine. In many states, driving with a suspended license is misdemeanor offense that can lead to a criminal conviction, violation of probation or parole, and additional fines and fees.

Reinstating a suspended driver's license can be an onerous process. Many states keep a suspension in place until you have either made full payment on your all criminal justice debts owed to the state or entered into a payment plan to do so. Some states also charge an additional reinstatement fee.

Contact the Department of Motor Vehicles in your state to find out what criminal justice debts resulted in your license being suspended and how to go about getting the license reinstated. Using this information, contact they appropriate court or state agency to whom the debt is owed. Ask how much you owe and whether you are eligible for a payment plan or payment alternatives like community service. If interest was accruing on the debt while you were incarcerated, you may ask to have the interest charges waived.

If your court debt is related to probation, parole, or a suspended jail sentence, you may want to check with a criminal defense attorney before contacting the court on your own. Although unlikely, it is possible that contacting the court about unpaid court debt could lead the court to take enforcement action against you.

PAYMENT PLANS AND OTHER WAYS TO DELAY OR REDUCE PAYMENT

Especially with the assistance of an attorney, you may be able to reduce or even cancel (often called "remit") your criminal justice debt, either in whole or in part. Alternatively, you may be able to enter into a payment plan—or modify a plan you are currently on—based on your financial situation or other relevant factors. In some states, courts may also be able to stop your payments altogether for a certain period if you are on public benefits or have little income.

Many states allow judges, based on financial hardship, to modify or cancel a criminal justice debt owed to the government. You can ask for this relief in a hearing to show cause for non-payment, in a probation or payment status hearing, or through an affirmative petition to the court to remit the debt.

A payment plan might be a good way to manage payment of a criminal justice debt that you cannot afford to pay off all at once. Only agree to a payment plan you can afford. Be honest about your ability to make future payments. Ask about payment plan options as soon as possible; your ability to get into a payment plan may depend on how long you have been behind on your payments. In some states you must request a payment plan before your debt is sent to a collection agency.

Sometimes lawyers can work things out with a probation officer or other monitoring official to gain you more time to make a payment. Again, this is easier to do if you raise it as soon as possible.

Community Service As an Alternative. If you cannot get criminal justice debts waived, and are unable to pay them, in at least some states you can ask the court to consider community service instead of a fine or fee. Community services can be an excellent option for you if the work will be meaningful, promotes useful job skills or connections, and is reasonably convenient. But it is not for everyone, particularly if you have physical or mental disabilities, substance abuse issues, lack of access to transportation, or inflexible schedules due to work or child care obligations, or other responsibilities. If you have debts from *different* courts, it may not be possible to complete community service for each of them simultaneously.

ASSERTING YOUR RIGHTS AGAINST COLLECTION

Statute of Limitations. In some states, after a certain number of years, you no longer have to pay your unpaid criminal justice debt. How many years this will be depends on your state—the answer is found in laws sometimes called "statutes of limitations" or "statutes of repose" or laws that say that after a certain number of years your criminal justice debt shall be "written off." Federal court criminal justice debt, on the other hand, can be collected up to twenty years after the debt is imposed or you are released from incarceration on the underlying charge, whichever is later.

Protecting Assets and Income Against Garnishment. While governments can seize part of your wages, your bank account, and other assets to pay your criminal justice debt, there are limits to their ability to do so. As explained in the prior chapter, federal law protects most of your wages, payments for Social Security, Supplemental Security Income (SSI), VA, and certain other federal benefits, from seizure to pay criminal justice debt.

Whether a state court or agency can seize your *state* public benefits, your bank account, or even your home, car, or other assets is a more complicated question. The assets that state exemption laws protect vary by state, but may include state public benefit payments, tools of your trade, your home and car up to a certain value, and even a certain amount of cash. Nevertheless, in some states these exemption laws do *not* apply to the collection of criminal justice debt. Your best approach is to find a lawyer to help you understand how much of your income and property can be seized to pay your criminal justice debts and how much is protected from seizure.

Filing for Bankruptcy. Bankruptcy is a powerful tool for dealing with criminal justice debt. Filing bankruptcy can eliminate some of your criminal justice debt entirely and provide an orderly way for paying those criminal justice debts that bankruptcy cannot eliminate.

Bankruptcy can also allow you to take advantage of state programs to expunge or seal your criminal record that may otherwise be unavailable to you due to your outstanding criminal justice debt. A bankruptcy filing can also protect your driver's license or vehicle registration from being suspended if that suspension is based on your non-payment of traffic fines or other court debt that you can discharge in bankruptcy.

The relief you will receive from criminal justice debt by filing bankruptcy will depend on whether you file under chapter 7 or chapter 13 (see the discussion in Chapter 25 for the difference between the two). The purpose of a chapter 7 bankruptcy will be to eliminate or "discharge" certain debts entirely. A chapter 7 bankruptcy can discharge only certain criminal justice debt, but not most other types. It cannot discharge traffic debts, parking debts, and other fines and civil penalties. Also not dischargeable in a chapter 7 bankruptcy are criminal justice debts flowing from a court order for you to pay restitution. Parents can discharge restitution debts based on the actions of a juvenile.

More complicated is whether debt based on "costs" and surcharges are dischargeable in a chapter 7 bankruptcy, such as costs of prosecution, indigent defense fees, costs of probation, and surcharges assessed to a defendant. Also complicated is whether forfeited bail and bond debt owed either to the state or a bail bondsman is dischargeable in a chapter 7 bankruptcy. You should discuss these issues with a bankruptcy attorney.

A chapter 13 bankruptcy will offer more effective options for dealing with criminal justice debt. When you file a chapter 13 bankruptcy, you submit a plan to repay your creditors all or part of what they are owed. When you have successfully completed your chapter 13 plan, you receive a discharge that typically resolves much of your criminal justice debt.

In a chapter 13 bankruptcy, you can spread out payment for all of your criminal justice debt in installments over the life of your chapter 13 plan, typically from three to five years. In addition, with the exception of punitive fines or restitution entered as part of a sentence in a criminal case, you typically do not have to pay 100% of your criminal justice debts over the life of the plan. Instead you may have to pay only 10 cents or even zero cents on the dollar if your income is low enough and your assets fully exempt. For punitive fines and restitution you have to make full payment, but you can do so in installments over the three to five year length of your chapter 13 plan.

Seeking Legal Advice. If you have low or no income, you may be able to obtain free legal representation on criminal justice debt issues, particularly if you are facing incarceration for non-payment. If you were represented by a lawyer in a criminal case in which the fines, fees, or other debts were imposed, you may want to contact that lawyer. Your lawyer may be able to represent you or at least counsel you about your options for dealing with the debt, or refer you to another lawyer who can. If you were not represented by a lawyer when the debt was imposed, you may want to look into whether legal help is available by contacting the court that imposed the debt or the local public defender's office.

Legal services offices, pro bono attorneys affiliated with local bar associations, and other civil attorneys may also play important roles in representing clients in collection-related proceedings—including when incarceration is a potential risk. Attorneys with expertise in debt collection actions and in representing indigent clients may provide a valuable service by defending clients in collection actions or representing them in hearings related to criminal justice non-payment. Additionally, legal services and pro bono attorneys may provide valuable representation in affirmative proceedings to modify a debt obligation or repayment plan.

23

Federal Income Tax Debt

TOPICS COVERED IN THIS CHAPTER

When your debt burden is overwhelming, you may find yourself behind on your taxes. Most people have a variety of tax obligations. The three most common are property taxes and federal and state income taxes. Advice on property taxes is found in Chapter 19. This chapter concentrates on back-due federal income taxes. Some of the information here also applies to state income taxes. Resources for getting help are listed at the end of this chapter.

You must give special consideration to your federal income tax obligations. If you can afford to pay the outstanding tax bill, you should do so in order to avoid accruing further interest and penalties. When you owe taxes to the Internal Revenue Service (IRS), the IRS will not ignore this debt, but instead, the IRS will press collection and seek penalties and interest. Outstanding federal taxes may be collected for ten years from the date assessed—a debt to the IRS can have a long life. The IRS also has far reaching authority to collect taxes—it can place a lien on property and levy (seize) property including bank accounts, wages, Social Security, and even pension payments.

FILE THE RETURN ON TIME EVEN IF YOU DO NOT PAY THE TAXES OWED

One of the worst things you can do if you cannot afford to pay your taxes is to not file your tax return. You must file an income tax return, in general, if you are a U.S. citizen or resident alien, and your taxable income exceeds certain amounts.

For the tax year 2018 (taxes due April 15, 2019), you have to file your return if:

- You are single and your taxable income exceeds $12,000.
- You are the head of a household and your taxable income exceeds $18,000.
- You are joint filers and your taxable income exceeds $24,000.
- You are self-employed and earn over $400.

These dollar amounts go up each year.

April 15th is the deadline for most people to file individual income tax returns and pay any taxes owed. Filing extensions are available, but this does not extend your time to pay.

If you fail to file either an extension or your tax returns by April 15, and you owe taxes, the IRS will prepare a proposed tax return, called a "substitute for return," which shows how much the IRS thinks you owe. You can dispute that determination by responding to the letter or filing a late return.

If you *file* late, the IRS will assess a late-filing penalty. If you owe taxes and are late in filing by sixty days, the penalty for *late-filing* is 5% of the taxes owed for each month or part of a month that your return is late, with a maximum penalty of up to 25% of the taxes owed. If your return is over sixty days late, the minimum penalty is the smaller of $135 or 100% of the tax owed.

Totally separate from any fee for filing late is the late-payment penalty. If you *pay* late, the IRS will assess a *late-payment* penalty. The penalty for late-payment is only a fraction of the larger penalty for not filing a return—it starts at only one half of 1% of the tax owed for each month late, up to a maximum of 25% of the taxes owed. You will also be assessed interest on the unpaid tax and penalty.

Getting an extension to file is also not the solution it might seem to be. Although the IRS will automatically give you a six-month extension if you request it with payment of the taxes you are likely to owe, keep in mind that this is only an extension of time to *file*. It does not give you more time to *pay* the taxes you owe, and you will be charged both interest and probably a late-payment penalty during the time of the extension if you have not paid in full by April 15. As noted above, if you can't pay the taxes due, it is a better idea to file the return, pay as much as you can, if anything, and then consider negotiating a payment option with the IRS (discussed below).

OPTIONS FOR PAYING TAX DEBT

If you cannot afford to pay your taxes, the solution is *not* to put the taxes on your credit card which you also will have trouble repaying. As described below, the IRS will give you a better deal than putting the tax payment on your credit card. Interest rates will be lower, there will not be a processing fee to pay, and you may even get the IRS to reduce your obligation.

When you file a return but cannot afford to pay the taxes due, you will generally have three options in dealing with the IRS:

- Enter into a monthly installment agreement;
- Negotiate for a smaller tax bill by seeking an "offer-in-compromise"; or
- Request a hardship determination, called "currently not collectible" status.

All of these options require IRS approval, although the IRS allows almost every taxpayer that owes less than $50,000 to enter into an installment agreement through a streamlined process available on their website. If IRS does not grant approval for any one of the three options, you then have the right to seek an appeal or ask for a review of your case. These actions often require you to submit IRS forms, that are available at www.irs.gov.

The Installment Agreement. The IRS allows you to pay taxes you owe in monthly installments over a period of up to six years. The IRS imposes a "user fee" of $149 ($43 for low-income taxpayers) to set up an installment agreement, the fee is reduced to $31 if you set up the agreement through the IRS website and you agree to pay using direct debit from your bank account.

Penalties and interest will continue to accrue until the balance is paid in full. The interest rate will be the federal short-term rate (presently a little over 1%) plus 3%, which is a lower rate than most rates for unsecured loans and credit cards. If you have an installment plan, the penalty for late payment is only one-quarter of 1% for each month. The IRS will waive penalties if you qualify under its First Time Penalty Abatement policy, or if you have a valid reason for your late payment or late filing. Use a Form 843 to request penalty abatement.

If you owe less than $50,000 and have already filed your return, you can complete an online application at the IRS website to apply for a monthly payment plan. You can also file IRS Form 9465: Installment Agreement Request, which you can mail in or attach to your return if you haven't filed it yet. You may also call the IRS at the phone number on your bill or notice. Be sure to ask for written confirmation of the installment plan you negotiated. The IRS charges a higher fee for requesting an installment agreement by mail (Form 9465) or by phone.

Generally, if you owe less than $25,000 and your installment agreement will fully pay the debt in six years or less, the IRS will not file lien against you. The IRS cannot execute a levy while the installment plan is in effect. (*See* **Steps the IRS Can Take to Force Payment**, below.)

Offer-in-Compromise. The IRS may accept payment for less than what you actually owe through its "offer-in-compromise" program. Reduced payment is permitted when the IRS determines that, under established financial guidelines, the taxpayer cannot afford to pay the full amount of taxes owed or where an exceptional circumstance exists such that collection of the tax would create an economic hardship or would be unfair and inequitable (for example, the assets that could be used to pay the tax debt are needed to pay for the long-term care of a seriously ill person).

There are special IRS forms you must fill out to request an "offer-in-compromise" (Form 656 and Form 433-A). You will also need to pay an application or "user" fee (presently $186) plus make a first payment of 20% of your offer amount (or the first payment of a proposed payment plan), unless your income is below a certain amount and you complete Form 656-A. Generally, an offer will only be accepted when the amount offered equals or exceeds your net equity in assets, plus your ability to make installment payments from future income.

It takes about six to twelve months for the IRS to review an offer-in-compromise. During that period, you will not be expected to make any payments on your tax debt. However, interest and penalties will continue to add up, so if your offer-in-compromise is rejected, you tax bill will grow during the time the IRS has your offer-in-compromise under review.

Non-Collectible Status. You may be eligible for a temporary hardship determination from the IRS, called "currently not collectible" (CNC) status. The IRS will only grant you this status if you do not have any assets you could use to pay your tax debt and you do not have any income left after "allowable expenses."

Allowable expense are listed on the IRS website (use the search box to find, "Collection Financial Standards") and are used by the IRS to determine allowable monthly living expenses. If your monthly income is less than the allowable living expenses, you will be eligible for the non-collectible status and the IRS will put your account on hold.

CNC status is not permanent, and does not mean the tax debt is forgiven or reduced. This status can change if your financial circumstances improve, if you file another return with a balance due, or if you do not file a tax return when you are required to do so. The IRS will monitor your tax returns and remove the hardship status if your returns suggest a significant financial improvement. Also, interest and penalties will continue to add up during this time.

To apply for CNC status, you should call the IRS at 800-829-7650 and specifically ask to be placed into "currently non-collectible status." If you do not ask for the status, the agent will generally ask you to set up a payment plan. When you ask for non-collectible status, the agent may send a Form 433-F: Collection Information Statement, for you to fill out, but in most cases, the agent will simply ask you questions in order to gather the relevant information to make the "currently not collectible" determination during the phone call.

If the IRS grants CNC status, it may file a lien with the county recorder's office (or similar agency) if you owe more than $10,000 even if you do not own any property. Generally, the lien will not appear on your credit report.

SPOUSAL DEFENSES

In certain limited cases, your responsibility to pay a tax may be cancelled when the tax is owed entirely by your spouse or ex-spouse. This cancellation may be available when your spouse or ex-spouse was solely responsible for failure to pay the taxes, the taxes are entirely attributable to your spouse's separate business, or if you were the victim of domestic abuse. This is true even if you filed a joint return. If you believe you are entitled to the IRS's "innocent spouse relief," you can file a Form 8857, but help from a tax professional is recommended. Resources for getting help are listed at the end of this article.

STEPS THE IRS CAN TAKE TO FORCE PAYMENT

If you do not set up a payment plan, negotiate an offer-of-compromise, or secure "currently not collectible status," the IRS can force payment. Before the IRS actually forces payment, it will generally send you a series of threatening letters, for instance a Notice of Tax Due and Demand for Payment or Final Notice of Intent to Levy.

These notices inform you that the IRS intends to seize or "levy" your property. The IRS can take any or all of your property, such as bank accounts, paychecks, and even homes, with the exception of certain exempt types of income and possessions.

Part of your wages are protected from being seized by the IRS—they are exempt from levy. A single filer can protect $230 per week, while a married couple filing jointly can protect $461.50 a week, meaning all of your salary will be seized except for the protected amount. Also exempt from levy are unemployment benefits, workers' compensation benefits, certain public assistance benefits, income needed to pay court-ordered child support, and certain pension benefits. Other protected property includes certain amounts of clothing, furniture, personal effects, and job-related tools. A state homestead exemption will *not* protect your home from an IRS tax lien or seizure. The IRS will not know about exemptions or defenses unless you or your advocate informs the IRS.

The IRS can also recover past-due taxes by seizing certain federal benefits and other payments, including Social Security payments (but not Supplemental Security Income payments). The IRS can levy 15% of your entire Social Security benefit. Unlike other forms of federal government seizures of benefit payments, the first $750 of your monthly income is not protected. In some cases, the IRS will levy even more than 15% of Social Security benefits.

Generally, the IRS will exempt low-income taxpayers from a levy on Social Security benefits. If your Social Security benefits are being seized, you should call the IRS at 800-829-7650 and specifically ask for them to remove the levy and place you in "currently not collectible" status or ask for a payment plan in a lower amount than the levy. Generally, the IRS will remove a Social Security levy if you are low-income. Resources for getting help are listed in at the end of this article.

When you receive a notice that your property is being levied or a lien is being placed on it, you can request a review of your case called a "Collection Due Process" hearing on Form 12153. You have thirty days from the date of the notice to request a hearing. The hearing request will result in a suspension of collection activities, including any levy, during the appeals process. During the hearing, you can request one of the payment options discussed earlier in this article—an installment agreement, an offer-in-compromise, or non-collectible status. In certain situations, you can dispute that you owe the tax.

Unless most or all of your assets and income are exempt from levy, it makes sense to negotiate for one of the three options for paying your tax debt to avoid seizure of personal property and income. Make sure any agreement is in writing. A good source for information about taxes is the IRS website at www.irs.gov.

EFFECT OF BANKRUPTCY ON YOUR TAX DEBT

Bankruptcy is not as effective a remedy when dealing with taxes as with other debts. In general, only old taxes debts can be discharged in a chapter 7 bankruptcy, for example, where the debt stems from a timely filed return that is more than three years old. Existing tax liens are likely to remain on your property even after a bankruptcy. In a chapter 13 bankruptcy, the full amount of the taxes owed can be paid in installments over a three-year to five-year period, and only the more recent (priority) taxes and not necessarily the entire tax liability and not tax penalties need be paid.

SEEKING HELP

You may be able to get help with your tax problems from a Low-Income Taxpayer Clinic. These are legal clinics based at law schools and legal services offices that help low-income taxpayers who have disputes with the IRS. Clinic locations are listed in IRS Publication 4134: Low Income Taxpayer Clinic List, and can be searched online at www.irs.gov/advocate/low-income-taxpayer-clinics/low-income-taxpayer-clinics-map. Another option may be your local legal services office, which can be located using http://lsc.gov/find-legal-aid.

In some cases, you can get assistance from the IRS Taxpayer Advocate Service, an independent organization within the IRS that helps taxpayers who have not been able to resolve tax problems through normal channels. You should fill out Form 911 or call 1-877-777-4778 to request Taxpayer Advocate Service assistance. IRS forms can be found at www.irs.gov.

24

Deciding Whether and When to File Bankruptcy

TOPICS COVERED IN THIS CHAPTER

Federal law provides the right to file bankruptcy for people with debt problems. Bankruptcy can be the right choice if you have no better way to deal with your debts. While you should consider other options first, do not wait until the last minute to think about bankruptcy. Important rights may be lost by delay.

WHAT BANKRUPTCY CAN AND CANNOT DO

Bankruptcy may make it possible for you to:

- Eliminate your responsibility for many of your debts and get a fresh start. When a debt is discharged at the close of a successful bankruptcy, you have no further legal obligation to pay that debt.
- Stop foreclosure on your house or manufactured home and allow you an opportunity to catch up on missed payments.
- Prevent repossession of your car or other property, or force the creditor to return property even after it has been repossessed.
- Stop wage garnishment, debt collection harassment, and other similar collection activities to give you some breathing room.

- Prevent termination of utility service or restore service if it has already been terminated.
- Lower the monthly payments on some debts, including car loans.
- Allow you an opportunity to challenge the claims of creditors who seek to collect more than they are legally entitled.

Bankruptcy, however, cannot cure every financial problem, nor is it an appropriate step for every individual. In bankruptcy, it is usually *not* possible to:

- Eliminate certain rights of "secured" creditors. A "secured" creditor has taken some form of lien on your property as collateral for a debt. Common examples are car loans and home mortgages. You can force secured creditors to take payments over time in the bankruptcy process, but you generally cannot keep the collateral unless you continue to pay the debt.
- Discharge certain types of special debts, such as child support, alimony, most student loans, court restitution orders, criminal fines, and some taxes.
- Protect all cosigners on their debts. When a relative or friend has cosigned a loan and you discharge the loan in bankruptcy, the cosigner may still have an obligation to repay all or part of the loan.
- Discharge debts that are incurred after bankruptcy has been filed.

UNDERSTANDING THE DIFFERENCE BETWEEN A CHAPTER 7 AND A CHAPTER 13 BANKRUPTCY

Your rights are very different depending on whether you file a chapter 7 or a chapter 13 bankruptcy. In a chapter 7 bankruptcy (called a "liquidation"), you eliminate most of your debts, but may lose your property other than "exempt" property—that is property the law says creditors cannot reach unless they take that property as collateral. For many families most of their property is exempt. In a chapter 13 case (called a "reorganization"), you keep all your property, and pay a portion or all of your debts in installments over a period of three to five years.

HOW A BANKRUPTCY CAN HELP YOU

An Immediate Stop of Foreclosures, Evictions, Repossessions, Utility Shut-Offs, Garnishments, and Other Creditor Actions. Your bankruptcy filing will automatically and immediately, without any further legal proceedings, stop most creditor actions against you and your property, at least temporarily.

Your request for bankruptcy protection creates an "automatic stay," which stops the continuation of or the start of repossessions, garnishments, attachments, utility shut-offs, foreclosures, evictions, and debt collection harassment.

The automatic stay provides you time to sort things out and address your financial problems. A creditor cannot take action against you or your property without bankruptcy court permission. Some creditors seek such permission immediately; others never seek permission.

Permission to continue collection activity is rarely granted to *unsecured* creditors. Secured creditors can get "relief from the stay" in a *chapter 7* case to continue foreclosure or repossession of their collateral. But an automatic stay will almost always continue to be in effect to protect you in a *chapter 13* bankruptcy case as long as you are making payments on the secured debt.

If the creditor takes action against you despite the automatic stay, the creditor may have to pay you damages and attorney fees and the creditor's actions against you can be reversed. For example, a foreclosure sale which is held in violation of the automatic stay can be set aside.

Discharge of Most Debts. When you successfully complete a bankruptcy, there is a "discharge" (that is, a cancellation) of many of your unsecured debts, such as medical bills and credit card obligations, which eliminates all debt collection and other actions concerning those debts. Certain debts may not be discharged, such as most taxes, liens associated with many secured debts, alimony, child support, and debts you incurred after the bankruptcy case was started. After bankruptcy, you will continue to owe those debts. Student loans can be discharged only if you can prove that repayment will be an undue hardship on you and your family.

Bankruptcy cannot prevent creditors from taking your home or car unless you make sufficient payments on your mortgage or car loan. The bankruptcy though prevents these creditors from seeking additional cash from you after they take the collateral. For example, if you do not pay a car loan, the creditor can seize and sell your car, but the bankruptcy prevents the creditor from seeking additional payment from you if the car's sale price does not cover the full amount of the debt.

Protection Against Wage Garnishment, Bank Seizures, and Enforcement of Judgment Liens. After you file bankruptcy, creditors are prohibited from garnishing your wages or other income or your bank account. Bankruptcy even stops government agencies from recovering Social Security or other public benefit overpayments, so long as your receipt of the overpayment was not based on fraud.

Bankruptcy also is an effective tool to deal with some types of court judgments against you. If a court judgment for money does not create a lien against your property, that judgment debt can be discharged in bankruptcy. If the judgment does create a lien on your property, you may ask the bankruptcy court to remove the lien if it affects "exempt property," and then the creditor can never touch that property.

Protection of Your Household Goods from Seizure. Most families' household goods are exempt from seizure—you keep them even in bankruptcy. This is the case even when a creditor has taken household goods as security for a loan, as long as that loan was not used to purchase those goods. If those household goods were taken as security to purchase those goods (such as when you purchase furniture on credit and the store takes the furniture as collateral for the loan), then see the next paragraphs on "secured creditors" where your rights are explained.

Added Flexibility in Dealing with Auto Loans, Mortgages, and Other Secured Creditors. Bankruptcy can help deal with creditors who take your property as collateral for their loans, such as car loans and mortgage loans. You still have to make payments on these loans if you want to keep the collateral. However, bankruptcy does provide added flexibility in dealing with these debts.

A chapter 7 bankruptcy lets you keep your car by paying the creditor the lesser of what you owe on the loan or the car's value. If your car is worth $1,000, and the remaining amount on your car loan is $3,000, you can keep the car by paying the creditor only the $1,000. The $1,000 payment usually must be made in a lump sum before the chapter 7 bankruptcy ends (usually after three to five months). Some creditors instead let you pay that amount in installments over a number of months even after the bankruptcy ends, but that is up to the creditor.

A chapter 13 bankruptcy gives you greater flexibility to keep your property. For example, if you are six months delinquent on a mortgage, filing a chapter 13 bankruptcy stops a threatened foreclosure and allows you to gradually catch up on the back-payments, over as many as three to five years. In some cases a chapter 13 filing also allows you to make lower monthly payments by extending the repayment period or lowering the loan's interest rate. But you have to keep making payments until the loan is paid off.

Utility Terminations. A bankruptcy filing stops a threatened utility termination and restores terminated service, at least for twenty days. To keep utility service beyond twenty days after the bankruptcy filing, you provide a security deposit (usually equal to approximately twice the average monthly bill) and keep current on new utility charges, but you need not pay the past-due charges incurred before the bankruptcy was filed. Often you can take sixty days to pay the deposit and some utilities may not require a deposit.

Driver Licenses. If your driver's license was or will be taken away because you have not paid a court judgment, such as one arising from an automobile accident, bankruptcy normally can discharge the obligation to pay the court judgment, and you then have a right to regain or retain the driver's license.

THE BEST TIME TO FILE FOR BANKRUPTCY

It is often stated that bankruptcy is a "last resort" for financially troubled consumers. This is not really true. In some cases, legal rights can be lost by delaying a bankruptcy. Be especially careful to get early advice about bankruptcy if you are concerned about saving your home or your car or protecting your bank account or wages from seizure.

For example, bankruptcy may not help you after your home is sold at a foreclosure sale or money in your bank account is seized. Bankruptcy can stop an eviction proceeding, but you have fewer rights in bankruptcy after a court has ordered you to be evicted. Act quickly to consider your bankruptcy rights.

While not ideal, all is not lost if you wait to the last minute before a foreclosure, repossession, or garnishment. Bankruptcies in an emergency can be filed with little preparation by filing only a brief petition, a statement of your Social Security number, and a list containing the names and addresses of your creditors. Additional forms must be completed and filed shortly thereafter.

But you must still complete an approved budget and credit counseling briefing before filing your bankruptcy. The counseling usually takes less than an hour, and can be done over the phone or over the internet.

On the other hand, if you are not facing immediate loss of property, but in the future you will incur new debts that you will not be able to pay, a bankruptcy filing should be delayed until you incur those new debts. New debts incurred after the bankruptcy filing are *not* discharged in that bankruptcy case—you will still be obligated to repay those new debts. If you file too soon and incur a lot of debt after the filing, you may be back to where you started from or even worse.

If you file a first bankruptcy too soon, you will find it more difficult to file a second bankruptcy to discharge the new debts incurred after you file the first bankruptcy. After you first file a chapter 7 bankruptcy, you have to wait eight years to file another chapter 7 case. There is more flexibility to file a chapter 13 case after first filing a chapter 7 bankruptcy. Thus it is a good idea to wait to file for bankruptcy until your debts have peaked.

If you decide to wait to file bankruptcy, avoid the temptation to go on expensive vacations or credit card shopping sprees that you do not intend to repay. In a chapter 7 bankruptcy, debts incurred in this way can be declared non-dischargeable. On the other hand, pre-bankruptcy expenses for medical care and other essentials are rarely challenged. Similarly, it may make sense before filing bankruptcy to purchase in installments needed medical or automobile insurance.

THE COST OF FILING BANKRUPTCY

Unfortunately, it is expensive to file bankruptcy. Bankruptcy is a legal proceeding with complicated rules and paperwork. You may want to get professional legal help, especially if you hope to use bankruptcy to prevent foreclosure or repossession. Most bankruptcy attorneys provide a free consultation to help you decide whether bankruptcy is the right choice. If the attorney takes the case, the attorney will expect to be paid, unless he or she works for a nonprofit legal services office or is doing the bankruptcy on a pro bono basis.

You also have to pay the court a bankruptcy filing fee—$310 for chapter 13 or $335 for chapter 7. The fee can be paid in four installments over 120 days (or 180 days with court permission). You can also ask the court to waive the filing fee in a chapter 7 case if your household income is less than 150% of the official poverty guidelines (for 2018, $24,690 for a family of two or $37,650 for a family of four). No waiver is allowed in a chapter 13 case.

In a chapter 13 case, you pay your debts over time, and you usually have to pay the trustee handling your payments a 10% commission on each payment. While this can add up, you will be paying far lower interest on your debts in a chapter 13 plan than if you had not filed bankruptcy. Even more significantly in a chapter 13 plan, you may only have to repay a small percentage of what you owe on most of your unsecured debts.

COMMON MISCONCEPTIONS ABOUT BANKRUPTCY

When You File Bankruptcy Typically You Will Lose Little or None of Your Property. People are wrong who believe that a bankruptcy filing results in the loss of most of their property. Everyone who files bankruptcy gets to keep some of their possessions, and most people get to keep *all of them.*

No matter the type of bankruptcy you file, unless property is collateral for a loan, you get to keep all your property that is protected by "exemption" laws. Exemption laws typically protect clothes, appliances, furniture, jewelry, and often even your car and home.

An exemption law may state that you get to keep property that is worth less than a certain amount. What that property is worth is based not on how much the property cost, but rather on your "equity" in the property: the amount that the property is worth in its present condition minus how much you owe on a loan for that property.

For example, if an exemption law protects a $2,000 motor vehicle, this dollar amount applies to $2,000 of your equity in the car, not to the total value of the car. If your car has a total value of $7,000 today with a $5,000 car loan balance, you have $2,000 in equity in the car. In this scenario, you can fully protect a $7,000 car with the $2,000 exemption. You will still have to repay the $5,000 car loan in the bankruptcy or the auto lender will take the car, but you won't lose the car to pay your other creditors.

What property and the amount of that property that is exempt varies widely from state to state and the application of exemptions in bankruptcy can be complex, particularly if you have moved within the last two years to a different state or bought a home within the last 40 months. You should discuss what property is exempt with a bankruptcy attorney, but the general rule of thumb is that, for most consumers filing bankruptcy, much of their property is exempt.

What property you keep also depends on the type of bankruptcy you choose—a chapter 7 or a chapter 13. In a chapter 7 case, you keep your exempt possessions, but other property may be sold, with the money distributed to pay your creditors. In a chapter 13 case, you keep all your property by paying their nonexempt value over time from future income under a plan approved by the bankruptcy court. If you have very valuable property, it might be sold in a chapter 7 bankruptcy, but you keep it if you pay its value to your creditors over a number of years in a chapter 13 plan.

The Effect of Bankruptcy on Your Credit Report. The effect of a bankruptcy on your credit report is of understandable concern. Most often, you should not worry about bankruptcy making it harder for you to obtain credit. If you are delinquent on a number of debts, this already appears on your credit record. A bankruptcy is unlikely to make your credit rating any worse, but instead may make it *easier* for you to obtain future credit.

New creditors will see that old obligations have been discharged in the bankruptcy and that you have fewer other creditors competing with them for payment. Creditors also recognize that you cannot receive a second chapter 7 bankruptcy discharge for another eight years.

After bankruptcy, your credit file will also list the outstanding balance as zero dollars for each of your debts. The credit file will list the fact that you filed bankruptcy and that certain debts at one time were delinquent, but creditors are most interested in what you owe now on each debt. That your credit report shows that you owe nothing on a debt improves your credit standing.

After your bankruptcy is complete, check your credit report to make sure all the debts you discharged in bankruptcy are listed as now owing zero dollars. File a dispute with the credit bureaus if your discharged debts continue to be listed as having a balance owed.

Bankruptcy also often will enhance the stability of your employment and income. Wage garnishments, continuous collection calls, car repossessions, telephone disconnections, and other consequences of an unaffordable debt burden are eliminated, and this should help you find and hold steady employment. Steady income is key to creditworthiness.

Bankruptcy will make it more difficult for you to obtain a new conventional mortgage to purchase a home. Even then, most lenders will not hold the bankruptcy against you if you re-establish a good credit reputation for two to four years after your bankruptcy.

After bankruptcy, some new lenders may demand collateral as security, ask for a cosigner, or want to know why bankruptcy was filed. Other creditors, such as some local retailers, may not even check your credit report.

Bankruptcies stay on your credit record for ten years from the bankruptcy filing, while your debts are usually only reported for seven years from their delinquency. If delinquencies on your debts are five or six years old, bankruptcy will not help your credit record. The debts will be deleted from your credit report within a year or two, while the bankruptcy will stay on your record for ten years.

If You File Bankruptcy, You Usually Do *Not* Need to Go to Court, unless something out of the ordinary occurs. You will have to attend one meeting with the bankruptcy trustee (not with a judge). Creditors are invited to that meeting but rarely attend. In the rare case that you do receive a notice to go to court, it is important that you go and also check with your attorney if you have one. Before your case is closed, you must also take a course in personal finances, which will last for approximately two hours.

The Effect of Bankruptcy on Your Reputation in the Community. Most people find their reputations do not suffer from filing bankruptcy. Bankruptcies are not generally announced publicly, although they are a matter of public record. It is unlikely that your friends and neighbors will know that you filed bankruptcy unless you tell them.

However, especially in a small town, where debts are owed to local people, reputational issues connected with filing bankruptcy may arise. In such a situation, weigh possible embarrassment and damage to reputation against bankruptcy's potential advantages. If you believe that your reputation in a small town is a concern, you may choose to voluntarily pay selected debts after bankruptcy, but you cannot leave selected creditors out of the bankruptcy process entirely.

Feelings of Moral Obligation. Most people want to pay their debts and make every effort to do so if payment is possible. If bankruptcy is the right solution to your financial problems, you should balance these feelings of obligation with the importance of protecting your family.

Bankruptcy is a legal right. A provision concerning bankruptcy is even contained in the United States Constitution. Big corporations like Kmart, American Airlines, Chrysler, and Macy's, and famous people like Toni Braxton, Tammy Wynette, Larry King, Mickey Rooney, Henry Ford, and Walt Disney have all chosen to file bankruptcy. The book of Deuteronomy states:

> At the end of every seven years thou shalt make a release. And this is the manner of the release: every creditor shall release that which he has lent unto his neighbor and his brother; because the Lord's release hath been proclaimed. (Deut. 15:1–2.)

Most importantly, during hard times, bankruptcy may be the only way to provide your family with food, clothing, and shelter. This book explores alternatives to bankruptcy, and these should be considered carefully. But it may be that bankruptcy is your best or only realistic alternative.

Potential Discrimination After Bankruptcy. The federal bankruptcy law offers you protection against being discriminated against because you have filed for bankruptcy. Government agencies, such as housing authorities and licensing departments, cannot deny you benefits because of a previous bankruptcy, including debts discharged in bankruptcy that were owed to those agencies. Government agencies and private entities involved in student loan programs also cannot discriminate against you based upon a bankruptcy filing.

Employers are not permitted to discriminate against you for filing bankruptcy. However, for some sensitive jobs which involve money or security, your bankruptcy may be considered evidence of financial problems which could be detrimental to your work. Bankruptcy law does not prevent discrimination by others, including private creditors, deciding whether to grant you any new loans.

WHEN BANKRUPTCY MAY BE THE WRONG SOLUTION

There are at least seven situations in which bankruptcy may not be the right option for you:

1. If all your assets and income are exempt, then you are "collection-proof." (See Chapter 21 for more information about what it means to be "collection-proof.") In that case, most creditors can do virtually nothing to harm you even if you don't filing bankruptcy. At which point, there may not be a compelling reason to file for bankruptcy. Waiting until you are no longer collection-proof is generally more prudent than filing right away, unless you are concerned with a home mortgage, car loan, or other secured loan.

2. The debts at issue are secured by your property—such as home mortgages or car loans—and you do not have sufficient income to keep up payments while also catching up on past-due amounts. Bankruptcy may not help you when the long-term expense of keeping your home or car exceeds your long-term income.
3. You have valuable assets that are not exempt in the bankruptcy process and you do not want to lose these assets. A chapter 13 filing may still help if you can afford the necessary payments.
4. Your main reason for filing bankruptcy is to discharge a student loan, alimony or child support obligations, court restitution orders, criminal fines, or some taxes. These obligations are difficult if not impossible to discharge in bankruptcy.
5. You have only a few debts and strong defenses for each. Instead of filing for bankruptcy, you can raise these defenses aggressively. Usually the disputes can be settled out of court in an acceptable way. If they are not settled, you can use bankruptcy later.
6. Because of a prior bankruptcy, you cannot receive a discharge in a chapter 7 bankruptcy. However, in most cases, a chapter 13 petition can still be filed.
7. You can afford to pay all of your current debts without hardship.

25

How the Bankruptcy Process Works

TOPICS COVERED IN THIS CHAPTER

This chapter summarizes how bankruptcy works. A far more detailed description for lawyers is found in NCLC's two-volume treatise, *Consumer Bankruptcy Law and Practice* (11th ed. 2016), *updated online at* www.nclc.org/library.

STEP ONE: GET THE RIGHT HELP WITH YOUR BANKRUPTCY FILING

Hiring a Bankruptcy Attorney. Generally, if you are considering bankruptcy it is best to consult an attorney who is a consumer bankruptcy expert. Select an attorney who will be responsive to your personal situation and is not be too busy to meet with you individually and to answer your questions. Before hiring an attorney, you should meet the attorney personally and make sure that you are comfortable with the attorney's style. At all points in the case, your attorney should take time to answer questions either directly or through an office paralegal. If an attorney does not respond to your telephone calls, you should keep trying and demand an answer.

The best way to find a trustworthy bankruptcy attorney is to seek recommendations from family, friends, the neighborhood legal services office, a volunteer lawyer's project, or other members of the community. To find a consumer bankruptcy attorney in your area, you can use the "Find an Attorney" search at the National Association of Consumer Bankruptcy Attorneys, at www.nacba.org. The lawyer advertising the cheapest rate is not necessarily the best. More tips to help you find an attorney can be found in Chapter 1.

Retainers and other documents should be read carefully so that you understand them. An attorney retainer is a contract under which you hire the attorney, governing what the attorney proposes to do and the fees for the proposed work.

The Wrong Help. Avoid document preparation services who offer to prepare the initial bankruptcy forms for a fee. These services are staffed by non-lawyers who cannot offer legal advice. They also offer no services after a bankruptcy case is started, so that you will have nowhere to turn for help later.

Others advertise bankruptcy-related services to take advantage of financially distressed consumers. Some advertise help with foreclosure when all they really do is charge enormous fees and put you into bankruptcy without providing any advice on how this will help or any assistance in getting through the process.

Others make promises that they cannot possibly keep. Do not pay money for debt counseling, credit repair, foreclosure assistance, or bankruptcy without being sure you are dealing with a reputable business. Debt consolidation and debt settlement agencies should also be avoided. If a deal seems too good to be true or if a solution to your problems seems too easy, it probably is.

Preparing to Meet with a Bankruptcy Attorney. Be prepared when first meeting a bankruptcy attorney to answer the following questions:

- What types of debt are causing you the most trouble?
- What are your significant assets?
- How were the debts incurred and are they secured by your property?
- Has any creditor started a process to collect any debt or to foreclose or repossess property?

Be prepared to report on the status of any pending lawsuits or foreclosures. Whenever possible, bring written information, particularly copies of your bills and any legal notices.

Your bankruptcy attorney may ask that you get a copy of your credit report. This helps the attorney understand how much is owed and to whom. It also provides necessary information such as account numbers and addresses of creditors.

Complete information is essential to an effective bankruptcy. If information is not complete, you will be the one to suffer. Expected tax refunds might be lost, major debts might not be cancellable, and you may unexpectedly lose property. Identify every possible debt, because debts not listed in the bankruptcy may not be discharged. Don't forget to even include debts where payments have not been recently demanded, debts that you cosigned, debts owed to friends or family members, student loans, public benefit overpayments, payday loans, and utility bills.

STEP TWO: EXEMPTION PLANNING

You can legally take steps that improve your position prior to filing bankruptcy, called "exemption planning." Exemption planning is an arrangement that allows you to keep the maximum amount of property after filing bankruptcy and lose as little as possible to creditors. It is similar to taking maximum advantage of tax laws, and, if done reasonably, it is perfectly legal.

You do this by making sure that as much of your property is "exempt" under applicable law and as little of your property is nonexempt. For example, you might sell nonexempt property and purchase exempt property. But an excessive transfer of property to create exempt assets can sometimes be found to be in bad faith. You cannot simply give away nonexempt property or sell it at nominal cost.

Any transfer of property within two years of filing must be disclosed. Improper transfers of property to third parties can be recovered and may be grounds for denying a discharge. The advice of your bankruptcy attorney can be key here.

STEP THREE: THE CREDIT COUNSELING REQUIREMENT

Bankruptcy law requires that before you file for bankruptcy you receive budget and credit counseling from an approved credit counseling agency and, on completion, file a certificate from that agency. First meet with your bankruptcy attorney because the credit counseling agency may try to dissuade you from filing bankruptcy. It is best to first hear whether your bankruptcy attorney thinks bankruptcy is your best option and why.

The credit counseling requirement is only met if the agency is an approved agency. A list of approved agencies is available at www.usdoj.gov/ust, at your local bankruptcy court, or from your bankruptcy attorney. Approved agencies can provide the counseling in-person, by telephone, or over the internet.

Most agencies charge between $10 to $40 for the pre-filing counseling (often the same amount for a married couple if both spouses are counseled at the same time). If you cannot afford the fee, ask the agency to provide the counseling free of charge or at a reduced fee. Reputable counseling agencies disclose their fee waiver policies up front, for example in a clear statement on their websites.

You can also ask the court in your initial filing to waive the counseling requirement because you are disabled, incapacitated, or on active military duty in a combat zone. Courts are very strict in granting waivers for the first two reasons, so in most cases it is not worth trying to get a waiver. If the court does not grant the waiver, your filing will be dismissed.

While it is possible to ask for a temporary postponement of your receiving counseling until shortly after you file bankruptcy (for example if you are rushing to use bankruptcy to stop a foreclosure), courts rarely grant such waivers because you can obtain counseling quickly over the phone or internet on an emergency basis. Denial of this waiver request will result in the dismissal of your bankruptcy filing, causing further delay, cost, and even more serious problems for your efforts to protect your home.

The counseling session usually takes less than an hour. The agency will prepare an income and expense budget and review it with you. Be realistic in describing your actual income and expenses. The session will go more quickly if you have written down your basic income and expense information in advance. Try to have a list of your debts handy, for example from a credit report. Spend time to gather all this information because you will need the same information later if you file for bankruptcy.

The agency will review with you any options short of bankruptcy, such as a debt management plan. As discussed in Chapter 12, before signing up for such a plan, carefully consider whether you can afford to make the suggested payments and whether such a plan will solve your financial problems.

If the agency initially convinces you to agree to an alternative to bankruptcy, make sure you get your certificate from the agency in case you change your mind. Then you can use the certificate to meet the bankruptcy counseling requirement as long as you file bankruptcy within 180 days of getting the certificate. The agency cannot refuse to provide you with a certificate because it believes your reasons for filing are inappropriate or not justified.

STEP FOUR: CHOOSING BETWEEN CHAPTER 7 AND CHAPTER 13

Bankruptcy law provides for two main types of consumer bankruptcies: chapter 7 and chapter 13. You should decide with your attorney which is the better chapter for you.

If a chapter 7 bankruptcy will accomplish your goals, it is generally the best choice because it is simpler and quicker than a chapter 13 bankruptcy. Once the papers are filed, unless unusual issues are raised, you will receive a discharge within three to five months.

Generally, chapter 7 is the best option when two factors are present:

- All or nearly all of your property is exempt; and
- The debts that are causing you problems are unsecured and dischargeable in chapter 7.

Even if some of your property is not exempt, you may be able to exchange small amounts of nonexempt property for exempt property before you file, as discussed above under exemption planning.

Where there are secured debts, a chapter 13 filing may not be necessary, particularly if you are current on your mortgage, car loan, and other secured debt payments. Then you can keep your home or other collateral, if it is exempt, even while going through a chapter 7 bankruptcy. A chapter 13 filing is generally preferable if you are delinquent on a secured debt (such as your mortgage or car loan) and want to cure this default over time.

The amount you will have to pay to your attorney will be considerably greater in chapter 13 than in chapter 7. However, the chapter 13 attorney fees can be paid over several years and the benefits of a chapter 13 may far outweigh the increased attorney costs if you are seeking to protect your home.

The most common reason for filing a chapter 13 petition is that one or more secured creditors (such as your mortgage or auto lender) cannot be dealt with satisfactorily in any other way. Few legal procedures create opportunities to deal with foreclosures and repossessions as quickly and effectively as a chapter 13 bankruptcy. Another reason to file a chapter 13 bankruptcy is to protect nonexempt assets, which would be sold in a chapter 7 case. However, the current value of the nonexempt property usually has to be paid over the course of the plan.

Other important reasons favoring a chapter 13 filing include:

- Some debts that are not dischargeable in chapter 7 can be discharged in chapter 13.
- Some creditors consider a chapter 13 filing, compared to a chapter 7, to be less harmful to your credit rating and reputation.
- If you obtained a chapter 7 discharge within the previous eight years, a new chapter 7 filing is not an option; only chapter 13 is available.

Even if you cannot afford payments to cure a default on your home mortgage, you can use the chapter 13 process to sell your home so that you can keep your equity and avoid the problems of a foreclosure sale.

You can change the type of bankruptcy you choose. Except in rare cases where the debtor engaged in some kind of fraudulent conduct in bankruptcy, it is easy to convert a case (at least once) from chapter 7 to chapter 13 or vice versa.

STEP FIVE: DECIDING WHETHER TO FILE BANKRUPTCY JOINTLY WITH A SPOUSE

If you and your spouse are living together and have debts that you are both responsible for, it is usually preferable for the two of you to file bankruptcy jointly. The filing fee is the same as if you were filing alone. If you file together, you will both get the advantages of a bankruptcy discharge. Since married couples often have joint debts, a spouse who does not file remains liable as a co-debtor and may be pursued by creditors.

You do not have to file jointly. If you want to file and your spouse does not (or vice versa), or if you and your spouse are separated, there is nothing to prevent a married individual from filing alone. However, the consequences of not filing jointly should be considered carefully.

Unmarried partners do not have the option of filing together. However, separate cases can be filed and administered by the court together.

HOW CHAPTER 7 BANKRUPTCIES WORK

Most Families Keep Most of Their Property Even in a Chapter 7. A chapter 7 bankruptcy case is often called a "liquidation," but that is inaccurate because most families keep most of their property in a chapter 7 bankruptcy. While the bankruptcy trustee will try to sell property for the benefit of creditors, federal and state law exempt much of your property from this sale.

Property that the bankruptcy trustee cannot sell and that you get to keep is called "exempt." In most consumer bankruptcies, nearly all your assets are exempt. If property is partly exempt and partly nonexempt, the trustee may sell it and pay you the value of the exempt part in cash. Or, if you have the money, you may pay the trustee the amount of the nonexempt value and keep the property.

Exemption laws vary from state to state and may be fairly complicated. You cannot make a final choice about bankruptcy without understanding the exemption laws for your particular state. While it is possible to research these on your own, the best course it to rely on a bankruptcy attorney.

The dollar amount that is exempt goes much further than you think because the dollar value refers not to the property's value, but the property's value over and above any loan you have that is secured by that property. This difference is called your "equity" in the property.

Consider, for example, if the state exemption for your home is $50,000, the home's value is $150,000, and you have a $100,000 mortgage. The home's equity or value over and above the $100,000 mortgage is $50,000, so that the home is totally protected by the state homestead exemption. The trustee cannot sell your home to pay off your other creditors, such as medical or credit card debt. Your mortgage lender (as opposed to the trustee) though can foreclose on the home if you do not keep up on your mortgage payments.

The trustee also is unlikely to sell your home for the benefit of other creditors if there is only a small amount of equity in the home. After deducting the exemption amount and realtor or other sales expenses, there will be nothing left to send to creditors. In the above example, the trustee is unlikely to sell your home even if it is worth $165,000 or even slightly more.

At the end of a chapter 7 case, you obtain a "discharge" of most of your unsecured debts. This means that you will no longer have a legal obligation to pay those debts. Generally, the discharge will include credit card debts, medical bills, utility arrearages, and other similar debts for which the creditor does not have collateral. Some unsecured debts, such as most student loans, debts based on fraud or malicious conduct, drunk driving debts, most tax debts, government fines, alimony, and child support are not likely to be discharged.

Chapter 7 bankruptcies rarely help with large secured debts, such as home mortgages, because the creditor keeps its rights in the collateral. The exemption does not apply to the secured creditor. While bankruptcy cancels your legal obligation to pay most personal debts, even secured debts, it does not prevent secured creditors from recovering their collateral if a debt is not repaid. This means that a chapter 7 case will not affect, except temporarily, the rights of a bank to foreclose on a home or repossess a car that is loan collateral. However, if you have received a chapter 7 discharge and a creditor later sells its collateral, the creditor may not sue you for any balance still owed.

Who Can File a Chapter 7 Bankruptcy? A "means test" makes it more difficult for wealthy consumers to file a chapter 7 bankruptcy. This test does not even apply to you if your income is below the median family income in your state. For 2018, for a family of four, the median family income ranged from a low of $67,486 in Arkansas to a high of $113,651 in Massachusetts.

A consumer with income above the median must fill out a form that compares the consumer's monthly income with actual and assumed expenses in a variety of categories. If this form shows, based on standards in the law, that the consumer should have a certain amount left over to pay unsecured creditors, the bankruptcy court may decide that the consumer cannot file a chapter 7 case, unless there are special circumstances. But chapter 7 should be available for virtually all Americans who are unable to pay all their bills.

What Are the First Steps? The first step in a chapter 7 bankruptcy is completion of a few basic forms, including an initial "petition" and a certificate from an approved credit counseling agency. At that time or shortly thereafter, with the assistance and direction of your attorney, you file your statement of financial affairs, statement whether you intend to keep your secured property, statement of monthly income and means test calculations, copies of any pay stubs you received from an employer during the sixty days before filing your bankruptcy case, and a set of schedules listing all your debts, assets, income, and expenses.

These forms should be filled out completely and accurately. Frequently overlooked assets include tax refunds, child support arrearages, security deposits, pledged goods at pawnbrokers, personal injury claims, other legal claims, and the cash value of life insurance policies. Often missed debts include debts that you cosigned, debts owed to friends or family members, student loans, public benefit overpayments, payday loans, and utility bills.

If requested, you must provide copies of certain tax returns, or a shorter version of the returns called "transcripts." Due to privacy concerns, no tax returns filed with the bankruptcy court will be available to the public and cannot be viewed on the internet.

At the beginning of the case you file a mailing list of all of your creditors. Bankruptcy courts often require that these forms be filed electronically in a particular format, but most courts allow consumers without an attorney to file in paper form or provide scanning and other equipment at the court that consumers can use to convert the forms for electronic filing. You should check with a bankruptcy specialist or your local bankruptcy court for a full list of filing requirements.

What Will Happen After Filing? Filing the petition triggers the "automatic stay." With few exceptions, this stops any creditor from taking collection action, pursuing a court case against you, or seizing your property based on debts that arose before you filed your bankruptcy petition. While the stay is automatic, if you are worried about a creditor action like a foreclosure or repossession, make a special effort to notify that creditor so that the action is stopped before it occurs.

If a creditor does take action against you other than in the bankruptcy court, including making collection calls or sending letters, you should politely inform the creditor about the bankruptcy. If you have an attorney, you should also tell your attorney about the contact. You may start a process to obtain damages for certain violations of the stay.

Within a few weeks after filing, the bankruptcy court or the trustee mails a notice of the stay and of the date and place for a "meeting of creditors." This notice will be mailed to all creditors, to you, and to your attorney, if you have one.

What Is a Bankruptcy Trustee? After you file a chapter 7 bankruptcy, a trustee is appointed to represent the interests of creditors. The trustee collects any property that can be sold, handles the sale, distributes the property to creditors with valid claims, and makes a final accounting to the court.

What Is the Meeting of Creditors? The trustee conducts a meeting of creditors, usually not at the courthouse, but rather at a separate government or office building. The meeting of creditors gives the trustee and others a chance to ask questions about your financial affairs.

Despite the name, few creditors will actually appear at the meeting. You, however, must attend. If you file jointly, your spouse must also attend. The meeting consists of a series of routine questions by the trustee and lasts from two minutes to half an hour. Beforehand, review the papers you or your attorney have filed with the court and bring any requested documents with you to the meeting, such as a copy of your most recent bank statements, a picture form of identification, or your most recent pay stub.

The Education Course Requirement. As part of the bankruptcy, and in addition to the credit counseling requirement before you file for bankruptcy, you must complete an approved educational course on personal finances. The fee is usually $20 to $50. If you cannot afford the fee, ask the agency to provide the course free of charge or at a reduced fee.

The course typically takes about two hours, and most course providers give you a choice whether to take the course in-person, over the internet, or over the telephone. The course generally covers budget development, money management, wise use of credit, and consumer information.

What Happens After the Meeting of Creditors and the Education Course? Unless there is an objection to the exemptions you have claimed, after the meeting of creditors you keep the property listed as exempt in your schedules. Property that is mostly, but not totally, exempt is usually abandoned by the trustee, which means that you also get to keep it.

If larger nonexempt assets remain, they are turned over to the trustee. You will usually be offered the option of paying the nonexempt value of the assets to the trustee in cash instead of turning over those assets. The trustee then sells any property collected, converts it to cash, and distributes it among the creditors.

During a chapter 7 bankruptcy, you will have to take steps to deal with your secured debts. You can surrender the collateral to the secured creditor or keep the collateral by paying the creditor in a lump sum the value of the collateral. You also have the option of "reaffirming" the debt to protect the collateral. In some situations, you can even keep your property by continuing to make scheduled payments.

What Is Reaffirmation and When Should I Consider It? Reaffirmation is your agreement during bankruptcy to remain legally obligated on some or all of a debt which you could have otherwise eliminated through the bankruptcy.

- If a creditor pressures you to reaffirm, you can say no. No law requires you to reaffirm a debt.
- Never reaffirm a debt just because a creditor offers to advance you some new credit or to keep your account in good standing. There are easier ways to obtain new credit than to agree to the expense of repaying a debt which bankruptcy can eliminate.
- If you really want, you can always pay any debts you want to pay after bankruptcy without signing a reaffirmation agreement. That way you cannot be sued if you stop paying.
- If for some reason you decide to reaffirm, negotiate the terms—the terms do not have to be the same as the original credit terms or the amount due.
- The court must approve any reaffirmation agreement. If the creditor tricks you into signing something, it has no effect until approved by the court.
- You can for any reason cancel any reaffirmation agreement for sixty days after it is filed with the court or any time before your discharge order.

You should never agree to reaffirm if:

- The debt is totally unsecured;
- The creditor cannot provide paperwork showing you that the debt is secured;
- The debt is secured and you have no interest in keeping the collateral;
- The debt is secured and you are hopelessly behind on payments, so that the property will be repossessed in any event.

You might consider reaffirmation if:

- The creditor gives you something valuable in return, such as an agreement to let you get caught up on a default in a manageable way or a reduction of a secured debt to the value of the property;
- You want to keep property used as collateral for a secured debt and your bankruptcy court will not allow you to keep it without reaffirming (and you

cannot afford the better alternative of paying the creditor the value of the property in a lump sum); or
- You can easily afford the payments on secured debt which will be required after bankruptcy.

What About Reaffirming Credit Card Debt? It is almost never a good idea to reaffirm a credit card debt. Generally ignore any offers the card company makes involving reaffirmation. You are better off eliminating that debt and getting a new card from another company. For some store credit cards, the company may threaten that it can seize purchases made on the card. Even if true, such threats are almost never carried out. Do not reaffirm a debt to protect property they will never seize.

A Bankruptcy Discharge Ends the Bankruptcy. The final step in most chapter 7 bankruptcy cases is the discharge that will eliminate many of your debts. In most places, if no one objects, the court enters the discharge without a hearing. You get the discharge order in the mail.

The discharge in chapter 7 covers all unsecured debts, including most credit card debt, medical bills, and back utility debts. Your discharge may not include:

- Certain taxes;
- Debts not listed in your schedules;
- Debts for alimony, child support, and family court property settlements;
- Most fines and penalties owed to government agencies;
- Student loans unless you can prove to the court that repaying them will be an "undue hardship";
- Debts incurred by driving while intoxicated;
- Debts incurred to pay taxes which cannot be discharged; and
- Debts you have formally agreed to reaffirm.

If a creditor asks the court within a strict time limit, the court may except from discharge:

- Debts incurred by certain types of fraud;
- Debts incurred while acting as a trustee for someone else's property;
- Debts for purposely causing injuries to individuals or property; and
- Certain debts for luxury goods or services or cash advances a few months before filing bankruptcy, unless you can show that you had good reason to incur the debt and that you were not intending to take advantage of the bankruptcy filing.

A few creditors (mainly credit card companies) make accusations of fraud even when consumers have done nothing wrong, intending to scare honest consumers to reaffirm the debt. Never agree to reaffirm if you have done nothing wrong.

It is illegal for a creditor to try to collect a debt discharged in bankruptcy. Contact your lawyer if you have been subject to collection efforts and you may be able to recover any damages.

HOW CHAPTER 13 BANKRUPTCIES WORK

The Initial Steps. Chapter 13 cases can be quite complicated. Definitely seek the help of an attorney specializing in bankruptcy as quickly as possible. Your delay may allow a foreclosure or repossession to proceed to the point where the chapter 13 bankruptcy can no longer help.

Unlike a chapter 7 that has some restrictions on higher income filers, any individual with a regular income can file a chapter 13 bankruptcy. An "individual with regular income" includes not only wage earners, but also recipients of government benefits, alimony, or support payments, or any other type of regular income. You cannot use chapter 13 if your debts are significantly in excess of $1 million, but this affects few consumers. Family farmers or fishermen can also proceed under chapter 12 instead of chapter 13, and this will often be a better choice.

Most of the initial steps in a chapter 13 case are similar to those in chapter 7 discussed earlier in this chapter. The bankruptcy begins with a petition and a certificate from an approved credit counseling agency. As with a chapter 7, additional forms and schedules must also be filed either with your petition or shortly thereafter.

The major difference with a chapter 13 filing is that a plan must be submitted at the same time that describes when creditors will be paid, how they will be paid, and how much they will be paid. In a chapter 13 bankruptcy, you will not lose any property as long as you have a plan to pay out all or part of what you owe over a period of years, usually from future income. You must begin making payments under that plan within thirty days after filing.

The filing immediately establishes the automatic stay, which prevents any further creditor acts against you or your property. Unlike a chapter 7, the automatic stay in chapter 13 prevents creditors from taking any action against your cosigners who have not filed bankruptcy, so long as your plan provides for payment of the debt.

A chapter 13 trustee is appointed and the meeting of creditors is held where the focus is usually on whether your plan meets legal requirements and whether you can afford to make the plan payments.

What Will I Have to Pay Under the Chapter 13 Plan? The heart of a chapter 13 case is your bankruptcy plan. This is a document outlining how you propose to make payments to various creditors while the plan is in effect. A chapter 13 plan normally requires monthly payments to the bankruptcy trustee over a period of three years, but courts can approve plans as long as five years.

Your payments are held by the chapter 13 trustee and not paid out to creditors until your chapter 13 plan is approved by the court after a "confirmation hearing," usually held roughly a month after the first meeting of creditors. Depending upon the terms of your proposed plan, or if required by the court, you may need to begin making payments directly to some secured creditors within thirty days after filing your bankruptcy case.

The court will inquire into whether your plan meets the requirements of chapter 13 and will hear any objections to approval of your chapter 13 plan raised by creditors or the trustee. If there are no objections, there may not even be a hearing and you then need not go to court. If the court does not approve your chapter 13 plan, the payments are returned to you after deduction of administrative costs.

How much you have to pay under your plan depends on whether debt is secured or unsecured and what the court will allow. Typically, after paying for necessary living expenses, you pay the balance of your income to the trustee while your bankruptcy proceeds. If you choose, this can occur automatically by wage deduction.

To keep your home, car, or other collateral for a loan, you must pay current and past-due payments in full under your plan, but you can spread those payments out over three to five years. Your unsecured creditors also receive a share of the payments made under the plan. By paying the nonexempt value of your property over a period of years, you get to keep all of your property under a chapter 13.

Depending upon the amount of your nonexempt property and income left over after paying necessary living expenses, your plan may pay unsecured creditors at less than the full amount they are owed, often as low as 5% to 10% of what they are owed. In most cases, consumers are no longer required to pay unsecured creditors for any interest, late fees, and other penalty charges that would otherwise come due after the chapter 13 is filed. If your income is above the state median family income, the amount you are required to pay unsecured creditors is based on a formula that considers the actual amounts you spend for some expenses and fixed amounts for other expenses.

What Does a Trustee Do in Chapter 13? The chapter 13 trustee has more to do than the chapter 7 trustee. The chapter 13 trustee may require that you provide additional documents, such as tax returns and documents showing that homes and cars are insured. The chapter 13 trustee collects your payments and distributes that money to creditors. The trustee will ask the court to dismiss your case if you fail to make the plan payments.

To get paid by the trustee, creditors file a proof of claim with the bankruptcy court. Both you and the trustee can object to the claim if the creditor overcharged you or if you have defenses to owing the money. The bankruptcy judge will decide how much the creditor should be paid.

The chapter 13 trustee's opinion is not necessarily the last word on any matter. You can raise any appropriate issue with the bankruptcy judge. Trustees are not judges and have no power to rule on disputes between you and your creditors.

What If I Don't Make My Payments Under the Plan? Once your plan is in place, your case is likely to be dismissed if you fail to make payments or keep up with any alimony and child support payments, and you could be back to where you were before bankruptcy. When this occurs, though, you still may have four options:

- *Hardship Discharge.* Bankruptcy law provides for a hardship discharge of debts if problems are caused by circumstances for which you are not responsible, such as serious deterioration of your financial circumstances.
- *Modification.* It is possible to modify a plan to address new problems, but creditors have a right to object to the modification, and, if so, the court will decide whether to allow the modification.
- *Conversion.* You have the right to convert a chapter 13 case to a chapter 7 case. After the conversion, nonexempt property is liquidated and you receive a chapter 7 discharge.
- *Dismissal.* Occasionally, dismissal is preferable to any of the other options. You have the right in most cases to dismiss your chapter 13 case.

What Debts Are Discharged After Completing the Chapter 13? The final step in a successfully completed chapter 13 case is the discharge. As with chapter 7, you must complete an educational course on personal finances before you will be given a discharge.

The discharge available in chapter 13 covers more debts than a discharge under chapter 7, including all debts provided for by the plan, except for support and alimony payments and long-term debts with final payments due after the completion of the plan. Other chapter 13 exceptions to discharge are most student loans (unless you can prove that repaying them will be an "undue hardship"), drunk driving debts, and criminal restitution debts.

A chapter 13 discharge eliminates legal responsibility on some debts that are not dischargeable in a chapter 7 case, such as claims for injuries to property purposely caused by you and debts from some property settlements in a divorce or separation proceeding. If you have caught up on any mortgage debt or other secured loan, the loan will be reinstated and the law requires the creditor to treat you as if you never fell behind.

BANKRUPTCY'S TAX CONSEQUENCES

Consumers are often surprised to learn that forgiven debt often is taxable to them. Bankruptcy is one exception to this rule. If debt is discharged in the bankruptcy process, you do not owe taxes on the unpaid amount of the debt.

Nevertheless, you may receive an IRS Form 1099-C from one or more creditors listing the amount you discharged in bankruptcy as canceled debt income. This form also goes to the IRS, and the IRS will treat this as a report of income to you, unless you explain it away. Attach an explanation to your tax form which includes your bankruptcy case number and the date of the discharge. Since tax laws are complicated, you may want to seek the advice of a qualified tax professional.

USING CREDIT WISELY AFTER BANKRUPTCY

Do not assume that, because you filed bankruptcy, you later will have to get credit on the worst terms. If you can't get credit on decent terms right after bankruptcy, it may be better to wait. Most lenders will not hold the bankruptcy against you if, after a few years, you can show that you have avoided problems and can manage your debts.

Be wary of auto dealers, mortgage brokers, and lenders who advertise: "Bankruptcy? Bad Credit? No Credit? No Problem!" They may give you a loan after bankruptcy, but at a very high cost. The extra costs and fees on these loans can make it impossible for you to keep up the loan payments. Getting this kind of loan can ruin your chances to rebuild your credit.

You should also avoid other credit offers that are aimed at recent bankruptcy filers. These may be an attempt to collect discharged debt in the form of a "disguised" reaffirmation agreement. For example, carefully read any credit card or other credit offer from a company that claims to own a debt you discharged or represent a lender you listed in your bankruptcy. This may be from a debt collection company that is trying to trick you into reaffirming a debt. The offer's fine print may require that some or all of the balance from the discharged debt is added to the new account.

Glossary

[Words in italics are separately defined in this glossary.]

Acceleration. When a *creditor* claims the total balance of a loan is due immediately. This cannot usually occur unless you have fallen behind on payments. In the case of a home mortgage, receipt of a letter stating that a loan has been "accelerated" is normally an important warning sign of foreclosure.

Amount Financed. The amount of money you are getting in a loan, calculated under rules required by federal law. This is the amount of money you are borrowing after deduction of certain loan charges that the *Truth in Lending Act* defines as "finance charges." You should think of the amount financed as the real amount you are borrowing. You will find the amount financed for a loan on the "disclosure statement" that is given to you when the loan papers are signed.

Annual Percentage Rate. The interest rate on a loan expressed under rules required by federal law. It is more accurate to look at the annual percentage rate (as opposed to the stated interest rate) to determine the true cost of a loan, because it tells you the full cost of the loan including many of the lender's fees. You will find the annual percentage rate for a loan on the "disclosure statement" that is given to you when the loan papers are signed.

Answer. In a lawsuit, this is a legal document that the *defendant* must file to respond to the claims being raised. There are often short time deadlines to file an answer. Failure to file an answer can result in a *default judgment.*

Arrears. The total amount you are behind on a debt. Usually the amount of all back-payments plus any collection costs.

Assignment. The transfer of a *mortgage* or *deed of trust* to another party usually evidenced by a document showing that the current mortgage holder (assignor) assigned its rights to the new holder (assignee).

Attachment. A legal process that allows a creditor to "attach" a *lien* to property that you own. Depending on state law, almost any kind of property may be subject to attachment, including your home, automobile, bank accounts, and wages. Once a *lien* is attached to the property, you may face further collection action on that property, including *execution, garnishment,* or *foreclosure.*

Auto/Car Title Loan. A short-term loan secured by a borrower's car title.

Automatic Stay. An automatic end to credit collection activity. Filing bankruptcy is the only way to get this protection.

Bankruptcy. A legal process available in all states that allows you to address your debt problems according to a set of special rules while getting protection from continued collection activity.

Bond. Amounts required by a court order to protect a party to a lawsuit while the case proceeds. A bond may be required in some circumstances to pursue an appeal.

Chapter 7 Bankruptcy. See *liquidation.*

Chapter 13 Bankruptcy. See *reorganization.*

Closing. The process of signing loan papers which obligate the borrower to repay a loan. This term is associated with the signing of a mortgage loan. It is also called the *settlement.*

Collateral. Property put up to secure a loan. If you have given a creditor collateral, that creditor can normally take and sell the collateral if you are not able to repay the loan. A creditor with collateral is normally known as a "*secured creditor.*"

Collection-Proof. Also known as "judgment-proof," this term is applied to people or businesses with property of minimal value, which can be entirely protected by *exemptions.* If you are collection-proof, it is difficult or sometimes impossible for any creditor to force you to pay a debt.

Complaint. A document beginning a lawsuit. A complaint normally includes a statement of all of the claims being raised by the person bringing the lawsuit.

Cosigner. A person who agrees to be responsible for someone else's debt. A cosigner is normally responsible for paying back a debt just as if he or she had received the money.

Counterclaim. A response to a lawsuit in which the person being sued raises legal claims against the person (or business) which started the case. For example, if you are sued by an automobile seller who claims you did not pay for a car, you might counterclaim that the car was a "lemon."

Credit Bureau, also called "consumer reporting agency" or "credit reporting agency." This is a company that receives information about a consumer's credit history and keeps records that are available to those seeking data about that consumer.

Credit Insurance. Insurance designed to pay off a borrower's mortgage debt if the borrower dies or is otherwise incapable of meeting the loan obligation.

Credit Report, also called a "consumer report" or a "credit record," is the information about a consumer that a *credit bureau* has on file that it can report to others. The report includes the credit history and current status of a consumer's monthly payment obligations and public information such as bankruptcies, court *judgments,* and tax liens.

Credit Score. A credit score (sometimes called a "FICO" score), is a number that summarizes your credit history. The purpose of the score is to help lenders evaluate whether you are a risky borrower.

Creditor. Any person or business to whom you owe money.

Cure a Default. If you have defaulted on a debt, this is a process for correcting the *default.* Most often, a "cure" refers to getting caught up on missed payments (paying the *arrears*). A cure may also be called *reinstatement.*

Debt Collector. The most common use of this term applies to anyone who collects debts. However, under the federal *Fair Debt Collection Practices Act* or "FDCPA," the term "debt collector" only applies to collection agencies and lawyers (or their employees) that are collecting debts for others. State laws may cover other types of collectors.

Debt Consolidation. Refinancing debt into a new loan. In the mortgage lending context, relatively short-term, unsecured debt is often rolled into long-term mortgage loans, putting the home at greater risk.

Debt Management Plan. Debt management plans are offered by many credit counseling agencies. Through debt management plans (DMPs), consumers send the credit counseling agency a monthly payment, which the agency then distributes to the consumer's creditors. In return, the consumer is supposed to get a break, usually in the form of creditor agreements to waive fees and to lower interest rates.

Debt Settlement. Negotiation and settlement services are different from debt management services (see *Debt Management Plan*) mainly because the debt settlement agencies do not send regular monthly payments to creditors. Instead, these agencies generally maintain a consumer's funds in separate accounts, holding the money until the agency believes it can settle a consumer's debts for less than the full amount owed.

Debtor. Any person who owes money to another. In *bankruptcy,* the term "debtor" refers to the person who begins a bankruptcy case.

Debtor's Examination, also known as "post-judgment process," "asset examination," and "supplementary process." This is normally a court ordered proceeding in which a debtor must appear in court or in an attorney's office to answer questions about current income and assets from which a *judgment* may be collected. In many states, failure to appear at a debtor's examination can result in an arrest warrant.

Deed. An instrument that transfers ownership from the seller to the buyer upon the closing of the sale.

Deed in Lieu. An agreement to turn real estate over to a lender as an alternative to *foreclosure.*

Deed of Trust. In some states, this is the term used for a pledge of real estate as *collateral.* It is similar to a *mortgage.*

Default. Failing to meet the requirements of an agreement. Most defaults involve failure to make required payments. However, other types of defaults are possible, including failure to maintain necessary insurance and failure to keep *collateral* in proper condition.

Default Judgment. A *judgment* in a lawsuit against a party who did not meet legal requirements in connection with the case. The most common reason for a default judgment is failing to file an *answer* or other necessary papers before deadlines specified by law.

Default Rate. The interest rate the creditor will charge once the borrower defaults on the loan. If a default interest rate is listed in a loan contract, is will always be higher than the contract interest rate.

Defendant. In a lawsuit, this is the person or business that is being sued.

Defense. A legal reason why a court should not award any or all of what is requested in a lawsuit. For example, a statement that the money is not owed is a defense to a collection lawsuit.

Deficiency. The amount a debtor owes a creditor on a debt after the creditor seizes and sells the *collateral*. A deficiency arises when the collateral is sold for less than the amount of the debt. Normally, a creditor must bring a lawsuit to collect a deficiency.

Discharge. A document that ends a debtor's legally enforceable obligation to pay a debt. It is common to get a discharge of a mortgage debt after the mortgage is fully paid off. In addition, most bankruptcies result in a discharge at the end of the case that applies to many debts.

Equity. Your equity in property is the amount of cash you would keep if you sold property and paid off all of the liens on that property. For example, if you own a house worth $100,000, but you owe $60,000 on your original mortgage and $10,000 on a second mortgage, you have $30,000 in equity. The same principle applies to cars and other types of property.

Escrow. Amounts set aside for a particular purpose. A formal escrow usually requires a legal agreement that covers permissible usage of the escrow and how and where the money is to be kept. One type of escrow is money you pay to your mortgage company to cover taxes and insurance. Escrow is also used when you have a dispute with a creditor. You may choose to set up an escrow to pay the debt in the event you lose the dispute.

Eviction. A legal process terminating the right to occupy a home, apartment, or business property. State law eviction proceedings are required before putting someone out.

Execution. The process of enforcing a court judgment by taking property from the *defendant*. Execution of a judgment of *eviction*, for example, involves the sheriff or a public official putting the tenants out. Execution of a *judgment lien* involves seizing and selling the property subject to the lien.

Exempt Property. Property that the law allows you to keep when you are being faced with collection on an *unsecured debt.* In *bankruptcy,* exempt property is protected from sale to satisfy the claims of creditors. Your exemption applies to your *equity* in the property after deduction for the amounts you owe to pay *liens* on that property.

Exemptions. These are laws that give you the right to keep your *exempt property.*

Fair Credit Reporting Act. A federal (national) law that regulates *credit bureaus* and the use of credit reports.

Fair Debt Collection Practices Act. A federal (national) law that governs the conduct of *debt collectors* and that prevents many abusive collection tactics.

Federal Law. A law of the United states that applies throughout the country. The *bankruptcy* law is an example of a federal law.

Finance Company. A company engaged in making loans to individuals or businesses. Unlike a bank, it does not receive deposits from the public.

Force-Placed Insurance. The insurance policy your lender will "force" you to purchase if your insurance is cancelled or if your lender does not have proof of your insurance coverage. Force-placed insurance is **very** expensive.

Foreclosure. A legal process to terminate your ownership of real estate that is *collateral* for a debt, based on a *mortgage* or *deed of trust.* In some states, foreclosure involves a court proceeding ("judicial foreclosure"), while in others foreclosure occurs by creditor action alone ("non-judicial foreclosure").

Fraudulent Transfer. Giving away property to keep it out of the hands of creditors. The law allows *creditors* to sue to get the property back.

Garnishment. A *creditor's* seizure, to satisfy a debt, of property belonging to the *debtor* that is in the possession of a someone else. Usually a court has to authorize the seizure in advance. An example would be seizure of money in your bank account to repay a court judgment. Wages owed to you can also be garnished in many states.

Guarantor. A person who agrees to pay another person's debt in the event that they do not pay. The term guarantor is often used interchangeably with *cosigner,* even though there are some minor legal distinctions in the collection process.

Hazard Insurance. Insurance that covers property loss or damage, usually paid for by borrowers and required when obtaining a mortgage.

Home Equity Loan. This term is generally used to describe any mortgage loan that is not used to finance the purchase of the home.

Home Ownership and Equity Protection Act (HOEPA). This is a federal (national) law that provides special protection to homeowners when they obtain home mortgage loans at high interest rates or with high fees.

Homestead Exemption. The right, available in most states and in the *bankruptcy* process, to treat your residence as *exempt property* that cannot be sold to satisfy the claims of *unsecured creditors*. In most states, the homestead exemption covers a certain dollar amount of your equity in your residence. A home cannot normally be sold to pay claims of your creditors unless your equity in the home exceeds the amount of the exemption. A homestead exemption will not normally protect you from *foreclosure* when you have voluntarily pledged your home as *collateral*.

Insolvent. A person or business that does not have sufficient assets to pay its debts.

Interest. The cost of borrowing money over time. Interest rates are expressed as a percentage.

Judgment. A determination by a court as to the outcome of a lawsuit, including any amounts owed.

Judgment Lien. A *lien* that attaches to property as the result of a *judgment*. For example, if you lose a collection lawsuit, the creditor normally has the right to an *attachment* on any real estate that you own.

Judgment-Proof. See *collection-proof*.

Levy. A process, in some states, for *attachment* of a *judgment lien* and/or *execution* of that *lien*.

Lien. Also called a "security interest," it is a legal interest taken by creditors in your property to secure repayment of a debt. A lien can be created voluntarily in connection with a loan, such as when you pledge real estate by giving a creditor a *mortgage* or *deed of trust*. A lien can also be created without your consent by *attachment* based on a court order. A creditor with a lien is called a *secured creditor*.

Liquidation. Sale of property to pay creditors. The term is also used as a shorthand name for the chapter 7 bankruptcy process, even though property is not always sold in that bankruptcy process.

Mortgage. An agreement in which a property owner grants a *creditor* the right to satisfy a debt by selling the property in the event of a *default*.

Mortgage Broker. An individual who offers to arrange financing for a consumer. Brokers are supposed to operate as agents for consumers, seeking the best products. States vary as to whether or not the brokers are regulated.

Mortgage Insurance. See *private mortgage insurance*.

Mortgage Servicer. A bank, mortgage company, or a similar business that communicates with property owners concerning their *mortgage* loans. The servicer usually works for another company that owns the mortgage. It may accept and record payments, negotiate *workouts,* and supervise the *foreclosure* process in the event of a *default.*

Negative Equity. Negative *equity* arises when the value of an item of property you own is less than the total you owe on all the liens on that property. For example, if you own a home worth $100,000 and borrow $125,000 to consolidate debts, you have negative equity of $25,000.

Non-Purchase Money Security Interest. A non-purchase money security interest arises when you agree to give a lender collateral that was not purchased with money from that loan. For example, a finance company may insist that you give a lawn mower or living room set as collateral for a loan you take out to pay for car repairs.

Non-Sufficient Funds (NSF). Fees are charged for non-sufficient funds (NSF) when a checking account is overdrawn. NSF fees are different than overdraft fees, which are charged for the extension of a loan using bank funds to cover the amount you would have overdrawn.

Note. This term is commonly used as a name for a contract involving the loan of money.

Notice of Right to Cancel. This document explains your right to cancel a loan in some circumstances. You should receive such a notice in connection with most door-to-door sales and for *mortgage* loans that are not used to buy your residence.

Notice to Quit. In most states, this is a notice given by an owner of property (usually a landlord) demanding that a tenant leave within a specified period of time or face eviction proceedings.

Overdraft Loans. Also called "bounce-check protection" or "courtesy overdraft protection," these are a form of high-cost, short-term credit. With these products, financial institutions cover their customers' overdrafts when they have a negative balance, and then charge them a fee.

Payday Loan, also called "cash advances," "deferred presentment," "deferred deposits," or "check loans." Payday loan customers write the lender a post-dated check or sign an authorization for the lender to take money out of an account electronically for a certain amount. The amount on the check equals the amount borrowed plus a fee that is either a percentage of the full amount of the check or a flat dollar amount. The check (or debit agreement) is then held for up to a month, usually until the customer's next payday or receipt of a government check. At the end of the agreed time period, the customer must either pay back the full amount of the check (more than what the lender gave out), allow the check to be cashed, or pay another fee to extend the loan.

Personal Property. Property other than real estate.

Predatory Lending. A term for a variety of lending practices that strip wealth or income from borrowers. Predatory loans are typically much more expensive than justified by the risk associated with the loan. Characteristics of these loans may include, but are not limited to, excessive or hidden fees, charges for unnecessary products, high interest rates, terms designed to trap borrowers in debt, fraud, and refinances that do not provide any net benefit to the borrower.

Prepayment. Paying off all or part of the loan balance before it is due.

Prepayment Penalty. A fee charged by a lender if the borrower pays the loan off early. The lender's rationale for imposing prepayment penalties is to cover the loss of costs advanced by the lender at the time the loan is made.

Pre-Sale. Sale of property in anticipation of *foreclosure* or *repossession,* usually with the lender's consent. A pre-sale is likely to lead to a higher sale price than foreclosure or repossession.

Principal. The amount borrowed.

Private Mortgage Insurance (PMI). Insurance provided by non-government insurers that protects lenders against loss if a borrower defaults. This insurance is usually required when a borrower makes less than a 20% down payment. When the borrower's equity in the property equals 20%, she may request that the insurance be cancelled.

Pro Se, also called "pro per." Representing yourself (without an attorney) in a legal case or bankruptcy proceeding.

Punitive Damages. Special damages that are sometimes awarded in court to punish a party who is responsible for serious misconduct.

Purchase Money Mortgage. The mortgage loan obtained to purchase a home.

Purchase Money Security Interest. A lien on property that arises when you agree to allow a lender to take as collateral the property you are purchasing with the loan.

Reaffirmation. An agreement in the *bankruptcy* process to pay back a debt that would otherwise be *discharged* in bankruptcy. Most reaffirmation agreements are a bad idea.

Real Estate Settlement Procedures Act (RESPA). The purpose of this *federal law* is to protect consumers from unnecessarily high settlement charges and certain abusive practices that have developed in the residential real estate market. The law requires disclosures before and at the *closing* as well as periodically throughout the term of the mortgage loan.

Redeem. Recovering *collateral* from a *creditor* by paying the entire amount you owe whether past-due or not.

Refinancing. The process of paying back old debts by borrowing new money either from an existing *creditor* or a new creditor.

Refund Anticipation Loan. See *tax refund anticipation loans.*

Reinstatement. The process of remedying a *default* so that the lender will treat you as if you had never fallen behind. See *curing a default.*

Rent to Own. Rent-to-own companies "rent" merchandise to a consumer for a stated period, after which the consumer owns the merchandise. A consumer pays much more than the value of the merchandise under a typical contract.

Reorganization (Chapter 13 Bankruptcy). This is a bankruptcy process to get relief from debts by making court-supervised payments over a period of time. The alternative is usually *liquidation* under chapter 7.

Replevin. The legal process in which a creditor seeks to recover *personal property* on which it claims a *lien*. Replevin is often threatened, but rarely occurs.

Repossession, often called "self-help repossession." Seizure by the creditor of *collateral* after the debtor's *default,* usually without court supervision or permission. Repossession is most common in connection with car loans.

Rescission. A right under some laws to cancel a contract or loan. The most common example of rescission arises in home equity loans and transactions to refinance a home loan. You have the right to rescind that loan within the first three business days after the loan is signed. In some cases, if the *creditor* has violated the law, your right to rescind may continue after the three-day period is up.

Retaliatory Eviction. An *eviction* where a landlord seeks to punish a tenant for exercising his or her legal rights (such as complaining to the building inspector or forming a tenant's organization).

Reverse Mortgage. A *refinancing* option usually available only to older homeowners who have built up substantial equity in their property. In a reverse mortgage, money is drawn based on the value of the property without an immediate repayment obligation, because the lender expects repayment by sale of the property at some point in the future.

Satisfaction. This is a legal document that states that a debt has been fully paid or that partial payment has been accepted as payment in full. A satisfaction is a type of *discharge.*

Secured Credit Cards. A credit card for which the card issuer requires that the card holder place a certain amount of money in a bank account with the card issuer. If the debtor does not repay the credit card, the card issuer can seize the money in the bank account.

Secured Creditor. Any *creditor* that has *collateral* for a debt.

Secured Debt. A debt for which the *creditor* has *collateral* in the form of a *mortgage, lien*, or *security interest* in certain items of property. The creditor can seize the property (*collateral*) if the *debtor defaults* in repayment of the debt.

Security Interest. See *lien*.

Self-Help Repossession. This is a process by which a *creditor* that has taken property as *collateral* can *repossess* the property without first getting court permission.

Servicer. See *mortgage servicer*.

Settlement. The *closing* of a mortgage loan. Also, the delivery of a loan or security to the buyer.

Settlement Statement (the "HUD-1"). The *Real Estate Settlement Procedures Act* requires lenders to give this disclosure at *closing* or one day in advance of closing if the consumer requests it. It should be the final statement of settlement costs.

Short Sale. A type of *pre-sale* in which the *creditor* agrees to let you sell property (usually real estate) for less than the full amount owed and to accept the proceeds of the sale as full *satisfaction* of the debt.

State Law. A law passed by an individual state that only applies to transactions in that state.

Statute. Another word for a law passed by a state or federal legislative body. Laws enacted by local entities, such as city councils, usually are called ordinances.

Subpoena. A document that is normally issued by a court in connection with a lawsuit, and that directs your attendance in a court or law office at a particular time. A subpoena may require production of documents related to the case.

Subprime Loan. A loan that is more expensive than a comparable prime loan. Subprime lending is generally defined as less than prime lending. This type of lending is designed to provide credit to borrowers with no credit history or past credit problems at a higher cost than conventional loans. Most of the *predatory loans* occur in the subprime market.

Summons, also called "original notice" or "notice of suit." This is a document that is provided at the beginning of the lawsuit to tell the *defendant* what is being requested and what must be done to respond to the *complaint*. The term "summons" is also sometimes used interchangeably with *subpoena* for other legal papers that direct a person to be at a particular place at a particular time.

Tax Refund Anticipation Loan. A loan to the *debtor* to be repaid out of the debtor's tax refund. The refund is often then sent directly to the lender. These loans can be very expensive.

Trustee. A trustee is a person or business that is responsible for managing assets for others. In *bankruptcy*, the trustee is a person appointed to administer the bankruptcy case and its assets to maximize the recovery for unsecured creditors.

Truth in Lending Act. A federal (national) law that requires that most lenders, when they make a loan, provide standard form disclosures of the cost and payment terms of the loan.

Underwriting. The process of applying established lending criteria to the qualifications of a particular loan applicant.

Unsecured Creditor. A *creditor* that has no *collateral* for the debt owed.

Unsecured Debt. A debt that does not involve *collateral.*

Usury. The practice of lending and charging the borrower interest, especially at an exorbitant or illegally high rate.

Variable Rate. Interest rate that changes periodically in relation to an "index."

Variable-Rate Mortgage. This is a mortgage loan on which the interest rate can change over time. The changes can affect the amount of your monthly payments.

Wage Assignment. An agreement to have wages paid to a person other than yourself. For example, some people assign a portion of their wages to be paid directly to cover a credit union bill.

Wage Garnishment. *Garnishment* of the *debtor*'s wages from the debtor's employer.

Warranty. Goods or services you purchase contain explicit and/or implicit promises (called "warranties") that the goods or services sold will meet certain standards. A seller's failure to live up to warranties often can be a *defense* to repayment of the debt.

Workout. This term covers a variety of negotiated agreements you might arrange with *creditors* to address a debt you are having trouble paying. Most commonly, the term is used with respect to agreements with a *mortgage* lender to restructure a loan to avoid *foreclosure.*

Index